John G. Morris

The Stork Family in the Lutheran Church

John G. Morris

The Stork Family in the Lutheran Church

ISBN/EAN: 9783337102128

Printed in Europe, USA, Canada, Australia, Japan

Cover: Foto ©Lupo / pixelio.de

More available books at **www.hansebooks.com**

REV. THEOPHILUS STORK, D. D.

REV. CHARLES A. STORK, D. D.

THE

STORK FAMILY

IN THE

LUTHERAN CHURCH:

OR

BIOGRAPHICAL SKETCHES

OF

REV. CHARLES AUGUSTUS GOTTLIEB STORK,
REV. THEOPHILUS STORK, D. D., AND
REV. CHARLES A. STORK, D. D.

BY

JOHN G. MORRIS, D. D., LL.D.,

AUTHOR OF "FIFTY YEARS IN THE LUTHERAN MINISTRY," "JOURNEYS OF LUTHER," "LUTHER AT COBURG," ETC., ETC.

PHILADELPHIA:
LUTHERAN PUBLICATION SOCIETY.

COPYRIGHT, 1886,
BY THE
LUTHERAN PUBLICATION SOCIETY.

PREFACE.

THIS volume is the first contribution to the series of biographies of some deceased ministers, which the Board of Publication has resolved to issue. It is singular in one respect, that it embraces the sketches of three men of the same name, and bearing to each other the near relations of grandfather, son and grandson. There are similar kinships in a few of the families of our ministers, but as the grandsons are still living, it is not likely that for years there will be another book published in which the lives of all three shall be narrated.

The writer of the present volume regrets that he was limited to so small a space for the full exhibition of the lives of these three most worthy men. He was compelled reluctantly to omit much that would have more fully illustrated their characters, but as a considerable portion of the writings of two of them has been published in books, reviews, magazines and church papers, he was not permitted by the committee of the Board to introduce any of them, even extracts, into their biographies.

The writer has availed himself of the help generously

furnished by relatives and friends ; but much of it he was obliged to lay aside for fear of enlarging the book beyond the prescribed limits.

It is hoped that other volumes, which have been assigned to competent writers, will rapidly follow this forerunner of the series.

J. G. M.

CONTENTS.

	PAGE
CHARLES AUGUSTUS GOTTLIEB STORK, ...	7
THEOPHILUS STORK, D. D., ...	29
CHARLES A. STORK, D. D., ...	128

PUBLISHERS' NOTE.

The publishers very much regret that they are unable to give the likeness of REV. CHARLES AUGUSTUS GOTTLIEB STORK, on the *Frontispiece*, with those of REV. THEOPHILUS STORK, D.D., and REV. CHARLES A. STORK, D. D.

A diligent inquiry among his descendants failed to find a daguerreotype or photograph of him. He lived in an age when "likenesses" were not as common as they have since become.

CHARLES AUGUSTUS GOTTLIEB STORK.

CHAPTER I.

BIRTH—PARENTAGE—SCHOOL AND UNIVERSITY LIFE—MINISTRY.

WHEN the intelligent son of a venerated father, after a visit to the scenes of his birth and boyhood a few years subsequent to his father's death, says, "I was unable to secure a single book or manuscript, or even an autograph, and I am left without the simplest relic of my father," the biographer is compelled to depend exclusively upon tradition for facts, the reports of cotemporaries, which are often exaggerated or perverted, the records of the churches which he served, the proceedings of the synod of which he was a member, or it may be some fragmentary document from the hand of the subject of his memoir, which has escaped the destruction of all his other writings.

This unfortunately is the case with the subject of this brief biography. There is nothing extant from his own hand relating to his life, except an imperfect manuscript detailing some incidents of his career, most of which are included in Dr. Bernheim's book on the German Settlements and the Lutherans in the Carolinas. All my information is derived from this admirable work, from Professor Stœver's Sketch in the *Evangelical Review*, Vol. viii, pp. 398-404, Sprague's Annals of the American Lutheran Pulpit, New York, 1869, which is almost entirely a reproduction of Professor Stœver's article. Besides these, I have some letters of gentlemen who knew Mr. Stork, or who lived within the limits of his pastoral district, and have known his character from report. All these combined furnish scant material for an extended biography, but we may be sure of their authenticity.

According to his own manuscript journal, quoted by the *Evangelical Review*, Vol. viii. pp. 398-404, and by Bernheim (p. 312), CHARLES AUGUSTUS GOTTLIEB STORK (originally *Storch*), was born in Helmstædt, Duchy of Brunswick, on June 16th, 1764. His father's name was George Friederich Storch, a merchant in that city, and his mother's name was Von Asseburg. The father afforded the son all the best educational advantages of the day. Helmstædt being a university town, furnished the best possible opportunities of instruction, and it was no doubt owing in great part to his early training, that he subsequently attained to such high proficiency as a linguist and theologian, which is attributed to him by all who knew him.

The pious parents were solicitous not only for the intellectual education of their son, but more especially for his religious culture. They lived in the time when the influences of Spener and Francke and their school of pietism flourished in its original purity, and their godly lives were conformed to the genuine gospel standard.

No wonder that under such parental teaching and pious example, their cherished son at an early period became deeply impressed with religious truth. The devoted pastor and professor of theology in the university, Rev. Mr. Velthusen, had special charge of the boy in his catechetical class, and at the age of fifteen he was confirmed, agreeably to the custom at that time universally prevalent in the Lutheran Church. This was in 1779.

About this time he was promoted from the parish school to a place in the high school, where he remained as a pupil for three years. At the end of that time, Professor Windeberg, the director of that institution, pronounced him fully qualified for admission into the university, which he entered in 1782. In his fragmentary journal as quoted by Bernheim, p. 312, he speaks of "having devoted himself three years to theological sciences," which shows that he had previously determined to serve God in the ministry.

Many of the most promising young men of those days, and also of the present, after having finished their university course, and having no other position as preachers or teachers, eagerly accept places as private tutors in respectable and wealthy families, until they are advanced to more lucrative positions. Indeed, many of these poor young men continue to serve in that capacity for years because they find no other means of support. Hence, not a few of them cease to be young men before they are appointed as pastors or professors, or secure other employment.

In 1785, young Stork was recommended by Rev.

Velthusen to the tutorship of a young nobleman, Von Hadenberg, whom he taught for a year until his removal from Helmstædt, "whereupon," says the journal, "I became the teacher of Mr. Friese's children, a merchant near Bremen." Here he remained two years.

We know nothing whatever of his life during his scholastic and university career, and must be content with the bare outline presented above.

A number of pious young ministers of the Spener-Francke school of Lutheranism had come over to this country as missionaries as early as 1733. The missionary spirit is the natural outgrowth of the revival of true religion.

In that day, the personal sacrifice of a voyage to America and of mission labors among the scattered Germans here, and the discomforts and perils of the enterprise, were far greater than a similar expedition to India or to the Sandwich Islands at the present time. The vigorous faith, Christian heroism, holy zeal and self-denying efforts which characterized our earlier ministers from Germany are deserving of all gratitude and admiration. No one can read the narrative of their toils, or contemplate the character of their piety, without instruction and profit. They were indeed devoted men, whose precious memory will be cherished by the pious throughout all time.

Young Stork, in his journal, as quoted by Bernheim, further says, "Having remained there (at Mr. Friese's) two years, I received the call and order from Rev. Velthusen to go as pastor to North Carolina; whereupon I was examined and ordained to the ministry and journeyed in May, 1788, from Germany, and arrived in America (Baltimore) about the end of June of the same year."

A petition from a number of members of the Lutheran Church in North Carolina had been received, accompanied by a communication from the Rev. Adolphus Nussman, who had been sent as a missionary to this country in 1733, and who had, for several years, been laboring in great poverty, earnestly imploring that additional help might be furnished to relieve the prevailing spiritual destitution. The request was forwarded to Rev. Velthusen, and his attention was immediately directed to Mr. Stork as a person eminently fitted to engage in such an enterprise. The young man, after due reflection, expressed a willingness to go, and at once made arrangements for his departure, at the same time receiving from his Sovereign a written assurance that if, for any reason, he might choose to return, he should still retain his claim to promotion in the fatherland. Young candidates for the pastoral office at that day received appointments to parishes only when vacancies were made by death or promotion, and then only, in most cases, in proportion to their time of service as teachers or vicars; but they lost this privilege by voluntary expatriation, and hence our young candidate judiciously secured himself against the forfeiture of this claim.

As a candidate for the sacred office he was then examined by order of the Duke, who was of course the civil head of the Church as well as of the Duchy. This examination was conducted by five professors, who it is fair to presume were somewhat more rigid and thorough than our examiners are of the present day.

He passed the ordeal creditably, which, as Velthusen says, was conducted in the strictest manner, and was ordained as a minister to North Carolina by his pastor, Velthusen, who had all along been his kind friend and generous benefactor. Thus, he was selected for this field as a minister before he was ordained or even examined. The practice of the Church in some, if not in all the Provinces and States of Germany, was not to ordain a man who had not received a call to some specific field of labor, and I think this would be found to be the Apostolic practice. Our custom in this country is somewhat different. Most of our Synods *license* candidates to preach and perform all the ministerial functions, and subsequent ordination confers no additional power, only entitling the candidate to a few unimportant additional privileges, and hence it is an empty ceremony. The *License* system was introduced into our Synods by these very fathers, who were trained under a system entirely different at home, but it was adopted here as a safeguard against the ordination of men of doubtful character or qualification in the early period of the Church in this country, but I think that danger need be no longer apprehended.

As has been stated, he arrived in Baltimore on June 27, 1788, and received from the brethren there a most cordial welcome. This must have been during the pastorship of Rev. Gotlieb Gerock, in Baltimore, but his name is not mentioned in Mr. Stork's report.

He remained in Baltimore about six weeks, and then he passed on towards his future field of labor. He traveled to Charleston by sea, and there purchased a horse, and, by an inland route, reached Pastor Nussman's residence in North Carolina in the month of September.

Mr. Stork, immediately after his arrival, was elected pastor of three congregations—one in Salisbury, where he took up his abode, and the others known by the name of the *Organ* Church, where he commenced his labors on October 26, 1788, and the *Pine* Church. He also soon commenced regular service in what was called the Irish Settlement. As the years passed on, he established other congregations in Rowan, Lincoln, and Cabarrus counties. Here he spent his days in a constant routine of most diligent and self-denying labor. He was repeatedly invited to occupy other fields, and some of them among the most eligible within the bounds of the denomination; but he declined them all, in view of the great want of ministers in the region in which he had planted himself. He lived in Salisbury seventeen years, and was privileged to witness the most gratifying results from his labors. During the first two years of his residence in this place, he was domesticated in the house of Louis Beard, whose daughter, Christina, he married on the 14th of January, 1790. They had eleven children, not one of whom is now living.

Once during his pastoral life he made a visit to the North, which in those days was a long and wearisome journey, and attended the meeting of the Synod of Pennsylvania, "to strengthen himself," as the record says, "to renewed exertion in the service of his Divine Master."

The Rev. Mr. A. Nussman, who had been settled for some years in North Carolina, and who hospitably received Mr. Stork, thus writes to Rev. Abbot Velthusen on November 12, 1788, which was only about six weeks after Stork's arrival: "Mr. Stork's sickness gave me much uneasiness and sorrow, for I love him on account of his learning, piety, temperament, and social qualities. . . . All persons who see and hear him love and honor him. But God has helped us; Rev. Stork is restored again, and may God preserve his health in future, so that whether I live or die, my expectations concerning him may be realized."*

A report was sent to the Helmstaedt Mission Society the following year (1789), from which Dr. Velthusen makes the following extract:

"Rev. Stork, as well as Mr. Roschen, is satisfied in the midst of the congregations. * * * He praises the people, who treat him with love and respect and supply him with the necessaries of life. * * * His congregation is building a house for him, and have offered him a loan for purchasing a plantation, without which one can not succeed there. He still lives in Salisbury, where an academy has been established in which there are some students, who receive instruction in Hebrew from him. In addition to that, he has also established a small German school. * * * He expects to confirm about fifty young persons next harvest season."

In a report from Mr. Roschen, who had preceded Mr. Stork in North Carolina a short time, but who returned

---

*Bernheim, 328. Ib. 330.

to Germany about the year 1800, there is recorded a little incident which deserves mention as being creditable to the character of the preaching in that district. He says: "Rev. Stork recently passed by the court house in Salisbury at the time a man was suffering the penalty of some crime by standing in the pillory. A German called us to stop awhile and see how the Americas punish rogues and thieves. Upon my asking him, 'The criminal is surely not a German?' I received the gratifying reply, 'Never has a German stood in the pillory in Salisbury; nor has ever a German been hung in this place.'"*

Mr. Stork suffered from alarming depression of spirits, which accompanied him in a greater or less degree of severity all his life. Mr. Roschen in this same letter remarks: "At first Stork in his hypochondria looked upon all things in a false light; besides, his arrival in America was unpropitious (that is, he was confined to bed soon after his arrival in North Carolina). Now he speaks differently. We all preach in black clothes and neck-cloth, but mostly without a gown, and often in our overcoats during bad weather in winter."

There is a singular proceeding reported in Dr. Bernheim's book, p. 338, in which Mr. Stork and four other German Lutheran pastors participated, and that was the ordination of a man to the Protestant Episcopal ministry. The ordination certificate is still extant, signed by five Lutheran ministers, in which it is expressly stated that "R. J. Miller is hereby declared to be ordained to 'ad-

---

* Bernheim, 332.

minister yᵉ sacraments and to have yᵉ care of souls, he always being obliged to obey yᵉ rules, ordinances and customs of yᵉ Christian Society, called yᵉ Protestant Episcopal Church in America!'"

These men gave their reasons on the reverse side of this certificate why they had ordained a man who was a member of the Episcopal church as a minister of that denomination. These reasons should be made known for a more unecclesiastical and un-Lutheran transaction is not to be encountered.

In a letter to Dr. Velthusen, dated Salisbury, February 25, 1803, Mr. Stork describes his condition:

"It is now nearly three years that I live in very sad circumstances; not only have I suffered during this time from various severe attacks of sickness, which brought me near to death, but likewise from an apparently incurable disease of the eyes, which seems to baffle all medical skill, and makes it impossible for me either to read or write. I am, however, quite restored from my sickness of last fall, a disease similar to yellow fever, and which rages in this vicinity with great mortality; I now feel tolerably strong and my eyes are somewhat better; nevertheless according to the physician I need not expect any permanent restoration of my health in this climate . . . . . . I still serve my old congregations, and I continue to preach the doctrines of Jesus Christ, the crucified, in simplicity, and have happily experienced the power of grace upon myself and others. The prevalence of infidelity, the contempt of the best of all religions, its usages and servants, the increase of irreligion and crime, as remarked, have occasioned me many sad hours. Nevertheless I have found consolation and courage in the thought

'So long as Christ protects His church,
May hell its rage continue,

and I hold fast to my faith, convinced that truth and religion will at last mightily raise up their head and prevail."

On the subject of the extraordinary manifestations of 1800 and 1801, called revivals by many, and which created such a deep interest in the churches of the South and West in those days, Mr. Stork thus expresses himself in a letter to Dr. Velthusen, February 25, 1803:

"By the side of this pestilence (infidelity) there prevails now, for over a year, a something, I know not what to name it, and I should not like to say *fanaticism*. Christians of every denomination assemble themselves in the forest, number four, six, and sometimes ten thousand persons; they erect tents, sing and pray and preach day and night, for five or six or eight days. I have been an eye-witness to scenes, in such large assemblies, which I cannot explain. I beheld young and old, feeble and strong, white and black, in a word, people of every age, position and circumstances, as though they were struck by lightning, speechless and motionless, and when they had somewhat recovered, they could be heard shrieking bitterly and supplicating God for mercy and grace.

"After they had thus spent three and many of them even more hours, they rose up, praised God, and commenced to pray in such a manner as they never were wont to do, exhorting sinners to come to Jesus, etc., etc. Many of those who were thus exercised were ungodly persons before, and we can now discover a remarkable change in them. Even deists have been brought to confess Christ in this way. Thus the affair continues to this hour.

"Opinions are various in regard to it; many, even ministers, denominate it the work of the devil; others again would explain it in a natural way, or in accordance with some physical law; whilst others look upon it as the work of God. Please, give me your opinion and explanation. The thing has occasioned me no little uneasiness. In our German congregations nothing of this kind has been manifested. . . . . . The enclosed published accounts will be interesting to you; the facts are similar to those which I myself have seen. The authors of these accounts are generally respectable men and worthy of belief."

The Synod of North Carolina was formed and held its first session in Salisbury on May 2, 1803; and Mr. Stork was elected first President, and was annually re-elected whenever he could be present.

During the latter period of his life he removed to a farm ten miles south of Salisbury, where he resided the remnant of his days. The last six years of his life, however, physical infirmities prevented him from discharging his ministerial duties publicly, but he suffered in calm submission to the will of God, and by his perfect resignation and patience exhibited the sanctifying power of divine grace.

For nearly thirty-seven years he served the church faithfully, and his memory will be blessed. He will be honored as one of the fathers of the Lutheran Church in North Carolina, and the day of his departure, the 27th of March, 1831, was a day of sadness and mourning to all the community in which he lived. His illness continued for nine weeks, and he frequently gave to his family and visiting friends the assurance of his hope of eternal life.

The Rev. Paul Henkel, for many years contemporary with Mr. Stork, in writing of the churches in North Carolina, says, " In the vicinity of Salisbury, Rowan county, there are three strong Lutheran congregations, which have been served by Rev. Charles Stork for nearly twenty years; but under many disadvantages, on account of the frequent and severe attacks of fever, which prostrated his energies, . . . and which apparently had several times brought him near to the grave. His numerous official duties lay often heavy upon him on account of his ill health, especially the administration of the Lord's Supper to 250 communicants at one time, so that his feeble powers of body were exhausted after having served all these people."*

The following inscription is engraved upon the tablet in the cemetery of Organ church, which marks the spot where this useful servant of the Lord was laid to rest: " Sacred to the memory of the Rev. Charles A. G. Storch, Pastor of the Evangelical Lutheran Church; who was born on the 16th of June, A. D. 1764, and departed this life on the 27th day of March, 1831. Aged 66 years, 9 months, and 11 days."

A local newspaper, in noticing his death, says : " The deep and unrestrained emotions of the assembly of his spiritual children at the grave of their departed friend evinced the magnitude of their loss and the extent of his worth."

He was a man of learning as well as of piety, as most of our earlier ministers were who received their education in Germany. He had the reputation of being a superior linguist, and besides being familiar with Hebrew, Greek and Latin, as all University-bred men were presumed to be, it is said that he spoke five or six languages.

It is also said that his library was valuable, embracing quite a number of celebrated German authors, whose theological works were usually written in Latin. The report was that he had bequeathed many of them to our Theological Seminary at Gettysburg, of which he was

---

* Bernheim, 367.

elected one of the first directors, and in the prosperity of which he had always showed the deepest interest. The most of his books, however, are in the possession of the College at Mt. Pleasant, North Carolina.

Among the many interesting incidents of his pastoral life, the following deserves mention: "During a communion season in the spring of 1821, when a large class of catechumens, numbering 77 persons, were confirmed, their aged pastor being present, but too feeble to stand during the ceremony, called all his catechumens to him, and gave them and the other members and friends of the church his last farewell. So affecting was the scene that the whole of that vast assembly was moved to tears, and long has been remembered the serious lesson which their aged pastor addressed to them at the time, whilst he held out his hand to each and gave them his parting blessing. He had introduced the Rev. D. Scherer as his successor. and who on this occasion administered the Sacrament."*

No one ever questioned the genuineness of his piety or the sincerity of his actions. Stern in his integrity, exemplary in his deportment, he awakened respect. The world acknowledged him to be an honest man, and paid to him as such its tribute of regard. He was a pious, humble Christian; cheerful, yet devout; zealous, without bigotry or fanaticism; sprightly, without levity; grave, without moroseness; a model of meekness and of every Christian virtue. No blemish ever sullied his conduct, no stain can tarnish the fair name he has left behind him.†

---

* Bernheim, 445.

† Prof. Stoever, Ev. Rev., vol. viii., 403.

LETTERS,

From some Gentlemen, relating to Mr. Stork.—The first two are taken from Sprague's "American Lutheran Pulpit."

LETTER FROM REV. THEOP. STORK D. D. TO DR. SPRAGUE.

BALTIMORE Jan. 20, 1862.

Dear Brother: I regret exceedingly that it is not in my power to furnish you with such personal recollections of my father, as would be worthy of him, or of the work in which you propose to incorporate them. I was but a boy when he died. Shortly after his death, I came North and have not since been associated with any of the family. Before I was old enough to take special interest in my father's library, it was distributed partly at least, among poor ministers at the South. Some ten years ago, I went South with a view of finding some of the books and manuscripts which had belonged to him, but was unable to secure a single one, not even an autograph. I am ashamed to make this acknowledgment, but it is a fact, and one over which I have no control. My exile from home in my boyhood, and the early departure of my brothers and sisters, have left me without the simplest relic of my father. So far as I can now recall him, he was tall, erect, of robust constitution, and had a real German face, with a mild, benevolent expression. He was regarded as one of the most learned and eloquent of the early German missionaries. He was said to be a remarkable linguist. I remember that Dr. Wilson, a Presbyterian clergyman from Mecklenburg county, used often to visit him, and they sometimes, to vary the scene a little, conversed in Greek. My father could speak some five or six languages fluently. He was eminently devoted to the great work of the ministry. But devoted as his whole life had been to Christ, he lamented, in his old age, that he had done so little for the souls purchased with a Saviour's blood.

I am yours truly in the Lord,
T. STORK.

FROM THE REV. D. P. ROSENMILLER TO DR. SPRAGUE.

LANCASTER, PA., May 21, 1862.

My Dear Sir: My acquaintance with the Rev. Charles A. G. Stork, of Cabarrus county, N. C., commenced in the spring of 1829, and continued until his decease, in the early part of 1831. During that time he was in a feeble condition, and unable to leave home, or to engage in anything that required either bodily or mental effort. His hospitable home was the favorite resort of many persons who honored and loved him as one of the excellent of the earth. He was living in the same community in which he had spent the whole of his active life; and it was not strange that those who had so long been witnesses of his pure and elevated example, and sharers in the good which he had accomplished, should have delighted to bear their grateful testimony to his character and influence.

Mr. Stork had received an excellent education in Germany, and was especially a proficient in the learned languages; and his well selected library was a proof that he kept pace with the theological literature of his time. In person he was tall and well proportioned, and his countenance was expressive of great meekness and benevolence. In his conversation he showed himself discreet and thoughtful, and evinced a delicate regard for the feelings of others. In social life he was highly interesting and attractive, but always kept at a great remove from every thing like unbecoming levity.

Several years previous to the commencement of my acquaintance with this excellent man, he had retired from all public duties, and the churches which he had served during his active ministry were under the charge of another pastor. The largest of his congregations were at Organ and St. John's churches. In my intercourse with his former parishioners, I often heard him spoken of as a very eloquent preacher, and a kind-hearted and attentive pastor. I frequently heard them cite some of his favorite sentiments, among which I remember the following— "The Word of God is a beautiful flower; but whilst the bee extracts honey from it, the spider draws from the same the most active poison."

Mr. Stork informed me that the churches he served were not the ones allotted to him when he was sent from Germany. He was designed for Lincoln county. But, after having endured a stormy voyage,* he arrived in the eastern part of the State— perhaps Guilford county—and thence communicated to his prospective churches the fact of his arrival, and asked them to send for him. The answer which he received was characterized by a freezing indifference. Perhaps it should have been excused, emanating, as it did, from a people who stood sadly in need of a missionary's labors; but the feelings of the newly-arrived pastor were deeply wounded by it, and he became anxious for a field in which he might labor with better prospects of sympathy and of success. Cabarrus county was accordingly assigned to him.

One peculiarity of Mr. Stork was his little knowledge of, and great indifference to, mere worldly matters. These he turned over to his faithful wife, in whose sagacity and prudence he had unbounded confidence. He had little or nothing of the spirit of worldly ambition. He never aspired to be a pastor in a city, though his learning and eloquence would have qualified him for exercising his ministry in the most cultivated and refined communities. He was contented to remain a plain country parson, mingling in peace and love with a plain and truly good people, whom he conducted, by word and example, in the path which the Good Shepherd had pointed out.

During one of my visits at Mr. Stork's house, a well-dressed gentleman called upon him, and stated that he was a refugee from Portugal, and had been an adherent of Don Pedro, who claimed his right to the Portuguese throne. But the party of Don Miguel had been too powerful for him, and the adherents of Don Pedro were compelled to leave the country, suffering the confiscation of their property. Mr. Stork was much interested in the tale of the stranger, and besides asking him to dine, made a pecuniary contribution to his relief, to which I gladly added my mite. He asked the name of the place in which the stranger resided; and when told that it was Montebello (Beau-

---

* By sea from Baltimore to Charleston, where he bought a horse and rode to North Carolina —[J. G. M.]

tiful Mountain), he dwelt much on the beauty of the name, and also upon the cruelties practiced by the usurper, Don Miguel. When I was about to leave, he requested me to remind the Rev. J. R——, of Salisbury, that he would be pleased to see him. "Tell him," said he, "that I would like to receive some of the crumbs."

With great regard, very truly yours,
D. P. ROSENMILLER.

FROM REV. S. ROTHROCK.

GOLD HILL, ROWAN CO, N C., Feb. 2, 1885.

Dear Dr. Morris: I regret that I cannot give you many facts in relation to Rev. C. A. G. Stork. He had died before I came to this county, consequently I had no personal acquaintance with him. There are but few persons living now that have much recollection of him. * * * * The congregation at Organ church numbered seventy-eight members, and promised him a yearly salary of forty pounds, North Carolina currency. He served Organ church as pastor thirty-five years.

In his style of preaching he appears to have been plain, affectionate and earnest. His sermons were well arranged, instructive and edifying. In his dress he was neat and precise. In his general demeanor he was dignified and affable, easy of approach by the humblest member of his flock. From the nature of his sermons he must have been studious in their preparation. I am not advised as to the extent of his library. In his habits of life he was very correct and exemplary. * * * * He was highly esteemed by his fellow-ministers, and I suppose him to have been sound in his theological faith. * * * * Mr. S. is said to have been a good musician, vocal and instrumental.

Yours truly,   S. ROTHROCK.

FROM REV. D. J. HAUER, D. D.

HANOVER, PA., March 4th, 1885.

Rev. Dr. Morris—Dear Brother: You have requested me to give you my recollections of the Rev. Charles Augustus Gottlieb Stork, of North Carolina. I regret that those recollections are not as perfect as I could desire, from the fact that half a century has elapsed since his death, and it was my privilege to know him only in his declining years, when his physical force was abated, and his vigor impaired by disease and the hand of time.

Our first meeting took place in the summer of 1827, at his home in Cabarrus county, nine miles south of Salisbury. It was upon my first visit to that section of the State, and as he was the oldest minister connected with the Lutheran Synod of North Carolina, and revered and beloved by his brethren and the community at large, I desired the privilege of his acquaintance, and as a young minister to pay him my respects.

He received me kindly, giving me a cordial welcome into the bosom of his interesting and agreeable family, which consisted of his wife and daughter, an amiable young lady, and his youngest son, Theophilus, whom he familarly called Gottlieb, and who was at that time studying the classics under his father's tuition.

His massive head was an index of a vigorous brain, his features were somewhat irregular, but his mouth expressed the firmness and decision which always characterized him. His character as a gentleman and Christian minister was irreproachable, and he enjoyed the confidence and esteem of Christians of all denominations. Affable in his manners, agreeable in his conversation, and easily approached, he never failed to gather about him groups of admiring friends.

Subject to fits of depression and melancholy, there were times when he would with the Psalmist exclaim, "All thy waves and thy billows are gone over me." Yet he was fond of social intercourse, and at times was cheerful and even vivacious. As a preacher he was plain, practical and forcible, rendering his teachings intelligible to his audiences, whose salvation and enlightenment he had at heart.

As a pastor he was kind and affectionate in his manner, ready to sympathize with the distressed and suffering, and to administer to the relief of the needy. He was studious, and prepared his sermons with care, adapting them to the condition of the people to whom he preached.

He was earnest in his ministrations, and commanded not only the attention but the confidence of his hearers. He was, under God, very successful in building up his churches: the membership of the Organ church in Rowan, and St. John's in Cabarrus county, were the largest in connection with the Synod. He was indefatigable in his efforts to win souls to Christ, as might be expected of one educated under the Christian influence of the Franckean school at Halle, Germany; and though his pastorate was large, he frequently visited vacant congregations and sought out the scattered Lutherans in other parts of the State—occasionally visiting the Lutheran settlements in the forks of the Saluda, in South Carolina, and ministering to the spiritual wants of old and young.

His library consisted of choice works, principally German and Latin, and he was well versed in the doctrine of our holy Christianity—ever ready to teach and defend the truth; he was a strong advocate of the divinity of Christ, and the efficacy and necessity of His atonement, and the cardinal doctrine of "Justification by Faith." He regarded the Augsburg Confession as a correct exposition of the fundamental doctrines of the word of God; and as taught in a manner substantially correct in its doctrinal articles.

He was liberal towards other denominations, believing in the communion of saints—not exclusive in his views, holding that in every nation those who "feared God and wrought righteousness are accepted of Him;" hence he enjoyed the friendship and esteem of Christians in general.

He was one of the founders of the Snyod of North Carolina, and it could be said that he was head and front of the Lutheran church in the South.

When the Episcopalians of North Carolina resolved to organize a convention under the direction of Bishop Moore of Virginia, the good bishop was anxious to secure the aid and co-operation of Father Stork, and he was pressingly invited to meet in the proposed convention and unite with them. This he respectfully declined to do, and in his reply gave them to understand that he was an Evangelical Lutheran, and not an Episcopalian : and that the doctrines of the Lutheran Church in minor points as well as in polity differed from the Episcopal.

He would not aid in the organization of an ecclesiastical body to which he did not wish to belong, yet as an evidence of his catholic spirit, he assured them that his church would be open to their ministry in their efforts to gather their dispersed members residing in the western part of the State, and to organize them into congregations. Such Christian liberality was worthy of the man.

He was the decided friend of an active spirituality, and rejoiced to see and hear of the conversion of souls. On one occasion of visiting him, I found him suffering from mental depression, and reclining upon his bed. As was his custom, he asked for news from the churches, and when told of a gracious work of grace in the congregation of Rev. Jacob Miller, of Stokes county, he arose promptly, and calling to his son Gottlieb to bring him his slippers, he sat up and expressed feelings of delight, rejoicing like the angels over the repentance of sinners, and commending the fidelity and zeal of brother Miller.

He was a father in Israel, and the friend and prudent counselor of young ministers, in whose welfare and success he manifested a deep interest, pointing out the dangers to which they were exposed, and giving them wholesome advice, that they might escape from temptation and maintain blameless reputations.

He was a decided friend of temperance, and as it was customary in that early day to offer the social glass even to ministerial guests, he advised young clergymen to set their faces against the custom, and kindly refuse this so-called expression of hospitality, adding, "that total abstinence is the only safeguard against intemperance."

He frequently related incidents connected with his ministry, some of which were quite ludicrous. On one occasion, when making a missionary tour among destitute Lutherans in South Carolina, he was obliged to improvise a pulpit. Finding a hogshead, he mounted thereon. While addressing his audience, he felt his foundation yielding, and in a moment his feet were upon the ground, and he was encased in the hogshead. Kind hands soon relieved him from this unpleasant predicament, amid the suppressed laughter of the assembly.

He continued to labor with earnestness and fidelity until the organization of the Tennessee Conference, whose members, by their opposition to the recently-organized General Synod, produced discord and schism in many of the congregations of North Carolina, including part of his charge, which depressed him very much; and as the infirmities of age were increasing, he was induced to resign his charge, contrary to the wishes of his people, whom he had faithfully served for many years.

As regards the time of his death and attending circumstances, I can say nothing, as it occurred after my removal from the State, but "his was the path of the just, shining more and more unto the perfect day," and doubtless, "his end was peace."

> "He needs no verse his virtues to record;
> He lived, he died, a servant of the Lord."

Truly yours,   DANIEL J. HAUER.

REV. THEOPHILUS STORK, D. D.

CHAPTER I.

BIRTH AND PARENTAGE—HOME TRAINING—COLLEGE AND SEMINARY EDUCATION—SOME OF HIS CLASSMATES—MANNERS AND DISPOSITION—DR. DIEHL'S MEMOIR—PREACHING IN HIS STUDENT YEARS.

IN the preceding biography I have traced the eminently useful career, as far as the limited sources of information would allow, of Rev. Carl Augustus Gottlieb Storch (which was the original German family name), and now I shall endeavor to present a portrait of his distinguished son, *Theophilus*, who was baptized *Gottlieb*, an expressive old German Christian name, but which was changed by himself into the beautiful and more euphonious Greek synonym, Theophilus. He was born near Salisbury, Rowan County, North Carolina, in August, 1814.* His mother's name was Christiana Beard, the daughter of the man with whom the father of Theophilus lived when he first came to this country in 1788.

We have very little authentic information concerning his early years. The boy grew up on the paternal farm, and had such educational advantages as the neighborhood

---

* The precise date I could not learn.

afforded. He must have made some progress, however, for he taught a school before leaving home for Gettysburg, and he could not have been over sixteen years of age when he wielded the country school-master's birch over the children of his father's parish. It is said that in early life he showed a fondness for reading, but it is presumed that he had little opportunity of gratifying his taste, for the lack of the kind of books which pleased him. His father's library consisted of nothing but theological and classical works in German or Latin, neither of which the studious boy could at that time read; and there were very few books of English literature to be found in that section of North Carolina fifty-five years ago, when young Stork was a plain country lad at home. His love for books which he delighted in could only be indulged in later years, when he came into contact with libraries and into the society of men of like tastes and pursuits to his own.

His youthful morals were of the strictest character, for his father's domestic discipline was of the good old German Lutheran type; but Theophilus was a boy of a naturally gentle disposition, who easily yielded to paternal control. He thus grew up to be a blameless man, whose fair name was never sullied by the breath of suspicion.

Theophilus entered what was then called the Gymnasium at Gettysburg, in October, 1830. This preparatory school was soon after elevated to the character of a college, of which he became a pupil with his classmates. He must have remained at Gettysburg six or seven years. He went there in 1830, graduated from college in 1835, and studied in the Seminary two years, which at that time was the prescribed time, but at present is extended to three years.*

Rev. Dr. Diehl, in a sketch of the life of Dr. Stork in the *Quarterly Review*, 1875, and who was contemporary with him in college, thus speaks of him: "It was in the winter of 1833: Mr. S. was then in his nineteenth year. He was tall, slender and graceful; always neatly dressed, genial in his association with the students. In boisterous sports he took no part. He was quite a favorite in society . . . among the students he was equally popular. He was dearly loved by his more intimate associates, and seemed to have no enemies. Even the rivalries incident to college life did not apparently awaken any malicious feeling towards him . . . He was considered a good scholar, holding a respectable standing in a class of great talent. He excelled in *belles lettres;* also in mental and moral science. He ranked higher in language than in mathematics."

At this time the College faculty was composed of Rev. Dr. C. P. Krauth, Sen. President; Rev. M. Jacobs, Professor of Mathematics and Natural Science; Rev. H. L. Baugher, Professor of Greek; Rev. W. M. Reynolds,

---

*The Theological Seminary was established in 1826. The Classical School to prepare young men for Theological study was opened in 1827, under the tutorship of Rev. D. Jacobs; in 1829, a scientific department under the care of his brother, Rev. M. Jacobs, was added, and the united schools were called the Gettysburg Gymnasium. Upon the lamented death of Prof. D. Jacobs, the Rev. H. L. Baugher was appointed Classical teacher in 1831; and the college proper was established in 1832.

Professor of the Latin Language and Literature; Rev. J. H. Marsden, Professor of Mineralogy and Botany.

Theophilus Stork was graduated in 1835, which was the second class that received diplomas. There were only Sophomore and Freshman classes formed the first year of the college. The valedictory was assigned to him, which was regarded as the first honor. He is said by those who knew him in those days to have been a beautiful speaker and a good writer, though somewhat too florid, which as a collegian's defect can easily be overlooked.

Two of his classmates were Samuel Sprecher and Ezra Keller, both strong and good men, and both became Presidents of Wittenberg College. Keller died young, but after rendering unspeakably great service to the Church; whilst Dr. Sprecher still lives, the honored survivor of a class of talented men, and maintaining a high rank among the theologians of our Church. Judge Dale, of Illinois, was another member of the class, who is still living and reflecting honor upon his *alma mater* by maintaining great reputation as a jurist and an enterprising citizen. Judge Dale attended the semi-centennial celebration of the college in 1882, where he met some of the men of his college generation and was received most cordially by all. David F. Bittle was the only other member of the class I have room to mention. He was an honored member of our ministry and a most industrious and successful worker in the Church. His founding of Roanoke college is alone the proudest monument that could be erected to his memory.

Young Stork was one of the founders of the Phrenakosmian Society in 1831, and the President of it in 1832 and 1834; anniversary speaker in 1835, and debater in 1833 and 1835.

During his college life his Christian character was richly developed, and the purity of his life had a wholesome influence upon his fellow students. He was not morose or even ascetic as a Christian, but loving, tender and meek.

He was not remarkable for close attention to his college studies, but he read extensively in English literature, and poetry especially. He had a good memory, and could easily commit numerous stanzas and striking passages. He was not considered a ready off-hand debater in the college society, but none could excel him in a written discourse or argument.

Though he was a graduate of both institutions at Gettysburg, and holding influential positions in the church, he never served as a Trustee or Director in either of them, and seldom or perhaps never attended the public exercises at the Commencements of the College or exhibitions of the Seminary classes. He did not heartily patronize either of them when it was in his power to do so, and when it would have been of advantage to him. I know myself that he did not admire one or two of the most prominent men in the Faculties, but he would not be convinced that this did not justify a withdrawal of his support from those schools which we were all laboring so hard to uphold. He sent his son Charles to the Preparatory school, but took him away after a few months.

I could nowhere find any record of the time and place of his conversion, at which we need not be surprised, for he was very reticent to strangers on the subject of his religious experience, although in his letters to the members of his household, as will be seen, he pours out his heart's emotions fully and tenderly. I doubt whether he would have been able to specify any peculiar circumstances attending the great change, but it was one of those gradual processes more felt than seen, and the natural outgrowth of his religious training at home. That it was thorough, his religious activity and godly life have signally exhibited.

IN THE SEMINARY.

In the fall of 1835 he entered the Theological Seminary, of which at that time Drs. Schmucker and Krauth were the only professors, and two years constituted the period of study.

His class consisted of thirteen, only one of whom, the Rev. Dr. C. W. Schaeffer, Professor in the Philadelphia Seminary, is now (1886) living. Among the others best known in the church were Michael Eyster, D. F. Bittle, and Ezra Keller.

His papers, which have been submitted to me, give no information concerning his life in that institution, and with all my efforts I have failed to procure any facts of an unusual or striking character. He is represented as being studious in his habits, exemplary in his life, and addicted to the same course of literary reading which he pursued in college. He was regarded as a fair *belles-lettres* scholar, possessing a fine poetical taste, and able to quote poetry on all occasions. His seminary exercises were always neat and beautiful, and whilst he was not a fluent speaker nor happy in an off-hand protracted argument, in which men of far inferior intellect may have surpassed him, yet he was solid even if ornate, and instructive even if diffusive. He secured the sincere regard and confidence of his fellow-students, and the respect of his teachers.

Dr. Diehl in the article previously quoted gives us a few interesting facts, which betray the character of our friend. He says: "During the second year in the Seminary, and especially in vacation time, he occasionally preached. His method at that time was to write his sermons with much care, and then to so familiarize his mind with the discourse as to deliver it without much use of the manuscript. His delivery had all the force and freedom of extemporaneous speaking. Nor did he confine himself to the written sermon. Under the influence of excitement he sometimes burst forth into impromptu eloquence of great power. An incident occurring to his eye would rouse him into indignation or melt him into sympathy, that called forth unwonted power of utterance. The people in the towns in Franklin, Washington and Frederick counties, in which he was accustomed to spend part of his vacation, long remembered some of his impromptu bursts of oratory. One occurred in Jefferson, Frederick county, Md., where he was spending several weeks with his friends. He was preaching one Sunday morning in the old Stone Church, when he observed a thoughtless young man talking to his companions in a disorderly manner. It kindled young Stork's indignation. With flashing eye he turned to the young man, and in tones of awful tenderness thundered out, 'Young man, I fear the first ray of light that will flash on your benighted soul will be reflected from the flames of hell!' On another occasion, preaching in one of the villages of Washington county, he noticed an aged woman weeping so sorrowfully during nearly all the sermon, that he supposed she must be crushed to the ground by an intolerable weight. His sympathies were deeply moved. He broke from the thread of his discourse and addressed her with so much pathos, and poured into the wounded spirit such a Christian consolation and hope, that the whole congregation was melted into tears."

CHAPTER II.

LICENSE TO PREACH—CALL TO WINCHESTER—MARRIAGE—SUCCESS AS PASTOR—LETTER FROM REV. DR. GILBERT.

IN August, 1837, he was called as pastor to the church at Winchester, Va., and accepted it even before he was licensed to preach. This course was not uncommon in those days, and in order to authorize young men to enter upon ministerial engagements under such circumstances, the Presidents of some of our Synods licensed them to preach *ad interim*, until they should be examined by the Synod at its next meeting, and then be regularly and permanently admitted to the ministry. Ezra Keller, D. F. Bittle and W. H. Smith were licensed at the same meeting with Mr. Stork by the Synod of Maryland.

Mr. Stork succeeded the Rev. N. Goertner at Winchester. Young Stork's fiery eloquence, suavity of temper and refinement of manners, secured the admiration of his people and the esteem of the whole population, which he maintained throughout his life.

Not long after his settlement he was married on November 16th, 1837, by Rev. S. W. Harkey, to Miss Mary Jane Lynch, daughter of William Lynch, Esq., then living near Jefferson, Frederick county, Md., and sister of Judge John A. Lynch, at present of Frederick.

Everything was favorable to Mr. Stork's ministerial

success in Winchester. He was a sympathizing pastor, a popular preacher, and a perfect Christian gentleman. His people were ardently attached to him and his wife, and gave him a generous support. They were proud of his growing reputation abroad and the admiration he gained from the influential members of other churches in and about Winchester. He was well spoken of as a preacher through the valley, and strangers staying over Sunday would go to hear Mr. Stork, of whom they heard so much as a first-class preacher. And thus he went on, year after year, gaining still greater reputation as a pulpit orator. As one of his classmates said, three years after Mr. Stork went to Winchester, "He has all the elements of a good preacher—person, voice, manner, magnetism, thought, sentiment, pungency and pathos."

Dr. Diehl, who was his hearer for eight months in 1840, and whose judgment is unbiased, says: "No competent judge will question that in the delivery of his sermons, in the gracefulness and propriety of gesture, in freedom, in rich and varied tones of voice, in the electric power flashing from his eyes, rarely turning to the manuscript but ranging over all the audience, in gushing thought and emotion expressed in every lineament of his face, he had few equals during the first five or six years of his ministry."

But this popularity as a preacher was not the whole of his success. It was not all which he aimed at. Doing good to the souls of men was his purpose; and this also, by divine grace, he accomplished. The fruits of his ministry were abundant. His church had been without a minister for several years. Some of the young people had strayed away, and some of the old ones were beginning to be careless. All the inconveniences of a church without a pastor were experienced, as well as all the disadvantages, but soon after young Stork became pastor a gratifying change took place. The attendance on public worship steadily increased. Those who had temporarily gone off returned, and those who had remained became more strongly attached. The young people resumed their places, and the number of catechumens increased. The Lord's Supper had more participants than in former times, and the addition of members by certificate was greater. The church was full of attentive hearers, and harmony prevailed in the congregation.

The following letter from the Rev. Dr. D. M. Gilbert, of Winchester, gives a picture of Mr. Stork's character whilst he was pastor of that church:

MAY 1st, 1885.

Dear Doctor: Dr. Theophilus Stork became pastor of our church here October 9th, 1837, being then in the 24th year of his age. He was, as you are well aware, from the time of his entrance upon ministerial life very popular and successful, both as a preacher and pastor, and greatly endeared himself to all classes of people in the congregation by his amiable disposition and his unaffected interest in their highest welfare. His labors were fruitful in good results, and his character and services are held in affectionate remembrance by all yet spared to us who were privileged to wait on his ministry. You have, no doubt, often noticed how some little foible or eccentricity of a man will be remembered and spoken of by his friends long after more important things are generally forgotten. I find it somewhat so in the case of Dr. Stork. No one has told me anything of any particular sermon he preached, but quite frequently have I heard instances given of his indifference in those early days with regard to matters of personal appearance.

The characteristics of his preaching which appear to be especially remembered are the beauty of diction, which throughout life marked everything that he wrote, and the earnestness of his delivery. A friend has recently told me that he well remembers hearing an old gentleman, long since gone to his rest, in speaking of different ministers, say something like this: "I like to hear Mr. Stork preach. If a man stands in the door of his house, gazing aimlessly about, and quietly ejaculating, as if talking to himself, 'fire, fire,' who pays any attention to him? But if he rushes out into the street, eagerly looking for those whose notice he would attract, and with uplifted arms shouting 'fire, *fire*, FIRE,' it is not likely that he will be very long in getting some response to his calls; and that illustrates just about the difference between Mr. Stork's style of preaching and that of some other men. He evidently feels the importance of his message, of the solemnity of the warnings it is his duty to give, and when he speaks them out to you from the pulpit his whole manner shows that he is in dead earnest about it." Everything that I have ever heard about Dr. Stork's preaching in the first years of his ministry fully accords with this testimony.

The congregation in Winchester was greatly strengthened by Dr. Stork's ministrations, and it was during his residence in Winchester that the ground was purchased for the building of a new church, which was completed and dedicated about three months after his removal.

The attachment which grew up between Dr. Stork and the people of this, his first pastoral charge, was very strong. His resignation, which was unexpected, appears to have been regarded by the congregation as of the nature of a serious calamity. He was formally urged in a long communication, signed by the members of the church council, to reconsider his determination and agree to devote his time and talents to the interests of the Winchester congregation still further, being assured that there would be no difficulty in arranging for increase of salary if that would prove a consideration of any weight in the decision. This document, a copy of which is before me as I write, expresses the highest regard for Mr. Stork personally, and an affectionate appreciation of his labors as a minister, as being "held not only by the congregation but by the whole community of Winchester;" and tells him that the council have resolved to take no action upon his resignation offered a few days before, until they have had opportunity to communicate more fully with him on the subject, hoping that he would ultimately decide to continue with them.

This appeal, in connection no doubt with many made by officers and members of the congregation in personal interviews, had the desired effect upon Mr. Stork. He was not prevailed upon not to go to Philadelphia, for he appears to have committed himself too fully to the people of St. Matthew's for that; but he was induced to enter into an engagement to return to the Winchester church either in the spring, or at furthest at the close of one year's service in St. Matthew's. This arrangement was concluded after Mr. Stork's departure, for I find in the records a copy of a letter from the council, addressed to him at Philadelphia in October, 1844, which says, "Your favor accepting again the charge of the church in Winchester was duly received," and in which Mr. Stork is assured of "the sincere and ardent satisfaction of the congregation at the prospect," etc. Our congregation here, in view of this engagement, engaged the late Rev. Jas. R. Keiser as a supply until the time appointed for Mr. Stork's return.

But the arrangement, as you know, was never carried out. At a meeting of the Winchester church council, held May 4th, 1842, a letter from Mr. Stork was presented, in which he asked to be released from his engagement for reasons therein set forth; whereupon, by resolution, he was unanimously released, and the council, "collectively and individually tendered him, as their friend and former pastor, their best wishes for a speedy restoration to health, and for his future usefulness in his present field of labor."

Yours truly, D. M. Gilbert.

CHAPTER III.

REMOVAL TO PHILADELPHIA—PASTOR OF ST. MATTHEW'S—REVIVAL SYSTEM—LETTERS FROM PARISHIONERS—HIS OWN LETTERS—SECRETARY OF GENERAL SYNOD—SCENE IN A COUNTRY CHURCH—LETTER FROM CHARLESTON IN 1850—DESCRIPTION OF A VOYAGE—FORMATION OF EAST PENNSYLVANIA SYNOD IN 1841—ORGANIZATION OF ST. MARK'S—CALL TO NEWBERRY, S. C.

EARLY in 1840, the second Lutheran church in Germantown, Pa., since served so many years by Rev. Dr. L. E. Albert, called Mr. Stork as pastor, but he declined accepting it.

In 1841, he was elected pastor of St. Matthew's church in New street, Philadelphia, as the successor of Rev. Mr. Mealey. This church was founded and built under the ministerial care of Rev. C. P. Krauth, sr., who began his arduous work in the upper room of what was then known as the Academy, corner of Fourth and Arch streets. It was a struggle from the beginning to the consummation. Mr. Krauth labored faithfully amid many discouragements, receiving no sympathy from the German churches, and very little from the only English one then in Philadelphia. Many men would have succumbed under this heavy responsibility and unpromising enterprise, but that man of delicate frame and feeble voice had an iron will, sanctified by divine grace, and a perseverance in the accomplishment of a good object that could not be intimidated.

Mr. Stork accepted this call and removed to Philadelphia in September, 1841.

He here had a wider field of operation—he was thrown into new associations—there were many other first-class preachers in that city but he had four years' experience, and he was young and vigorous and ardent. He had a holy ambition to succeed in his new field, and he had the happiness of seeing his church growing steadily, and many strong friends gathering around him. It was at that time the only English Lutheran church in Philadelphia, besides St. John's in Race street, and was not in a locality most favorable to progress; but with this disadvantage, and others which need not be mentioned, he soon filled his house of worship with an attentive and attached congregation. He took an active interest in the religious movements of the day, and freely co-operated with other ministers in the promotion of our common Christianity.

It was the day when the revival system was popular in nearly all the churches, and when remarkable religious excitement extensively prevailed. Numerous meetings were held all over the country; and although extravagances among a certain class of people seemed unavoidable, and some ministers even were sometimes drawn into the use of measures of doubtful expediency, still there is no doubt that thousands of persons heard the truths of the gospel impressively set forth who were not regular church goers, and many were induced to ask how to be saved, who before were indifferent. Even if hundreds of professed converts did not keep their vows, yet hundreds more did, and died or still live in the faith. Superficial profession and presumed conversion are inseparable from extensive religious excitement, and the great mistake of those days, and indeed of any "revival," is the neglect of teaching these converts the doctrines of the gospel as catechumens before admitting them to the full privileges of the church. If we who practiced the system to a greater or less extent had formed catechetical classes of these people and taught them as we do our catechumens, we would not have had so many apostacies to lament.

When Mr. Stork accepted the pastorate of St. Matthew's, he adopted the revival system with vigor. A pious mother in Israel remembers the time, "when in that church, heads of families and young and old were irresistibly drawn to the altar, and the aisles were filled up with anxious, penitent souls. Strangers, even young and thoughtless, could hardly remain in their pews, so evidently was the power of the Holy Ghost manifested. This state of things continued during his whole pastorate, until the new church in Spring Garden street was completed, and there he continued his earnest appeals to sinners, and he could not rest satisfied unless he felt that the presence of God was with his labors. The people were devoted to their pastor, and would walk long distances to attend every service during the week."

This witness to his fidelity thus continues: "I have felt it to be my duty for a long time to bear testimony for the glory of God and to encourage my dear pastor by telling what divine grace can do and has done in answer to our prayers, and especially to a mother's, and how God has blessed a mother and her eight children. Consecrated to God by prayer and baptism, and when they were capable of receiving instruction, they were taught the doctrines of the gospel and their duties as Christians from Luther's Catechism by Mr. Stork, and confirmed by him, and ever since they have followed Christ."

EXTRACTS FROM A FEW OF THE MANY LETTERS WRITTEN BY DR. STORK TO HIS FORMER PARISHIONERS AT WINCHESTER.

PHILADELPHIA, January 12, 1841.

After some apologies for his delay in answering the dear sister's letter, he proceeds:

I must tell you what the Lord has done for us here. I have been having a protracted meeting for nearly three weeks in St. Matthew's, and the Lord has blessed us, beyond even the measure of our faith. During the meeting there have been upward of fifty anxious souls who have asked "what they must do to be saved." Nearly forty have professed a change of heart. And last Sunday I received upwards of thirty into the church by confirmation, baptism, and certificate. The work is still going on—preaching every night, and anxious meeting every afternoon. I believe there were sixteen at anxious meeting this afternoon.

But with all this good news, I am sorry to say I have been much afflicted in body for the last three weeks. In fact, my lungs are affected. I have scarcely had an undisturbed night's rest during the meeting. My general health is bad. Next week I intend to have my chest examined by one of the best physicians in this country, and if he should confirm my present apprehensions, I do not know what I shall do.

Well now, I suppose you desire to know when I intend coming to Winchester. What shall I say? I am not unwilling to fulfill my promise, but if my health continues to decline, I could do but little good. But spring will determine the matter. I have not yet told any of the congregation here of my engagement, for fear it would injure my usefulness.

Have C., H., and V. become pious? I have prayed for them all. O, that they would remember their Creator in the days of their youth. Several about the age of V. came out during the meeting here, and are now rejoicing in the Saviour.

* * * * * * *

PHILADELPHIA, December 10th, 1842.

Your kind letter came to me as a comforter in the gloomy hours of affliction. For the last three or four days I have been confined to my chamber and bed, with a bilious attack. You must never consider your letters as an intrusion; no, they are to me the most welcome messengers. They, as if by one magic touch, open up the whole of the reminiscences of Winchester. I feel soothed; it is a luscious melancholy like that produced by the sweet and simple songs of my childhood. I assure you that I am exceedingly delighted to receive a letter from any of my friends, but more especially from one who always sympathized with me in my ministerial difficulties, and gave me so many tokens of friendship and Christian affection. It is true I am not always prompt in responding to letters that I receive, but that is owing to the incessant pressure of ministerial duties, and sometimes to a natural negligence which has nothing to do with the heart.

As you rejoice in the conversion of sinners everywhere, I must give you a little account of our meeting. I kept up a meeting in St. Matthew's for three weeks without interruption. We had not as extensive a work as last winter, but we have reason to be thankful for what has been done. Eighteen or twenty professed conversion during the meeting, and the church was greatly revived. But at present I am unable to preach, and indeed my system for some time has been prostrated. I expect I will have to go to the country yet, and take a charge where I would have riding on horseback and exercise in the open air.

It would be useless for me to say that nothing would afford me more real satisfaction than to be present and participate in the solemn exercises of the consecration. O, it would indeed be an intellectual and spiritual feast! But what could I do as I now am? I would be utterly unable to engage in the exercises of the occasion.

I would write more, but my head feels as if it were bursting.

* * * * * * *

PHILADELPHIA, February 19th, 1844.

Nothing can give me such unmingled satisfaction as to hear from time to time of one and another of my old friends giving themselves to the Lord. I rejoice in the intelligence that Mr. J. H. and Mr. P. M. have professed their faith in the Son of God. Congratulate them for me, and tell them for me to endure hardness as good soldiers of the cross, and I will pledge myself, by the grace of God, to meet them, and all my pious friends in Winchester, at the right hand of the Judge, and stand together upon Mount Zion, inhaling immortal joys.

I was gratified with the effusions of piety in your letter, and you must pardon me when I tell you that I repeated some of the sentiments of your letter in our prayer-meeting. Of course, I did not mention your name. When I was in Virginia a few weeks ago, I cast a longing look towards Winchester, but it was impossible to indulge the luxury of a visit at that time. I was on a wedding excursion, and was obliged to return before Sabbath.

* * * * * * *

I am happy in knowing that you are now supplied with a pastor whose labors are universally satisfactory, and which, by the blessing of the Great Head of the Church, will be productive of great and permanent good. And I feel some satisfaction in the reflection that I did all in my power to secure his valuable services for the church so dear to my heart.

We are, I think, in a healthful and prosperous condition. But in consequence of my health, I have not been able to hold any protracted meetings this winter. The doctor urged upon me the necessity of leaving the city, and taking some charge in the country. But how can I again rupture the ties that have been formed? And yet, if there is no change for the better, I will be compelled to submit. If I remain here, how gladly will I welcome you in our midst, and do all in my power to make your stay the most happy.

PHILADELPHIA, June 24, 1844.

Since the receipt of your letter there has been quite a revolution in my temporal position—I have at length entered upon the hitherto untried pleasures of housekeeping. I am now comfortably lodged and boarded in my own house, and as the old saying is, place my feet under my own table. I assure you I find it quite a change for the better. I have everything that I desire of this world, and if kind Providence will now deign to add the blessing of heaven to the grace of God, enable me to glorify *Him*, who loved me and gave Himself for me, I shall have all for which I care and pray. One of the greatest pleasures of housekeeping, is the opportunity it furnishes for the exercise of hospitality. I have felt it already, and I can assure you, nothing will afford me greater pleasure than to entertain any of my Winchester friends in whose kind rich hospitality I have so richly shared. * * * * * * * * *

This is quite a chapter on housekeeping—but as it is quite a novelty with me, you will excuse this exuberance of feeling.

I am happy to hear from time to time of your increasing prosperity in the church. Bro. S—— is a man whose worth will increase in your estimation the longer you know him. He has rare excellencies as a man and preacher. And I am sure, from what I know of you all, you will appreciate his merits and love him most dearly. Our church matters are prosperous, though nothing special. I expect to have quite an addition at our next communion. There seems to have been rather a spiritual barrenness throughout the churches during the last year. But I think God has been teaching us a lesson which it was important for the church to learn, and which will ultimately be attended with greater and richer blessings to Zion.

I would gladly accept your invitation to spend part of the summer with you. But it is probable I shall not be able to travel this summer. I must be more economical. If I leave at all, it will be only for a few weeks. So that I shall not enjoy the happiness of spending some time in Winchester *this* summer.

HOME CORRESPONDENCE.

NEW YORK, May 13th, 1848.

Sunday Evening: We had (at the meeting of the General Synod) a most precious and soul edifying Sabbath. In the morning Dr. Bachman, of Charleston, preached a most thrilling and rousing sermon. He is in the evening of life, but seems to possess the fervor, and fire, and enthusiasm of youth. In the afternoon we had a Synodical Communion. There, around the altar, knelt about fifty ministers of Jesus Christ—the hoary headed and the young from all parts of the United States. To me, and I believe to all, it was deeply affecting and impressive. I wept like Mary at the feet of Jesus, and I rejoiced like Peter on the Mount of Transfiguration. Harris remarks, "The nearer we are drawn to the cross the closer we are bound to His people." I felt this to-day. Just as in the natural world, the nearer the great centre of gravitation the greater the power of cohesive attraction, so the nearer the cross, the great central point of spiritual gravitation, the closer the affinity and cohesion of souls.

I shall be full of business and perplexity while here, as the Synod has appointed me Secretary—it is a very laborious business.* I hope to return on Wednesday, so as to give me Thursday to finish my lecture on Poetry in the evening.

HARPER'S FERRY, Aug. 4, 1848.

I am here—a place which Jefferson said was worth a trip across the ocean to see. I rose this morning early to see the sun rise over the mountains, and as the rosy morn flushed with a golden radiance the summit of the hoary mount, I thought of Coleridge, who, as he stood in the vale of Chamouny, looking up at the sky-pointing Alps, exclaimed: "Who sunk thy sunless pillars deep in earth?" etc.

My soul was filled with silent praise as I stood at the base of the mountain and looked up to its top, all sparkling in the morning sun. There was something profoundly humiliating,

---

* The Doctor had the misfortune to lose a good portion of his manuscript, and parts of the Proceedings were made up and printed from memory.—J. G. M,

and yet sublimely elevating, in the thought that I through Christ was permitted to feel myself a child of Him, "who looketh upon the mountains and they tremble, and toucheth the hills and they smoke," and, with filial endearment and trust, to look up through all the beauties and sublimities of nature, and say, "My Father made them all. Behold what manner of love the Father hath bestowed on us, that we should be called sons of God."

BALTIMORE, August 22, 1848.

Sabbath: I was detained up the country; went to church in a most retired part of Baltimore county, enjoyed the Sabbath very much. In the evening I went to a Methodist church; the minister did not come, the members conducted a prayer-meeting. An *old Israelite* got up and gave out the hymn—"A charge to keep I have," etc. He made some very simple remarks, and my heart melted, and I wept. Then they sang—"When I can read my title clear," etc., to a good old tune. I could stand it no longer; I rose from my seat, and went forward to the man conducting the meeting and told him I would like to say something. I felt an irresistible impulse to speak something of *Jesus* to the people. I spoke, I believe, nearly three quarters of an hour with tears and affection. One of Dr. Plumer's members from the city was out staying at the same hotel with me. He told me afterwards, it was one of the happiest meetings he was ever at—that he wept like a child all the time, and that all around him were bathed in tears. It seemed to *me* that God *moved* me to go to that meeting and to speak. I felt as if I could never tire of speaking to people of the wonders of redeeming love *yesterday*. I had a long talk with a poor old negro man about the Saviour. He was very ignorant, but I tried to urge him to seek Jesus by turning from all his sins, and loving Him with all his heart. He seemed very much affected, and promised me to begin to pray that night. I assure you, dearest, I would rather be the poorest minister of Jesus than to be emperor of the world. I believe I felt a thrill of pleasure and sublimity of joy beside that old negro man, such as no earthly distinction or glory could ever impart.

In 1850, he was a member of the General Synod, which met in Charleston, S. C., and this is the proper place to insert the following:

LETTER TO MRS. STORK.

CHARLESTON, April 27, 1850.

The fresh and balmy breathing of the ocean, and the songs of the morning birds, remind me that I am writing to my wife, from the sunny South. But you are anxious to know about our trip, and the first impressions of Charleston. I felt sad after leaving you, lest you should be lonely when I was gone. And yet you appeared so happy that I was reconciled to what was before me. At Washington we met twelve or thirteen of our ministers on their way to Synod, and with such company the hours fled as rapidly as the rolling cars. We traveled all day and night. At Wilmington, N. C., we took the steamboat about two o'clock p. m., on Thursday. From this point we had one hundred and sixty miles on the ocean. This was unexpected by me. It was a glorious sail upon the ocean. It was moonlight, and everything above us and around us was rich and vocal with the glory of God. Some of the brethren wished me whilst standing upon the upper deck, with the gorgeous heavens above us pearled round with glittering stars, and the hoar ocean, with its wild waste of waters and eternal roar, was rolling beneath and around us—under these circumstances, the brethren wished me to repeat that sublime apostrophe to the ocean, by the English bard, beginning,

> "Roll on, thou deep and dark blue ocean, roll. . . .
> Thou glorious mirror where the Almighty's form
> Glasses itself in tempests," etc.

And then that couplet in which the poet expresses the unchangeableness of the ocean, I think one of the finest specimens of the truly poetical:

> "Time writes no wrinkles on thy azure brow;
> As creation's dawn beheld thee, thou rollest now."

It was to me a night of unusual enjoyment: my soul seemed to expand and swell with devout astonishment and praise at the wonderful works of the Lord. I felt the insignificance of man in the presence of these outshadowings of the Almighty, and yet an unspeakable delight, yea, ecstasy in the thought, "My Father made them all."

But yet there is only a step often from the sublime to the ridiculous. When the passengers began to feel that strange impulse from within to pay their devotions to Neptune, it was ludicrous enough to all but the victims. After the early part of the evening passed, and I had been wrapped in thoughts and feelings such as described above, I was taken sick, and spent a miserable night. I was too sick almost to live. It was dreadful: wearily passed the sleepless night; the sea was rough, and the ship rolled and tossed upon the dashing billows. We arrived here about nine o'clock on Friday morning.

FORMATION OF EAST PENNSYLVANIA SYNOD.

When he settled in Philadelphia in 1841, there was but one Lutheran Synod in that State east of the Susquehanna. The proceedings at the meetings were for the most part conducted in the German language, which some of the young clergy did not clearly understand; but this of itself would not have been regarded as a sufficient ground for a division.

A "Broadside," with the title of "Thoughts on the Formation of a New Synod in the Eastern District of Pennsylvania" (said to have been written by Prof. Reynolds), was circulated, which contained what were regarded as very strong reasons for the proposed measure.*

The first meeting for the purpose of considering the expediency of forming this new Synod was held in Lancaster, May 2, 1842, during the meeting of the parent

---

* This document has become very scarce, but a copy may be consulted in the rooms of the Historical Society, Gettysburg.

Synod, at which ten ministers and three laymen were present. A memorial to the Synod of Pennsylvania was adopted and presented, but the Synod resolved that " they would in nowise consent to a division of this body, but should any brethren consider it desirable to separate from us, an honorable dismission shall be given them as individuals, if they so request."

Upon this action of the mother Synod, nine ministers and two lay delegates withdrew to the lecture-room, when the Evangelical Lutheran Synod of East Pennsylvania was organized, and all provision was made for a permanent constitution and all other features of a regularly-constituted ecclesiastical body.

It was resolved to meet as a new Synod in Lebanon,* on September 15, 1842. At the first regular meeting eleven ministers and four lay delegates were recognized as members.

At this meeting a communication to the President of the new Synod from the President of the Synod of Pennsylvania was submitted to a committee, which animadverted sharply on its spirit and contents. This of course gave offence to the old Synod, which, with other presumed or real grievances, led it to refuse the reception of the delegate of the new Synod to the old, and this delegate was Dr. Stork himself.

At the next meeting of the new Synod he presented a report conveyed in moderate and conciliatory language, although he considered the treatment as very harsh. The action of the Synod upon his report was anything but re-

---

*It was afterwards changed to Pikeland, Chester county.

taliatory, but the breach was widened, and a long controversy ensued.

I dwell so long upon these facts for the purpose of showing Dr. Stork's connection with them, for he subsequently bore a conspicuous part in the protracted newspaper discussion, and thus brought upon himself the severe condemnation of some influential men. But time heals many feuds, and before Dr. Stork died he had the happiness of seeing the revival of a more fraternal feeling between the two Synods, as well as between individual members of them.

As early as 1849, Mr. Stork became dissatisfied with the location of his church in New street, although the congregation was large and the Sunday-school flourishing. Some of the members had moved to the northwestern section of the city, where there was no Lutheran church, and the expediency of establishing one was considered. The result was the purchase of a lot on Spring Garden street, near Thirteenth, and the erection of a splendid house of worship, surmounted by a very tall spire.

He resigned his pastorship of St. Matthew's on August 1, 1850, after eight years' service, and entered upon his duties as pastor of St. Mark's, as it was called.

He was succeeded at St. Matthew's by Rev. Mr. Hutter. At the Synod of October, 1851, he reported a communion list of 120 members, which increased to 205 in 1852.

He resigned his pastorship of St. Mark's in the latter part of 1858 in answer to a call to the Presidency of Newberry College, S. C.; and in the winter of 1859 he proceeded to Newberry, S. C., arriving there on February 22d. He at once entered upon his duties, but he was not inaugurated as President until the meeting of the Synod in the fall. Dr. J. A. Brown was Professor in the Theological department, and these two men, to some extent, interchanged their labors—Mr. Stork giving instruction in Church History and some other theological subjects, while Dr. Brown rendered an equivalent in Greek in college.

During his residence there, Mr. Stork was also elected pastor of the church in the village. He held this position for about six months.

All my efforts to procure information concerning Dr. Stork's special labors and incidents during his brief residence at Newberry, from residents, colleagues and students, have failed.

CHAPTER IV.

ORGANIZATION OF ST. MARK'S IN PHILADELPHIA—RETIREMENT FROM THE PULPIT FOR A YEAR—LETTERS—INCIDENTS.

ORGANIZATION OF ST. MARK'S.

THE following facts connected with the organization of St. Mark's are obligingly furnished by one who took an active part in the enterprise.

Dr. Stork was unanimously elected pastor of St. Matthew's on July 19, 1841, and took charge of the church at a salary of $800 a year. His introductory sermon was on the words 1 Cor. ii. 2: "For I determine not to know any thing among you, save Jesus Christ and Him crucified," which he lived by example and precept all through his life. When he came to us, the Lutheran churches in Philadelphia were not in the most prosperous spiritual condition; but before long Mr. Stork infused new life and energy into St. Matthew's, and raised up a congregation of loving, devoted, useful Christian worshippers. Through his influence and prayers, the Lord sent His Spirit among us. More than forty souls were added to the church, and from that time forward the congregation flourished spiritually as well as financially. He organized Friday evening prayer-meetings, which were well attended; the next step was a Sunday morning prayer-meeting of young men, which resulted in much good. Many young men boldly and honestly came out as leaders in prayer. After two years of his ministry his wife died at Germantown, and he was left with two sons, Charles and William. This was a heavy affliction for our pastor, but he did not murmur against the decree of heaven, but endured it with calm Christian resignation. After the lapse of several years he married Miss Emma Baker, of Philadelphia, a most estimable, intelligent Christian lady.

About the year 1844, Mr. Stork conceived the idea that the people of St. Matthew's should extend their borders in an effort to organize a Sunday-school in the northern section of the city, and several brethren were appointed to carry out the work. They met with encouraging success, and within five years a very fine brick church was erected, and a very respectable congregation gathered, and all this was the result of Mr. Stork's untiring energy and fervent Christian zeal.

In the beginning of the year 1850 he held a consultation in reference to organizing a new enterprise in the western part of the city. An interest was at once awakened in it, and we agreed to call a meeting through the public papers, inviting all Lutherans and others who felt concerned to meet us. The first meeting was attended by twenty-four persons. The second call brought out a larger number. At this meeting a man and his wife, entire strangers to us all, met with us, and she was the only woman present. We made ourselves known to them, and treated them very politely. He told me that he had not been inside of a church for thirty years, but that he had noticed this call, and stranger as he was to us all, he had determined to attend. The kindness we showed him impressed him deeply, and he resolved to cast his lot among us. He became one of our most active, useful and exemplary members.

Our first measure was to establish a Sunday-school in Brotherly Love Hall. This was about March, 1850. The school continued to prosper until we moved into the lecture-room, which was consecrated on the second Sunday of February, 1851, by Rev. Dr. B. Kurtz.

From that time our school and church membership increased rapidly, and it was not until then that Mr. Stork was called to take charge of the church, although it was thus intended. The majority of the people of St. Mark's was made up of the district surrounding it; a number of Methodists, a few Presbyterians, and one Roman Catholic, united with us. The number of families from St. Matthew's, the mother church, which joined us was not over twelve or thirteen, although the whole congregation generously stood by and encouraged us; the credit of financial help principally belongs to St. Matthew's, although a portion of the funds also came from other sources.

The church named St. Mark's was completed and consecrated in the summer of 1851. All went on very smoothly until 1854, when Doctor Stork's health began to break down from overwork, and he resigned. Doctor Charles A. Smith was called to supply his place. In the course of a year or two, Doctor Stork's health was partially restored, and the congregation desired that he should return, and he yielded to their wishes.

His standing as a minister among other ministers and

denominations was very high, and he was an eminently useful man.

The following, without place or date or name of person addressed, evidently has reference to the new enterprise of St. Mark's, in Philadelphia:

TUESDAY (no date).

I must meet a committee of St. Mark's to-day. I feel that to unfold my heart to them would dispel the clouds that seem to hang over my soul. There is an unaccountable tendency to depression. The future is full of darkness. My only refuge is in God, and my soul is refreshed in the shadow of the Cross. After prayer this morning it seemed as if all my sadness were gone. I feel happy. I have such a clear conviction that God is going to take me through a school, for the disciplining of my spirit and the perfection of my Christian character. And even trials, and disappointments, and crosses, seem as blessings. I feel happy that, through even such a process, my proud heart may be humbled and my lofty imaginations be made low. Pray for me, that I may not only succeed in building up a new church for Christ, but in doing that I may gain a new heart, and my soul be renovated and purified, and made a temple indeed for Christ, beautified with salvation and adorned with all the grace of the Spirit. This, I had such a sweet assurance this morning, is what the Lord is going to do, that I could not tell you the happiness I feel.

LETTER TO HIS SON, THEN A STUDENT.

PHILADELPHIA. Nov. 14, 1854.

DEAR CHARLES * * * * *

I am glad too, that you feel how unfit and unworthy you are in prospect of the holy office of the ministry. If you did not feel so, it would argue in you a want of a due estimate of the work, and would indeed evidence a moral unfitness for the ministry. You say you cannot go alone. You are not required; Jesus still says, "Lo, I am with you." You are nothing in your own strength, but you have God's truth, which is mighty, to proclaim, and you have the promise of the Holy Ghost to give efficacy to that truth, and Jesus the Almighty Saviour, to be with you and help you in every time of need. I would rather be the humblest minister in the land, to preach the gospel to perishing sinners. One soul won to Christ and heaven, is worth more than all the world, beside which the honors and wealth of the world are but weeds and rags. But never mind the future — only cultivate faith and love, and all piety and prayer, casting all your care upon God, and take no thought for the morrow. Improve your time both in the culture of the mind and the heart, and leave the rest to God.

RETIREMENT FROM THE PULPIT FOR A YEAR.

In the spring of 1854 he began to feel the effects of constant and protracted labor, and he was advised by his physician to abandon his pulpit ministrations and pastoral work for a year, and engage in some employment which would compel him to live much of his time in the open air. He assumed an office most uncongenial to his tastes, against which his friends should have vehemently protested. The idea that the poetical, the imaginative, the versatile Stork should have been content for a whole year to tie himself down to a subject of common facts and figures, and repeat them every Sunday, was absurd. However useful and important the cause may be, he was the last man in the world to be entrusted with it. The irksomeness of repetition was of itself enough to break him down; and although he had a different audience every time he presented the subject, yet it was the same unvarying theme, and this palled upon his refined sensibilities. He had not the incentive of daily bread to stimulate perseverance, nor the wants of the needy at home to urge him on to energetic action. Nor did the necessary absence from home, which this work required, suit his domestic tastes or his habits of reading, or his sense of duty to those he loved to meet at the home fireside. He soon gave it up, a wiser if not a better man. We are not all fitted to all kinds of Christian work. Many a most efficient tract society secretary would have been as much out of place in Mr. Stork's pulpit as he was in the performance of the routine work of a secretary's office, or in the presentation of the same subject five or six times in a month.

Rev. Charles A. Smith served St. Mark's for the year of Mr. Stork's unsatisfactory engagement with the Tract Society. He resumed the pastoral care of St. Mark's in the summer of 1855, and the following year he reported a communion list of 375 members. It was here also that the "New Measure" system, then so popular, was practiced, and large numbers attended these extra meetings. He was highly esteemed by his own people, and gained the admiration of many who were not members of his church.

He was not backward in promptly rebuking what he deemed unseemly conduct in the house of God, as we have already seen when speaking of him while yet a student, and a correspondent from Illinois communicates the following instance which is worthy of insertion. He thus writes: "On my first visit to Philadelphia, now thirty-three years ago, I sought out the then youthful congregation of the popular preacher, Mr. Stork, in Spring Garden street. To my great disappointment another man preached, and closely read a long sermon, and the people seemed to be impatient, especially when Mr. Stork rose and began some announcements and general remarks relative to the church. The people became more uneasy and restive, indicating a desire to be dismissed without delay. This unbecoming manifestation roused him, and he settled them down more quickly and effectually than I have ever seen before or since. He rose to his full height, and elevating his right hand, he exclaimed in ringing tones, 'You can sit in theatres and concerts till 11 or 12 o'clock at night and show no signs of weariness, but when the unspeakable interests of your souls are being considered, your patience is soon exhausted.' Immediately all was silent as death—no motion, no cough, not a stir—and he calmly proceeded to speak to a very attentive congregation."

The following letter belongs to this period:

PHILADELPHIA, March 4th, 1856.

I have an earnest desire to be a sincere and faithful minister of Jesus Christ. I think I have lost all aspiration for mere fame—it is but a bubble. But a true, a devoted disciple of Jesus, to be a faithful preacher of His gospel, this is now the burning desire, the highest ambition of my heart. Pray for your unworthy husband. I say unworthy, because I feel such a painful consciousness that I am not worthy of the love of my friends, much less worthy of the infinite love of God.

* * * * * * *

I never had such deep self-abasement before God as in prayer last night, and yet the communion was sweet and refreshing.

INCIDENTS.

Doctor Stork had a brother who was a successful business man, and who wished him to become a lawyer, offering to defray his expenses and to establish him in an office, but he felt his call to the ministry to be imperative.

This brother at his death bequeathed to Doctor Stork and his sister, the only surviving members of the family, a large estate, but by some mischance little of it found its way to the pockets of either.

A curious accident befell the little sum that came as the Doctor's share. The bank note was divided into two parts to be sent North, and each part was sent separately to avoid risk of loss. Through his carelessness one-half of the note got into the waste-basket, where the housekeeper found and rescued it.

At another time, he made an engagement to preach in a church at one of our popular seaside resorts. The church was crowded; all were waiting patiently for the sermon; but just at that moment the unfortunate preacher discovered that a stout brother had sat down upon his spectacles and smashed them. This was indeed a dilemma. But he was equal to the occasion, and performed his task, if not to his own comfort, at least to the satisfaction of all who listened to him.

A cherished friend had presented him with a neat diamond breastpin. He used to say: "You know how I feel about that pin." Well, he summoned courage to wear it once or twice. The last time was on a lecture occasion. He was about to rise up to speak when he suddenly remembered that pin, and what did he do, but snatch it out and put it into his vest pocket?

Usually, mornings and evenings were devoted to study

and writing, afternoons to pastoral visits. He was like an electric bell at the call of duty, so prompt and ready.

It was often quite amusing to see his delight when he would say, "I have now settled all my debts," and even if not a cent remained in his house, he was content. He often said, we all had as much as we needed of this world's goods, and he was thankful for and satisfied with his allotment. He took great comfort in his children, and it was his pleasure to train and educate them for their life work.

DECEMBER, 1857.

DEAR CHARLIE:—I have received intelligence of the death of my only sister, Mrs. Brougher; she died in the triumph of faith, exclaiming "Come, Lord Jesus, come quickly." All the members of my father's family are now in heaven except myself, and I hope by the grace of God to meet them, and then we shall constitute a renewed family—no wanderer lost—a glorious hope.*

---

*Mrs. B———, lived in Mississippi. Students of Pennsylvania College in 1841-46, may remember a tall young Southerner in college of this name. He was the son of the lady here spoken of, and of course the nephew of Mr. Stork. There could not have been more than 10 years or so difference in their ages. It surprises some to hear that a young man all the way from Mississippi, very distant at that day, should come to Gettysburg to college. But his father was one of the first subscribers to the *Lutheran Observer* in its beginning, and always cherished a warm interest in the church and sent his son all the way to Gettysburg to school.

CHAPTER V.

PRESIDENT OF NEWBERRY COLLEGE—REASONS FOR ACCEPTING—LETTERS TO HIS WIFE—HIS EXPERIENCE AND TRIALS—HIS HEALTH FAILS—VISIT TO THE NORTH—LETTERS—RESOLVES NOT TO RETURN—DR. STORK AS AN OBSERVER OF THE LORD'S DAY—LETTERS.

PRESIDENCY OF NEWBERRY COLLEGE.

THERE was a college, as well as a theological seminary established at Newberry, South Carolina. In 1858, neither was provided with a President. Both institutions were governed by the same Trustees, and they earnestly urged Dr. Stork to cast in his lot with theirs, and allowed him the privilege of assuming either position, deeming him well qualified for both. He preferred the college Presidency and accepted the call. He did not like to give up the pulpit, and it was the universal opinion of his friends that the pulpit was his legitimate place. They knew he could preach, but they doubted whether he could manage a school. They doubted also whether the monotony of carrying out the old-fashioned college curriculum would suit his tastes, always concerned about the inspiring and the new.

But his health began to be seriously impaired about this time, and a painful nervousness, occasioned by an accident, induced him to believe that a residence in the South would be beneficial.

The following letter from a member of his family is pertinent. It may be interesting to know the circumstances which led to Dr. Stork's acceptance of the Presidency of Newberry College, South Carolina. His health received a severe shock—the result of an accident during his summer sojourn in Chesnut Hill—which is detailed in the following letter:

LETTER RELATING TO NEWBERRY.

PHILADELPHIA, Nov. 5, 1858.

My Dear Charles: I am happy to find you so responsive to my suggestions in relation to the South. I feel a longing for some position in which I could prosecute my studies, and at the same time be devoted to the church and the glory of God. Such a position is now offered to me, and I feel disposed to accept it. It will cost a painful struggle to break the bonds that bind me here. But having my whole family with me, I think I should be perfectly happy almost anywhere. I expect to go South next week and view the place and property, and after my return will decide the matter. Let us pray, Charles, that God may guide us in this important decision. * * * * * * *

Yours in the bonds of fatherly love, T. STORK.

Nov. 22.

P. S.—I have been to the South. I was delighted with almost everything. The town of Newberry is a very pleasant place. The college building is beautiful. They will have nearly $50,000 endowment and the building paid for—a fair beginning. They expect a large number of students. They want an assistant in the preparatory department by the first of January. How would you like the position? You can get it if you want it. Let me know your feelings about going South. It is a hard struggle for me to decide. How can I leave my people? If I knew the Lord's will I would not hesitate one moment. Write to us soon, and give us your opinion. If I go I wish to have my whole family. Newberry has the best society in South Carolina, and that is saying a good deal.

Mother has been poorly. Physicians think a Southern climate would be advantageous to her. Write. Mother and Willie send their love to you.

Yours affectionately, T. S.

LETTERS TO HIS WIFE.

NEWBERRY, January 26, 1859.

Dearest: I have been trying to live near to the Cross—with Jesus abiding in me—I do hunger and thirst after righteousness. That text, the other morning, has subdued me to humility and tears before God. "As the Father hath loved me, *so* have I loved you"—O the height and depth of the love of Jesus—O that I could feel my soul filled with this love—Emma, pray for me. My highest *ambition* now is to be a *true, devoted* living servant of Jesus, that Christ may be all in *all.* Last night the Phrenakosmian Society of College had an exhibition in College chapel. The college was lit up—fine effect—the chapel was crowded. If I had not known where I was, I might have supposed myself at Concert Hall; as fine a set of ladies and gentlemen as I ever saw in a Philadelphia concert. It was beautiful—performers all German. The speaking was highly creditable, students all well dressed, and I felt proud of Newberry College.

NEWBERRY, May 24, 1859.

Charles tries to help me, and when any of the Professors are unwell he takes their place. He heard the Greek class for Mr. Brown. He was delighted with him. Mr. Brown says he can recommend him fully for the Greek professorship. He will have only Greek. He will have time to finish his theological studies and preach on the Sabbath. He is very much pleased with Newberry.

FRIDAY EVENING.

We had an excellent meeting on Wednesday night. There was a good deal of solemnity—O, that the Lord would come into our midst and revive His work—O, that the many careless and impenitent sinners here might be brought to Jesus!

NEWBERRY, S. C., May 9, 1859.

I was 14 miles in the country. Had an immense gathering. The people everywhere received me with the most cordial greeting, and so far as they can help, will sustain our Institution. I came across a man settled in life—with four children—who feels called to preach the Gospel. He is wealthy, with a splendid plantation, and everything around him in the most comfortable style. But, he says, he must give up all for Christ, and I believe he will come to our Institution and study several years. Mr. Brown and I have begun our protracted meetings here. Preaching every night this week, and communion next Sabbath. With our other duties this is pretty hard work; I feel exhausted at night. Pray the Lord for our meeting, that some souls may be given to the Saviour.

College buildings are paid for. About $50,000 endowment. *One hundred and twenty students*—quite a number of talented and promising young men.

Theological Seminary.—Four theological students in actual preparation, four or five in college who are looking forward to the ministry. The Seminary has an endowment of its own of $23,000. I have letters informing me of a large number of students from Charleston, Georgia, and Mississippi, for next fall.

NEWBERRY, S. C., May 31, 1859.

We had our second communion yesterday. There was a crowded church and great solemnity. . . . . . The Lord was with us. There are many in this community deeply impressed. On Sunday morning, after church, I felt prompted to go and visit a very genteel-looking colored man who had been attending all our meetings. I found him concerned about his salvation, and I spoke to him of Jesus and salvation. He was deeply moved, and promised to give his entire attention to the deliverance of his soul. . . . . . We now have morning and evening prayers in the chapel. This new feature in the college gives new interest to our daily duties. . . . . . I am kept very busy from morning to night. I have so many speeches and essays to criticise that my hands are full.

NEWBERRY, S. C., June 8, 1859.

Things proceed rather monotonously here—in the outer world; the inner world of thought and feeling is in constant change. In my daily studies novelties present themselves at every step. In my religious experience I trust that daily there is to my soul some new phase of the Divine love. Here, after all, is the only true and satisfying portion. The man is truly blessed who can say from a sincere heart, and joyfully: "Whom have I in heaven but Thee, and there is none upon earth that I desire beside Thee."

By the way, Charles preached on Sunday night, on the text—"Seek ye first the kingdom of God and His righteousness, etc." It was a beautiful, I may say masterly, production. He wrote it in a very short time, sitting in my study. Mr. Brown is very much taken with Charles. . . . . . He has very refined feelings, and seems devotional—in reading the Scriptures and in secret prayer. He will think for himself, and will not be governed by the opinions of persons who are swayed by prejudices.

NEWBERRY, S. C., June 15, 1859.

I believe this separation, though painful, will do me good. Yes, it has done me good, I feel drawn to the Lord—to my Saviour—in my loneliness, and I can, in some humble way, say as Jesus: "And yet I am not alone, for the Father is with me." I long for that perfect love which casteth out fear; for that joyous assurance—that abiding in Christ—that conscious *oneness* with Christ—that I may always be happy, feeling that whether living or dying I am the Lord's. O, that I could reach the spiritual attitude of Paul, when he said: "For me to live is Christ, and to die is gain."

We had a hard week—I mean the last. We preached every night, and employed the intervals of the day not engaged in college, in visiting the people and talking to them on the subject of religion. The Lord has answered our prayers and blessed our labors. On Sabbath the church was overflowing—the galleries, usually appropriated to the blacks, were half devoted to the white people for want of room below. Seventeen persons were added to the church. There is, I believe, quite a religious interest in the community. Indeed, we had quite a Pentecostal season. O unite with me in praising the Lord for His goodness, and for His wonderful works to us and this little church.

Next Sabbath I go down to St. Paul's to preach. We think of having another meeting here, and communion. You see I have enough to do; yes, there is a great work to be done here. Pray for me.

He finally concluded that his impaired health would not permit him to remain at Newberry, and he determined to leave. His family was not with him at the time, as the following letters will show; but whether they remained in Newberry or were in Philadelphia, does not appear from the copies of the letters which were put into my hands. Neither is the date of his leaving Newberry given.

LEESBURG, April 24, 1860.

Well, here I am at last after a weary and exhaustive tour. Had I known all the discomforts of such a trip, I should not have left Newberry in such a state of health. I suffered more the last week than during the three weeks of my previous sickness. I staid in Raleigh on Friday night and met a friend from Philadelphia. Saturday, I went to Richmond and remained over Sabbath. I was not able to go further; besides, I could not have reached Washington without breaking in upon the Lord's day, and you know I am a strict observer of that day. I felt very lonely in a city with no acquaintance or friends; indeed, I thought at one time during the day, that I must give up to die, my respiration was so difficult. I committed myself to Jesus, and He brought me through. I went to church and heard a sermon on the "love of Christ passing knowledge." Oh! it was precious to me, the love of Jesus! I could say from my heart, "Had I ten thousand hearts, O, Lord Jesus, I'd give them all to Thee." In the momentary ecstasy of my feelings, I forgot all about my poor lungs, and seemed to breathe the air of heaven, and to see Jesus whom my soul loveth; and I felt, O, if I get well again how I should like to preach:

"To tell poor sinners all around,
What a dear Saviour I have found."

On Monday, I went on to Washington. My friends think I should not go back to South Carolina this session. It is not likely I shall be able to resume my duties before next fall. I feel much relieved and breathe more naturally. I slept well and feel refreshed. The doctor whom I consulted in Washington said there was a tendency to congestion of the lungs, but if I am careful it would pass away. He says I must avoid excitement and speaking for a time, as my heart was implicated by sympathy.

LEESBURG, April 30, 1860.

Thanks to the Lord, He has healed our diseases. I hope we are both better. I bless the Lord I can say to you I am better. But since I began taking medical advice here I have been improving. My chest is very weak—my right lung is laboring under some difficulty. The doctors all agree that it is in part from the fall—there is a painful weakness in that lung, and I fear I shall never be myself fully again. I have had a serious time on Friday night; I was in such a nervous condition, trembling, palpitation of heart, that I thought my time was come. I have rested sweetly in Jesus. He is my strength and portion. O, what a Saviour, for life and death!

His allusion in the preceding letter to his observance of the Lord's day renders the insertion of the following, from his wife, proper at this place:

In Dr. Stork's home-life, *reverence* for holy things, and a strict regard for the holy Sabbath, were marked. At the family altar, and at *meals*, his prayers were always earnest and devout; levity and trifling were instantly checked, although *cheerfulness* and *considerateness* for all around him prevailed. It is remembered that on a little excursion to Chesnut Hill he, with a few friends, visited one of our churches. Some of the lively sisters mounted into the pulpit and began sounding out their voices. Dr. Stork at once testified his disapprobation to the irreverence in the holy place. The rebuke was never forgotten. With him the sanctity of the Sabbath was an imperative duty. He disliked to have *milk* even served on Sunday, and he endeavored to change the custom and give the milkmen opportunity of attending church. Also household work—he objected to have pavements swept off on Sunday, chiefly on account of several families around him, who were *careless* in their observance of the Day of Rest. It was remarkable in one of his genial and impulsive temperament, and the young son, Charles, would come smiling, and say: "Father is having a good time with his friends—how they do enjoy themselves—how *happy these ministers* are."

No interruption was ever allowed to prevent family prayers; no hurry of travel or business caused a neglect of this daily duty. It was a powerful magnet, drawing his children in fondest affection to him, and indeed his entire household. As his health became more impaired, it was pitiable to see his disappointment and his distress when he was unable to attend Divine service. It was a heart-break when his physicians told him he *must* give up preaching—that meant death to his ardent soul. He was most submissive and patient, and said: "Doctor, *my work is done*." His end was peace; his entrance into glory was almost visible, as his countenance beamed with the glad transition as he changed from the mortal to the immortal. One of the watchers said: "*He sees Jesus*"—such a light shone upon his face as the *spirit left the casket.*

It is nowhere stated when he arrived at home from the South, nor where he spent the summer. The following letter will show where he was in November:

LITITZ, November 2, 1860.

I am tried. I fear my friends think me too fickle—but I have always had to contend with a feeble constitution, and you know what a trial it is to work with mind and body, when both are languid and enfeebled. I want to work, and will work while I have strength. I wish to spend and be spent in the service of my Lord and Saviour. I believe the Lord will open new places where I can win souls to Christ, and His blessing still rest upon my feeble labors. The time is short, and we should be willing, in self-denial, to work while it is called to-day. Though often sad, have had precious seasons of communion with God in Christ.

I had quite a return of my difficulty of respiration, keeping me from sleep. It is strange that the pain in my back and the difficulty of breathing come together. I have suffered from both this week. But there is no no use waiting to get perfectly well—I must go to work. I promised to be in Baltimore on Wednesday or Thursday night and preach for them on Sunday. I think I should prefer the *Observer* on your account as well as my own.

I have just received a letter from Brother Hutter informing me of the departure of Dr. Baker.* Alas! such a life! For him, there is nothing to regret; he was a good and faithful man; his work is done, and he has gone to live with Jesus, which is far better . . . . . This news has somewhat saddened me.

DR. STORK REFUSES TO PRINT A VOLUME OF HIS SERMONS.

Among his papers I found the following scrap faintly written in pencil :

A minister from the interior of the State wishes to know whether I could not publish a volume of my sermons.

1. I say emphatically, No! I have scarcely a single sermon that I could publish without re-writing. I never wrote my sermons fully out. I left open places for extempore speaking and illustrations.

2. I think my correspondent is mistaken about the present good they might accomplish. It is one thing to hear a sermon from the pulpit, and another to read it. When you take away the man, the voice, the occasion, the congregation, there may not be much left, at least not enough to justify putting it in

---

* For many years a Lutheran minister in Lancaster, but removed to Philadelphia, where he died in 1860.

print. I remember that once a minister asked me to let him read a sermon which I had preached in his presence. In returning it he said: "I thought it was a very fine sermon when I heard it, but I find it is not much after all."

3. I have now a pulpit to fill in our Monthly,* and all my time is taken up in writing and gathering material for that journal.

I am sorry that I must differ from the brother, and hope he will subscribe for the Monthly and circulate it among his people, instead of wishing a volume of my sermons.

A friend of Dr. Stork's requests me to insert the following fact: "The Doctor once preached a sermon on the authenticity and evidence of the Bible, and the house was crowded by people from different churches, who were so well pleased that many of my Scotch Presbyterian friends asked to have it repeated. With many other interested parties we prevailed on him, and it was repeated with more additional evidence, and the house was jammed."

Another little incident we recall to mind: The Doctor happened to meet one of his charge who seemed to be very much excited about some incident that troubled him, and in his excitement used some naughty words, when the doctor kindly remonstrated with him for giving way to his temper. The man turned and looked at the Doctor, "Why," said he, "Dr. Stork, I have controlled more temper in one week than you have controlled in your life time. Why, Doctor, you never had a temper to control."

---
* He was editor of the *Lutheran Home Journal.*—J. G. M.

CHAPTER VI.

REMOVAL TO BALTIMORE—HISTORY OF ST. MARK'S—LETTER—STATE OF HIS HEALTH—HIS SON CHARLES HIS ASSISTANT—LETTER OF THE COUNCIL—LETTERS—RESIGNATION—RETIRES TO PHILADELPHIA—MISSIONARY ENTERPRISE—CLOSE OF HIS PASTORAL WORK—LETTERS.

REMOVAL TO BALTIMORE IN 1860.

THE First English Lutheran church in Baltimore, then located in Lexington street, between Howard and Park, became vacant by the resignation of the pastor, J. G. Morris, in June, 1860. Immediate steps were taken to elect a successor, and the two principal candidates were Dr. Stork, of Philadelphia, and Dr. McCron, of the Third Lutheran church, on Monument street, Baltimore. Twenty-two ballotings were held before either received a constitutional majority; but after a long and rather excited struggle, Dr. McCron was elected as a temporary supply by a small majority.

One hundred and one of the members were dissatisfied with this result and withdrew, upon which Dr. McCron was chosen permanent pastor by those who remained.

On October 23, 1860, those who separated themselves from the First church held a meeting in the lecture room of the Second Lutheran church on Lombard street, when one hundred and thirteen persons signed a paper declaring their purpose to unite in the organization of a new English Lutheran church.

A provisional Church Council was appointed, and also a committee to invite the Rev. Dr. Stork to become pastor of the new organization about to be formed.

After the adjournment of the meeting, the committee met at the house of Dr. Kemp, when it was determined that there should be no delay in perfecting the new enterprise, and measures were taken to secure a place of worship immediately. In a few days thereafter, the Committee succeeded in renting the Third Presbyterian church in Eutaw street. The Sunday morning and Wednesday evening service was determined to be a joint one between the Lutherans and Presbyterians. The Sunday evening was to be exclusively Lutheran, and the lecture room on Sunday afternoons was free for the Lutheran Sunday-school.

Under this arrangement, the first service of the congregation was held on Sunday evening, November 4, 1860. Rev. Dr. Morris, late pastor of the First church, preached on Gen. xxiv. 56—*Hinder me not, seeing the Lord hath prospered my way.*

Dr. Stork was notified of his unanimous election November, 1860, and was urgently requested to accept it. To the unspeakable gratification of all the members, he gave his consent, and he took charge as pastor on December 1, 1860.

The Presbyterian church on Eutaw street was bought for $10,500, and full possession of it was taken by the congregation in February, 1861.

Dr. Stork now entered upon a new field of labor, and one of peculiar difficulty and uncertain success. True, he had a faithful and devoted membership of over one hundred, but they had just purchased a house of worship at a sum which would perhaps be a burden for years—it required a considerable outlay to renovate it, and superadded to this were the support of the minister and the other expenses of maintaining the worship.

But the people had full confidence in the ability and piety of their pastor, and in reliance upon God, they prayerfully and resolutely engaged in the work.

Dr. Stork fully answered their expectations, and the congregation gradually grew. Their church council were men of energy and prudence; the ladies of the church were active and persevering; their Sunday-school, under the efficient superintendence of the veteran Dr. Kemp; the sympathy of the Second and Third churches; the cordial good will of other evangelical congregations in the city, all cheered this new organization with the hope of ultimate success.

The pastor soon secured the confidence of many of the city ministers, with whom he coöperated in every good work. His amiable disposition, refined manners and godly life gained him friends everywhere, and he soon attained a high rank among all who had the good fortune to know him. He was chosen a member of the boards of management of various religious societies, and showed a lively interest in their work. He was at different times invited to address these societies at their anniversary meetings.

The following letter belongs to this period:

BALTIMORE, November 21, 1861.

* * * * * * * *

I have been very happy for the last three or four days. I think after a great spiritual conflict—after much prayer—I am now peacefully sitting at the feet of Jesus, resigned to His will, ready to suffer for His sake, or to be used in any way for His glory. I feel very happy in the thought that God is chastening me, and is determined to make me more humble and holy. He is touching me in some of my weak points (such as ambition, love of distinction), and taking away the occasions of pride and self-glory, and making me to glory only in Christ. O, if only this results from my trials—I will praise the Lord. For I do feel a yearning to be holy—to be entirely devoted to the Lord—and to rejoice in hope of the glory of God. If only I can be settled, I shall be truly happy. Now that I am fully resigned to the Lord, I feel that He will bless us. Our church is getting on well . . . . . I see some signs of good—here and there the truth is having effect, and I think we shall have some souls for Christ. Glory to God!

LETTER TO HIS COUNCIL—CHARLES, HIS ASSISTANT.

His health suffered from his arduous labors and anxieties, and on February 21, 1862, he thus wrote to the council:

Owing to a chronic affection of my throat and great nervous excitability, I am usually exhausted by one service on the Sabbath. The second is generally arduous and prostrating.

From my past experience, I am led to believe that I ought not to preach more than once on the Sabbath, and that a persistence in two services will shorten the period of my ministerial activity. In view of these facts, I desire an assistant. At present, I have become assistant editor of the *Lutheran Observer*, partly with the view of securing an assistant without any additional expense to the church. I shall thus be able to serve the church in an extension of her usefulness and the cause of truth and righteousness. And if the proposed arrangement meets with your approbation, it will be a grand relief to my mind, as well as enable me, I believe, to prolong my active service in the church and also to be useful through the instrumentality of the religious press. I submit the matter to your prayerful consideration, hoping that you will act deliberately, and do what in your honest judgment will promote the best interests of the church.

This proposition was acceded to, and at the same meeting the Rev. Charles A. Stork was nominated for the position and unanimously approved. It was submitted to a congregational meeting on February 26, 1862, and ratified by all present. It was understood that Dr. Stork generously agreed to pay the salary of his assistant out of his own funds.

HIS RESIGNATION.

For three years this joint pastorship was happily and successfully maintained, when finally Dr. Stork was reluctantly compelled to resign his position, which he did in a very touching letter on May 25, 1865.

Among other things, he says to the Council:

I can assure you that this step has cost me much painful and tearful regret, for my connection with the church has been one of almost unmingled pleasure and satisfaction.

I have received from the people the most gratifying tokens of confidence and affection. I cannot recall a single instance of unkindness to shade the pleasant memories of the last five years. We have labored together in mutual sympathy and affection in the building up of the church and the extension of the Redeemer's kingdom, and the Lord has crowned our united labors with His richest blessing. I shall ever hold the people of St. Mark's in grateful remembrance, and cherish my association with the church among the most pleasant memories of the past.

From this expression of my feelings, you may easily suppose that this step is taken with great reluctance and sincere sorrow. It has been taken from considerations of health; my inability to assume the entire labors of the charge, and my conviction that the best and permanent interests of the church will be promoted by the undivided labors of one pastor. . . . . . . Allow me to assure the council that I shall always feel the deepest interest in the prosperity of St. Mark's. . . . . .

The feelings here expressed by Dr. Stork were heartily reciprocated by the entire congregation, and the parting was mutually sad. But the acceptance of the resignation was unavoidable, for none of the causes given for this course by the pastor could be removed. Complete cessation from all pastoral work, especially owing to his increasingly distressing bronchial affection, was absolutely essential to the preservation of his life.

If there had been no prospect of an acceptable immediate successor, the difficulty and the embarrassment of the separation would have been enhanced, but his accomplished and popular son, Charles, was his assistant, and ready to assume all the duties so ably and satisfactorily performed by his distinguished father.

The son was immediately nominated by the council, which was unanimously ratified at a congregational meeting held on June 14th, 1865.

The reply of the council to Dr. Stork's letter of resignation is here inserted in part:

BALTIMORE, July 5, 1865.

Rev. and Dear Sir: Your resignation as pastor of St. Mark's . . . tendered a few weeks since, having gone into effect on the 1st instant, the Church Council, in behalf of those whom it is their honor and pleasure to represent, beg leave to express to you their profound regret in sundering a tie so endearing as that which has bound us together for nearly five years as pastor and people. Our hearts are too full to calmly sit down and call up in memory the many pleasing incidents of the past—your ministrations in the pulpit every Lord's day, at the weekly meeting, in the schools of the church, at our homes, in every-day life—without feeling overwhelmed and heart-sick in view of the separation.

We can only reconcile ourselves to the event by accepting it as the ordering of the Great Disposer of all things, and humbly pray that it may be sanctified to your good and ours.

We separate as we came together, of one mind and one heart, determined to press on vigorously and trustingly with our new pastor in building up St. Mark's, praying that the Master will bestow upon his labors the same blessing and success which He vouchsafed to his predecessor.

You bear away with you our most ardent wishes for your own and your family's welfare; and if, in the inscrutable ways of Him who doeth all things well, we should be destined to meet no more, God grant that Heaven may witness our reunion!

RETIRES TO PHILADELPHIA.

Dr. Stork retired to Philadelphia, the home of his wife, where he had numerous friends, his former parishioners, and where he could pursue his literary labors without interruption. It was not necessary for him to work for a livelihood, so that he had abundant leisure to follow his own inclinations. But he could not long remain inactive —he always cherished schemes of church progress—he was out of his element when he had no religious enterprise on hand—his nervous temperament demanded incessant action. He was not the man who could devote his whole attention to books or retirement of any character, but he must be stirring, or he would lapse into melancholy.

He conceived the project of establishing a new congregation in the vicinity of Broad and Arch streets. A hall was rented, and soon a small assembly gathered around him, which he organized into a church, which he called St. Andrew's, on New Year day, 1865. The increase was sufficient to authorize the purschase of a lot of ground, which is now occupied by Dr. Seiss' church of the Holy Communion. Some progress was made towards its erection, but difficulties occurred concerning the title to the property, and the enterprise was abandoned. It is doubtful whether, in the condition of his health, he would have been able to endure the labors, anxieties and vexations necessarily growing out of an undertaking of the dimensions contemplated. It was a great relief when he was compelled to abandon it. It would have overtaxed his strength and shortened his days.

Dr. F. W. Conrad was at that time pastor of the Church of the Messiah, and Dr. Stork and his members of St. Andrew's were invited by the people of the Messiah Mission to unite with them, under the joint pastoral care of these two men. This arrangement continued for about a year, but it was found to be inexpedient. Both men were engaged in editorial and other literary pursuits, so that active pastoral work, so essential to a mission, was out of the question, and Dr. Stork retired in 1871;—and here end the pastoral labors of this earnest and warmhearted servant of God, which were prosecuted with success for thirty-six years.

CHAPTER VII.

HIS EDITORIAL AND LITERARY CAREER—DEATH AND BURIAL.

IN 1855, he and Rev. C. A. Smith were editors of a monthly periodical which was called *The Home Journal*. It was intended for plain family reading, and its pages sparkled with gems furnished from the fertile imagination of Dr. Stork; but he was not the man to be perplexed by the drudgery of business or the dull routine of office duties. He soon grew weary of any annoying service outside of the pulpit, and the monotonous yet compulsory work of furnishing at a certain time a specific quantity of literary matter, was irksome. If he could have remained in his study and have been perfectly free to write when he felt the inspiration, and had not been annoyed by business calls or engagements, he would have dashed off the most charming articles for his magazine to any extent desired. The publication was suspended.

About this time the *Lutheran Observer* fell into incompetent hands, and it was conducted in so slovenly a manner that the patronage declined alarmingly. Rev. Dr. B. Kurtz, who had temporarily retired from the editorship, observing this disheartening condition of things, and apprehending that his old favorite, which he he had labored so long and so hard to sustain, would suffer irrecoverably until he went to the rescue, resumed the management of the paper in 1861, as he said to me, "to save it from ruin." To give it greater efficiency, and to enliven its columns with rich and instructive articles, he entered upon an engagement with Dr. Stork as assistant editor. After the paper had been reëstablished upon a solid basis and the confidence of its patrons had been re-secured and the number increased, Drs. Stork and Diehl purchased the *Observer* in 1862, and they sold one-third interest to Dr. Conrad. Dr. Stork being resident editor in Baltimore, had a large share in the management of the literary department, and this relation he sustained until his removal from Baltimore in 1865.

When the *Observer* was transferred to Philadelphia, and it became the property of the *Lutheran Observer Association*, on New-Year day, 1867, Dr. Stork once more became a member of the editorial staff, a position which he held for several years, retiring in July, 1869.

Four years after, near the close of 1873, he issued a prospectus for a family magazine, and published the first number with the title of *Lutheran Home Monthly*, in January, 1874. After issuing three additional numbers, he was taken suddenly ill, and never recovered.

Dr. Stork was the author of nine publications in book form, and of two small works in pamphlet form. A volume of his sermons, edited by his sons, was published two years after his death. His writings are chiefly on Biblical subjects. He reveals in them his devout and loving heart, a wide range of reading, and fine æsthetic talent.

The following is a list of his works in the order of their publication:

1. The Children of the New Testament, 1854, pp. 185.

2. Luther's Christmas Tree, 1855, pp. 32.
3. Jesus in the Temple, 1856, pp. 31.
4. Home Scenes in the New Testament, 1857, pp. 296.
5. Luther at Home, 1871, pp. 148.
6. The Unseen World, 1871, pp. 148.
7. Luther and the Bible, 1873, pp. 208.
8. Afternoon, 1874, pp. 360.
9. Sermons, 1876, pp. 339.

There were besides, published from his pen, two Hymns for the Soldier, 1867; sermon on Maternal Responsibility, 1858.

Numerous other articles for the church papers and the Review were contributed by him.

The degree of Doctor of Divinity was conferred on him by Pennsylvania College in 1851.

Dr. Stork was twice married. His first wife has been previously mentioned. She died in Germantown in August, 1846. Two years after, he married Miss Emma Baker, of Philadelphia, who survives him, and is the mother of his youngest son, Theophilus Baker Stork. His children by the first wife were William L. Stork, now of Baltimore, and Rev. Dr. Charles A. Stork, deceased.

DEATH, BURIAL AND MEMORIAL EULOGIES.

Dr. Stork died in Philadelphia on Saturday, March 28th, 1874. The following account of his funeral is taken from the *Lutheran Observer*:

"Tuesday, the 31st of March, was set apart for conveying his mortal remains to the tomb, and the occasion was unspeakably impressive. The funeral was appointed for 11 o'clock in the morning, at the residence of the deceased. As the hour approached, large numbers of relatives, friends and acquaintances began to arrive, and after taking a last and tearful look at the form of him whom in life they cherished so tenderly, distributed themselves through the large mansion until all its apartments were filled with sorrowing relatives and mourning friends, who came to manifest their sympathy with the bereaved, and their respect and esteem for the departed.

"About mid-day the funeral services were commenced with the singing of a beautiful hymn in soft and plaintive notes by the choir of St. Matthew's church, after which Dr. L. E. Albert, of Germantown, read appropriate passages from the sacred Scriptures. Dr. W. M. Baum then delivered a touching tribute to the memory of the deceased, setting forth in fitting terms the character, leading events and labors of his life. He was followed by Dr. J. G. Butler, of Washington, D. C., who, in a brief and tender impromptu address, bore testimony to his worth, devotion and usefulness. Dr. C. P. Krauth, of this city, offered an impressive prayer, commending the stricken widow and the fatherless children to the guardian care of their covenant-keeping Father in heaven.

"A double procession in carriages and on foot was then formed, and proceededed to the old cemetery of St. John's Lutheran congregation, near the church, on Race between Fourth and Fifth streets, where the body, in charge of a committee from St. Matthew's church, was deposited in the vault of the Baker family, with the relatives of his wife. Dr. J. A. Seiss, the pastor of St. John's church, impressively read the burial services. Then the benediction was pronounced, and the mourners and the multitude, who had followed a loving husband, a fond father and a dear relative, a Christian brother, a devoted friend and a faithful pastor, to his final resting place, returned sadly and thoughtfully to their homes.

"The obsequies of Dr. Stork are worthy of more than a mere passing notice. He had lived in this city a quarter of a century, and held the pastoral relation in four different congregations, at different periods, for more than twenty years. The seals of his ministry are counted by hundreds, and those who were edified by his discourses and writings by thousands. His spiritual children, his former parishioners, his ministerial brethren and his personal friends came together with one mind and one heart. They bore a united testimony to his artlessness, simplicity and tenderness as a Christian man, and to his earnestness, ability and fidelity as a pastor and minister; and while they recalled his spiritual graces, they cast the mantle of charity over his human imperfections. They loved him with the most tender and ardent affection. The heart-strings of all present were so tuned with sympathy, that they need but be touched by the truths read from the Scriptures, or the words uttered by the preacher, or the petitions offered in prayer, or the sentiments breathed in song, to give a response in sighs and tears. When 'Jesus wept' at the grave of Lazarus, the Jews said: 'Behold how he loved him.' By a similar interpretation of the tears shed around the bier of

Dr. Stork, we may also exclaim: 'Behold how they loved him!'

"Death levels all human distinctions" and unites all again with their kindred dust. Death has also a sweet harmonizing influence upon the living. We were struck with this at the funeral of Dr. Stork. There were seventeen Lutheran clergymen present, seven of whom, viz., Drs. Krauth, Seiss, C. F. Schaeffer, C. W. Schaeffer, and Revs. Bickel, Geissenhainer and Kunkleman, belong to the General Council; and ten, viz., Drs. Morris, Butler, Albert, Baum and Conrad, and Revs. Dimm, Sheeleigh, Holman, Yeiser and Steck, belong to the General Synod. Of those who officiated, two pertained to the former and three to the latter body. Dr. Krauth had succeeded Dr. Stork both as pastor at Winchester and at St. Mark's, Philadelphia. Dr. Baum had succeeded him as pastor in Winchester and in St. Matthew's, in this city. Rev. Kunkleman succeeded him at St. Mark's, Philadelphia; his own son Charles A. followed him in St. Mark's, Baltimore. Dr. Conrad was associated with him as editor in Baltimore, and as both editor and pastor in Philadelphia. All of them were once united in one general ecclesiastical body; and although that body was subsequently divided and they became ecclesiastically separated, they alike responded to the call of death and gathered around the bier of their departed classmate, and predecessor, and associate, and synodical colleague, and ministerial brother, and buried him in the unity of 'the faith once delivered to the saints.'

"Although a Lutheran, Dr. Stork was not a sectarian, but a catholic Christian. He not only acknowledged the orthodoxy of the evangelical Protestant denominations, but he practiced altar and pulpit fellowship with them. He took part in the general ecclesiastical movements of this city, was at home in union meetings, and was widely known and universally esteemed by the ministers and members of other denominations, many of whom attended his funeral, and united their testimony to his Christian charity and catholic spirit, with that borne by the members of his own household of faith.

"All present at these obsequies felt that 'it is better to go to the house of mourning than to the house of feasting,' 'All things are yours,' says Paul—'death' as well as 'life.' Life to consecrate to Christ—death to ponder and improve for Christ. From that coffin, as his pulpit, death proclaimed that it is appointed unto men once to die; that they know neither the day nor the hour when the summons to appear before God shall come; and that it becometh all men to be ready to depart and be with Christ. On that solemn occasion, memory recalled many endearing associations and precious recollections of the departed—many deeds of charity and mercy, parting counsels, last farewells, and dying testimonies to the supporting grace and presence of Jesus, unutterable in words, but beaming from his eye, and lighting up his face with joy, when already 'quite on the verge of heaven.' All present on that impressive occasion realized that 'the memory of the just is blessed.' And the Scriptural admonition to all is: 'Remember them * * * who have spoken unto you the Word of God; whose faith follow, considering the end of their conversation.' 'They that turn many to righteousness shall shine as the brightness of the firmament, and as the stars forever and ever.' 'Work while it is called to-day, for the night cometh wherein no man can work.' 'Be thou faithful unto death, and I will give thee the crown of life.'"

CHAPTER VIII.

REMINISCENCES—MEMORIALS—TRIBUTES OF RESPECT.

Lewis L. Houpt writes:

Philadelphia, March, 1885.

Dr. Stork's peculiar attraction was his earnestness and sincerity. He was very eloquent at times, and his discourses were beautifully illustrated and emphatically delivered. He was specially gifted in prayer, and all were drawn to him by his affectionate manner, his child-like simplicity, and humble Christian character. There was a personal magnetism about him that won all hearts alike, and people of all churches gladly sat under his ministry, and listened to the Word from his lips. They came and attended and connected themselves not so much with St. Mark's Lutheran church as with Dr. Stork's church, by which name it was universally known in his day.

REV. DR. C. W. SCHAEFFER.

Germantown, March 23, 1885.

My relations to Dr. Stork were such as enable me to speak of him only in general terms. He entered the Theological Seminary at Gettysburg only after I had left it; so that I saw very little of him there; yet knew him, all along, as occupying a position of prominence, for the excellence of his character and the value of his talents and attainments, as a student of Pennsylvania College.

Upon his coming to Philadelphia, as pastor of St. Matthew's, he took an active part in the organizing of the East Pennsylvania Synod. Although my personal relations with all the early members of that Synod were quite intimate and perfectly friendly, yet the fact of our belonging to different synods resulted in my having very little official intercourse with Dr. Stork.

Yet, I may say that I knew him well, having often met him in private life, and, very often, in the prosecution of the arduous and self-denying business which continued for years, and which resulted in the establishment of the "Board of Publication" at 42 N. Ninth street, Philadelphia. I may speak moderately, and yet come behind none, in testifying concerning his purity of character, his genial spirit, the refinement of his manners, his hearty and persuasive eloquence in the pulpit, the devotion and tender sympathies that so strongly marked his pastoral activities.

My personal recollections of him are altogether pleasant; and I cherish his memory fondly, as that of an eminently good and useful man. I am glad that you have undertaken the work you have on hand; I wish you all success in it, and that it may be followed with the blessing that cometh down from above.

FROM REV. DR. R. WEISER, DENVER, COL.

May 3, 1885.

* * * * When young Stork came to Gettysburg at about 16 years of age, he was a slender youth and apparently in delicate health.

He took a high position as a diligent and successful student of the Classics. * * * After he had entered the ministry, I met him at protracted meetings in Frederick, where I heard him preach several of his spendid sermons. After his removal to Philadelphia, I became associated with him in East Pennsylvania Synod, and often heard him preach, and met him at the General Synod at various places. * * * * *

Soon after the death of his first wife, the East Pennsylvania Synod met at Milton. He had preached on several occasions with great power and pathos, his heart had been mellowed by affliction, and the realities of the invisible world seem to have laid hold of his mind in an unusual manner; for the moment he opened his lips to speak, a wave of excitement seemed to roll over the congregation. At the close of the Synod Dr. Stork was requested by a resolution to return the thanks of Synod to the members of the church who had entertained us so handsomely.

When Brother Stork rose up to speak, a deep solemnity pervaded the whole large assembly, for all expected to hear something unusually interesting, and we were not disappointed, for a more thrilling and pathetic address none of us had ever heard. After speaking most affectionately and impressively to the people, and thanking them for their kindness and hospitality, and hoping they might be rewarded, he then turned to the preachers and with deep feeling said: "And now my dear brethren we have spent a pleasant season together; we have been cheered and comforted by the presence of the Lord—our hearts have been knit closer together—we have sat together in heavenly places in Christ Jesus. But we must now separate. You, my dear brethren, will return to your homes, your loved ones will receive you with joy and gladness—but where am I to go? I have no home on earth! The Lord has broken up my home." At this point he was so overcome by his feelings that he broke down, and we all broke down with him, and the whole vast audience in a moment had become a Bochim (a house of weeping). Never had I seen such an outbreak of feeling—we all loved Brother Stork, and our deepest sympathies were with him, and it took some time before he could finish his address. This was on the 26th of September, 1846: I recollect it distinctly.

It is scarcely necessary for me to state that Brother Stork was much beloved by all his clerical brethren, for he was an amiable and lovable man, full of tenderness and sympathy. As a preacher he was eloquent and very impressive, he never failed to gain the attention of his hearers; his sermons were all carefully written, and he generally read them, but he was an elegant reader. He paid, perhaps, more attention to rhetoric and elocution than any other man in the church. His cadences, and gestures, and the modulations of his voice, all seemed to have been carefully studied. This some of his best friends thought was not natural, and detracted somewhat as they supposed from his power in the pulpit. But these were the very points that constituted his strength in the pulpit. In any other man than Rev. T. Stork, the modulation of the voice, and its peculiar intonation would have been looked upon as affectation; but in him it was perfectly natural. He was mild, conciliatory, and forgiving. His preaching was always acceptable and instructive. His aim was to do good. Nor did he labor in vain. The fruits of his labors are all the churches which he served; his memory is still cherished by those who enjoyed the benefit of his labors. He spent the evening of his life in writing rather than in preaching. His style is clear and elegant, highly finished, and always fresh, lively and vigorous. I loved him as a man, admired him as a preacher, and cannot speak too highly of him as a writer of entertaining and instructive books. I would say of him, as Halleck said of Drake:

> "Green be the turf above thee,
> Friend of my early days:
> None knew thee but to love thee,
> None named thee but to praise."

I send you this faded chaplet, which you may hang upon the tomb of an old and departed friend and brother.

A JUDICIOUS ESTIMATE OF DR. STORK AS A SERMONIZER.
(From the Observer.)

The volume of sermons of Dr. T. Stork, edited by his sons, and issued by our Board of Publication, appeared at a time of all least favorable to arrest public attention. It was in the very midst of the stir and bustle of the Centennial, and of a most exciting Presidential election. The minds of most people were occupied with other things than the reading of sermons. But the Centennial is now over, and a President has been elected; and we may turn our minds to the more common but more enduring subjects of thought.

It may be regarded as somewhat of a venture at almost any time and by any one to publish a volume of sermons. Few such volumes succeed in gaining or holding the attention of any considerable number of readers. The most attractive preachers in the pulpit are often very dull in print: and "as dull as a sermon" has in certain circles passed into a by-word. We think that a great deal that is said about sermons and preaching is more commonplace and dull than any preaching can well be; and yet it cannot be denied that, as a rule, sermons are not the most interesting reading. For this some better reasons than those ordinarily offered might be given were it necessary, but this is not our purpose.

This may be regarded as a rather awkward and cumbersome introduction to a few words on a volume of sermons. Very well. Let it be so regarded. We want to say that this volume of sermons by Dr. Stork cannot be considered dull or commonplace, but will be read with interest and profit by all who love divine truth, and may be studied with advantage by those whose business it is to preach the gospel. It deserves a place in the minister's library, and in the choice reading of the family. It will serve as a quickener of thought and of piety.

It is not our purpose to attempt any careful analysis of this volume, or to offer any extended criticism. Our main object is simply to call attention to it, in the hope that many will be induced to procure the volume and study it for themselves, and in the assurance that they will be amply rewarded. To avoid misapprehension, we will say that if any one obtains this volume with the expectation of finding learned discussions, or faultless homiletics, he will likely be disappointed. The volume cannot be commended for these qualities. But it has qualities—the very qualities that made Dr. Stork among the most attractive and impressive of preachers—that must commend the volume, and make it worthy of a careful study. In attempting to note a few points which strike us in reading the volume, we mention—

The absence of just those qualities which too often make sermons, written or preached, dull. There are no trite utterances, which mean nothing at all, or unmeaning sentences that seem to be spoken just because something must be said. Sometimes we are tempted to say as we read or hear, This is all true, but what of it? To find a volume free from such studied dullness is no small merit, and is a great relief in reading.

Again, there is no tedious prolixity. Some preachers when they hit upon a good idea, beat it to death. They seem to be so pleased with it that they handle it until all life and beauty are departed. Under the pretense of presenting it under different points of view, they exhibit it until we are tired, and the mind wanders after something else. There is nothing tedious in these sermons. Their brevity is explained from the fact that they were left in an incomplete condition; but had they been much longer it would not have altered the case—they lack the common quality of tedious prolixity.

The qualities thus stated are rather negative than positive, and it would do injustice to these sermons to leave the impression that they are lacking in positive excellencies. Some of these we should name, as freshness, simplicity, beauty, aptness of illustration, spirituality, and fervor. Without any great claim to originality, there is a freshness about these sermons that is attractive. Truths are put in a strong and striking light. There are sharp, incisive sentences, and vivid pictures scattered through them, which relieve them of everything like tameness, and make them a pleasure to read. Take this at random from the sermon, " Christ's Sigh:" "There may have been something in the dangerousness of the faculty he was about to bestow upon the man that made him sigh. It was language. He knew the power of speaking was specially the power of sinning; that no member was so difficult of control and so liable to offend as the tongue . . . It was a perilous gift. It may help us to keep the door of our lips to remember that Christ sighed when restoring this faculty." That is equal to a whole sermon on the danger of the tongue.

With this is joined a charming simplicity and beauty. We do not mean either superficiality or meretricious decorations. The idea which some people attach to simplicity in style or speaking is that it has no depth of meaning. But they mistake emptiness and superficiality for genuine simplicity—to which it has no resemblance. And their idea of beauty corresponds with the present idea of dress—the more ornamental work the more beautiful. But good taste spurns such excessive adornment. Dr. Stork had the taste to combine simplicity with beauty, as we find them in the natural world. While there are sparkling beauties in conception and expression, they do not destroy the simplicity of his style. He never wearies with a profusion of ornament.

Many of the striking illustrations with which Dr.

Stork's preaching abounded it is known were introduced on the occasion, and are not found in his printed discussions. But we have enough here to give some idea of his aptness at illustration and in the application of Scripture.

A crowning excellence in these sermons is their spirituality and religious power. The preacher, one feels, is in sympathy with his subject, and is aiming to draw his hearers to the Saviour. In the pulpit he seemed to be standing near the cross, and from it to sound out the invitations of mercy and peace. They are gospel sermons —not dry discussions of doctrines or moral essays, but teeming with rich treasures of divine truth.

We feel quite sure that more preaching like that in these sermons would help to render the pulpit more effective and the world better.

REMINISCENCES OF THE REV. T. STORK, D. D.

(From Rev. Dr. S. W. Harkey.)

As I knew Theophilus Stork in his boyhood in North Carolina, and as a student during his entire course in the college and seminary at Gettysburg, I may perhaps be able to give a few facts of interest to the general reader.

I can remember the name of old grandfather Stork (written Storch in German), the revered father of Theophilus, for more than sixty years, as the embodiment of almost everything that was valuable to the Lutheran church in the central counties of North Carolina. The same class of people, of our household of faith, were found here as in Pennsylvania. In fact, numbers of them had immigrated from Pennsylvania, going south through the "valley of Virginia," and across the "Blue Ridge" into Guilford county, where Salem, a Moravian town, has existed from the early times, and then into the good lands along the Yadkin and Catawba rivers. The Germans seem always to find the good lands. Over all these portions of North Carolina, German Lutherans were scattered even before the times of the Revolutionary war.

Old father Stork did more than all other men, a century ago, to seek out these scattered sheep of our fold, and gather them into congregations. Many of the churches which he organized still exist, some of which I have known personally, as the one in Salisbury, the "Organ Church," some twenty miles south of Salisbury, and the St. John's church, formerly called the "Red Meeting House," some miles east of Concord in Cabarrus county.

Father Stork owned a farm some five miles west from the Organ church, where he spent the evening of his days in retirement, after disease compelled him to relinquish the active duties of the ministry, and where Theophilus passed his childhood and youth. When I was eighteen years of age I taught a school in this neighborhood in the winter of 1829–30, and also gathered the young people together to practice singing on Sunday afternoons when there was no service. One Sunday afternoon Theophilus, who was then a lad fifteen or sixteen years of age, came to my singing-school and insisted that I must go home with him, as his father wished to see me. It was a distance of about ten miles, and he had come on horseback. We rode the horse turn-about, and soon made our way to the home of the venerable patriarch. They had heard that I had a desire to go to Gettysburg to study for the ministry, and as Theophilus was also to go, they wished to see me about it. Father Stork was now disabled from all labor, and confined to his room by dropsy. I saw him sitting in his large arm-chair, unable to walk or move around, except as that chair was moved. I remained over night, and Theophilus and I talked over and over the whole matter of our going to Gettysburg to study for the ministry, and laid plans for its accomplishment. It was indeed a grave question for us. It was a long distance from our home, nearly five hundred miles from that part of Carolina to Gettysburg. We were young, and knew nothing about the world or a course of education for the ministry. And worst of all, I had no money to pay my way, though Stork had some means.

Theophilus was the youngest son of Father Stork, "the son of his old age," and he was anxious that this son should be devoted to the work of Christ—in some sense to take the father's place in the church when he was gone. We were called into the old gentleman's room in the evening for family worship. Neither of us could pray extemporaneously, but we could sing and read. So we sang a hymn, and Theophilus read a prayer from the liturgy. Father Stork then asked me about going to study for the ministry, and said he wanted Theophilus to go to Gettysburg the coming fall; he was now going to a high school nearer home, but by next fall he should go to Gettysburg. He urged me to go as soon as I could get ready. I told him the difficulties in my way —that I was young and inexperienced, was my father's oldest child and he needed me at home on the farm, and that my parents could not possibly raise the money to support me; otherwise they were willing I should go. He said: "Tell your parents such things *must* be—they MUST be! God will help you. They must let you go." I told him there were two other young men of whom I had heard who wanted to go, and perhaps I could go with them. He said I must go, and he would write to Professor Schmucker, and prepare the way for me. The agreement was made that I should go as soon as I could get ready, and should write back and tell how things were at "the Seminary," and in a few months Theophilus should come. I parted from the good man, having received his blessing, and I never saw him again. But that blessing abideth yet, and all that he said, and much more than any of us could hope for has come to pass! My school closed about March, 1830, and I had made a little money with which I could pay my way to Gettysburg, and for the future the good Lord must help—and He did. The other two young men and myself "fixed up" a little one-horse wagon, with a top to it, called a "carry-all," and came to Gettysburg, leaving home on the 24th of May, 1830, and arriving at our journey's end on the 10th day of June, at an expense of $3.55¼ each, or $10.65¾ for all three of us, a distance of five hundred miles! Theophilus Stork was exceedingly anxious to go with us; but for good reasons his father thought best that he should wait and come in the fall.

It was then, as yet, a "day of small things" at Gettysburg. No seminary or college buildings, or Professors' houses, existed. There had been theological classes organized, and the "Gymnasium," and in all some thirty odd students were in attendance. The exercises were held in the old Academy, an humble two-story brick building, containing a library room, a small chapel, and three recitation rooms. Rev. Prof. S. S. Schmucker was there, and Revs. David and Michael Jacobs. I well remember the pale and sickly face of David Jacobs, to whom I recited my first lessons in the Latin Grammar. He left the Institution that summer, and took a trip to the South for the benefit of his health, but only got back as far as to Shepherdstown, Virginia, where he died.

The same fall, in the month of October I think, Theophilus Stork came to Gettysburg, making the trip in the stage; a ruddy youth of sixteen, full of life and hope. One of the first things he asked me was, "How much have you learned since you are here? Can you read any Latin?" I took up a copy of Cæsar, and read a paragraph or two near the beginning, which I had about committed to memory. "Why, you can read Latin better than I can," said he, "and I am surprised at you!" "Come on," said I, "we are here now at Gettysburg, and we must make it tell." Of course we were fast friends all the time during our student days, and during all his life. You will observe from these statements which I know to be true, that some errors have been committed by a writer in the *Review* who furnished a sketch of Dr. Stork's life. He did not go to Gettysburg after his father's death, but *before*, and was called home when his father was dying, and returned to Gettysburg in the fall of 1831. It is not correct to say, as that writer has done, that his father urged his "delicate health as an insuperable obstacle," for the pastoral office; but, on the other hand, the father gave his full consent, and even insisted upon this course. I am perfectly familiar with all these *facts*.

He was a faithful student, a good young man, and I think entirely free from the usual college vices. He remained at Gettysburg several years longer than I did, and graduated in both college and seminary.

A TRIP SOUTH.

During the summer and fall vacation of 1832, *three* of us North Carolina students took it into our heads to make a trip back to the old home. But how was it to be done? No railroads in those days, nor any way of going except by stage or on foot. But stage fare was high, and we had no money with which to pay it even if it had been low. After much deliberation and planning, we determined to attempt the journey on foot! Each of us would make up a small bundle of such clothing as we must have, in the shape of a knapsack, and, as the roads were good, we could go on slowly from day to day, and surely in *three weeks* we could make the 500 miles! Theophilus Stork was one of the trio, and eager to make the start. "Good-by, Gettysburg!" for awhile, anyhow —hope to return in a couple of months! The first day we tramped from Gettysburg to Hagerstown, and the second from Hagerstown to Martinsburg, in Virginia; and then we called a "council of war," for Theophilus declared he could go no farther. His feet were terribly sore, and he was completely "used up." What should we do? The whole subject was duly considered, and it was determined that Stork should take the stage and return to Gettysburg, and the other two of us shouldered our knapsacks and went "marching on." And we made the 500 mile trip, and in due time were at our places again in Gettysburg, and found Brother Stork all right. How we made the trip—how we walked, and when and how we rested—what sights we saw in the valley of Virginia, at the *Natural Bridge*, and in the mountains we crossed—and how one of our number, though he had been at Gettysburg only two years and had no license to preach yet, did preach all around in the old Carolina churches, and produced quite "a sensation"—all this and a great deal more it is no business of this article to tell. Only Brother Stork never started on another such trip on foot, nor did the rest of us.

After all, the failure of dear Theophilus to accompany us to Carolina at that time, proved a most sad and serious loss to him, subsequently causing him much grief. He never got to see the face of his good mother again. How deeply this distressed him I perhaps got to know better than any one else. His father had been called home the year before, but his mother was yet living when we made the trip, but died rather suddenly the next year, and he saw her no more. Afterwards it was made his sad duty to visit the old homestead, to aid in settling up matters—but O, how changed! The old farm and house were there, but all he loved most dearly on earth were gone. I asked him about it when he returned. "Ah! yes," said he, "I was at the dear old home. The house and the barn and the shade trees in the yard, and the garden, all are there as they used to be; the kitchen, dining room, study and parlor, all remain; but O, the loved ones all are gone! I examined everything carefully. The little horse I had carved on the kitchen-door with my penknife, is still there; and the spring branch where I used to fish with a pin hook—all still there. The birds sing among the branches of the trees as sweetly as ever; but the whole seemed a mockery, where no sweet voice of the dear departed was now to be heard."

From Lutheran Observer, April 3, 1874—Editorial.

Dr. S. was an attractive and forcible preacher, always interesting and often presenting truths in a most beautiful and striking manner. He was especially successful in pressing the truth upon the impenitent, and many extensive revivals of religion took place under his efficient ministrations of the gospel in nearly all his pastorates.

Personally, he was genial and companionable, and his attachment to and interest in personal friends was very warm and tender. He devoted a considerable portion of his time to authorship and has published a number of works, some of which have passed through several editions. * * * As a writer, Dr. Stork displayed a lively imagination and poetic fancy, as well as a cultivated and literary taste; and our readers are too well acquainted with his attractive style to require any characteristic of it here.

From the Lutheran Home Monthly.

DR. STORK IS DEAD. We do not speak of the editor, the writer, the Doctor of Divinity, but of the *man*. Doubtless every Lutheran journal in the land will bear testimony to Dr. Stork's worth, and many a one who has no connection with our church, or indeed with any church, will have some words of compliment to speak or write; but who can tell a tithe of the good man's goodness and amiability and benevolence and beneficence?

Let others talk of him in his public life, let yet others publish what he was to them socially; grant us, dear reader, the sad privilege of boasting of our close intimacy with this excellent man for the past six years. Every day, during that time, unless absent from the city or ill, he spent some two hours with us at the Publication House, aiding us by his advice, by his exquisite literary taste, by his means, and still more by his countenance and personal influence—all this done as President of the Board, lovingly, unselfishly, and without any remuneration whatever.

Time and again we have been asked, "Why do you publish books for Dr. Stork and not for *us?*" Waiving the fact that Dr. Stork's reputation as an author made his books eminently desirable to any Publishing House, we are now at liberty to answer—his death has unsealed our lips—" Because he assumed a large part of the labor, and, on account of our inadequate capital, all the expense."

On the other hand, the inquiry has been made, and with some reason, "Why did he not let the Publication Society publish his last two books?" We feel at liberty now to reply to that query: It was his intention to give those two books to the Publication Board, and all the preliminary labor, including the stereotyping, and even the purchase of the paper, was done by us to that intent; but alas! his attention was called to some unkind remarks with regard to the Board's publishing books for him and not for others; also that he took advantage of his position as President to give his own books a precedence.

These strictures, so unfounded and so unjust, made in many instances by persons who knew nothing of the Doctor, and in every case by those who knew nothing of the circumstances, wounded his sensitive heart to a degree not sufficient, it is true, to induce him to defend himself from the baseless charge, and yet enough to make him feel that "it might be better" (his own words) to have his books published elsewhere — the Publication House being no loser by the change.

Our cheek burns as we write these words, and we do it only from a sense of justice to the dead. Our testimony is, and we write it advisedly, that the Publication Society, during our time, owes much more to Dr. T. Stork than to any other one man.

The *Lutheran Home Monthly* is the last proof of his unselfish love for the Church, and for its Publication

House. His money and his energy have given it life and being. It has afforded him great anxiety, and has necessarily cost him a goodly sum beyond its receipts.

"Took advantage of his position!" Yes, Dr. Stork *did* take advantage of his position, but not in the way charged. The advantage consisted in this one good man's bearing far more than his share of the work of the Publication House.

At another time we hope to write further on this subject; at present we feel inadequate to the duty.

The last editorial written for the *Home Monthly* was "I am Now Ready." Dr. Stork *was* ready to leave his work, unfinished here, to be continued in heaven. We mourn our loss in him, even though we call to mind his own beautiful language in his last book:

"The departure of loved ones is a sorrow which shades the earth, but opens heaven. Every Christian friend departed may in spirit be walking with us by the way, causing our hearts to rejoice within us by opening to us the deep things of God, though, like the disciples of old, our eyes are holden that we see it not."

The following tender and touching article written for the *Observer* soon after Dr. Stork's death, by his youngest son, now an attorney in Philadelphia, presents his poetical tastes and social character in an attractive light:

IN MEMORIAM.

"Nay, if you read this line, remember not
  The hand that writ it; for I love you so
  That I in your sweet thoughts would be forgot
  If thinking on me then should make you woe."

Who can ever forget those tender lines of Shakespeare? An American essayist has tried to separate the love and sweetness of the great poet's soul from his greatness. But Shakespeare's own true lover, Leigh Hunt, with an instinct truer than the critic's, has shown the greatness of the poet's genius in the delicacy and tenderness of his love-songs. Would that there were room to quote the warm-hearted appreciation of the gentle Hunt.

Men are wont to consider a loving, trusting nature as a weak one, and of an inferior rank. There could scarcely be a greater mistake. The loving soul is the grandest, highest type of man's nature. In Shakespeare his truest greatness was his capacity for true and noble loving, as shown in his sonnets. It is man made after the image of his Creator, who Himself is love.

This power of loving and this benignity and kindliness of soul may be seen running through the genius of all ages. When it is wanting one misses the most precious gift of genius to men—that sunny, trusting spirit of good will, and kindliness, and love. What would this world be, unlighted by its divine radiance?

It was with such thoughts that we read Dr. Stork's dedicatory stanzas in *Afternoon*. They, too, in a smaller degree, partake of the same loving tenderness of soul as Shakespeare's sonnets.

>Friends of our passing life and ways—
> Now present to our view;
>These garnered thoughts of leisure days,
> We dedicate to you.

> We ask not for posthumous fame
> From loving friends apart,
> But kindly thoughts about our name,—
> The memory of the heart.

It is the same spirit, expressed mayhap less perfectly—his was not the poet's power of song—but he gave what he had, he spoke as well as he could the longing of his heart for love and kindly memories.

Sometimes a man writes down his whole character in one or two brief sentences. In this the whole man, his spirit and life, are expressed. This, Dr. Stork, we think, has done in these dedicatory stanzas. Every one that knew him will recognize the sentiments and perceive how characteristic they are of the man. He asked not for posthumous fame; we all know how little ambition he had; he never expressed a regret at losing a high position; he often left it of his own accord. But when any one spoke ill of him or felt unkindly toward him, it grieved him to the heart. It is this, the most prominent trait of his character, that gives his life its highest dignity, that speaks his kinship with far greater spirits than his own. We shall never forget how he looked as he wrote those little verses which he put in "*Afternoon.*" He wrought them over and over, re-modelling and revising them with lingering fondness, and then he turned to us, when at last he had satisfied himself, and with that smile of quiet pleasure beaming on his face (just as his friends had seen him often greet them) read them over to us.

It is a sad pleasure, now and then, in one's reading to come across in his books the passages he loved to quote

—the sentences pencil-marked, the page turned down. He used to be very fond of bits of poetry. Here is one from Tennyson that he would often quote:

> "A thousand suns will stream on thee,
> A thousand moons shall quiver,
> But not by thee my steps shall be,
> Forever and forever."

He liked Tennyson much, and enjoyed especially the "Brook Song" which a young friend sang to him several times. There is, too, in the Idyls of the King, in the "Morte d'Arthur" a soliloquy that we remember reading to him which pleased him greatly, he never having noticed it before. And we recollect his telling us afterward how he quoted it once in a lecture, but the people, he thought, did not appreciate it. The lines were those beginning:

> "And slowly answered Arthur from the barge,
> The old order changeth, yielding place to new,
> And God fulfils himself in many ways
> Lest one good custom should corrupt the world."

The whole speech is fine, but when we came to

> "Pray for my soul. More things are wrought by prayer
> Than this world dreams of. Wherefore let thy voice
> Rise like a fountain for me night and day.
>   *   *   *   *   *   *   *   *
> For so the whole round earth is every way
> Bound by gold chains around the feet of God."

His face lit up in that rare way it would when he was pleased. "Let me see that," he said, and I handed him the book.

His consideration for the feelings of others was excessive. He was as thoughtful for the enjoyment of the servants in his house as he was for himself. At Christmas time—which he always observed with the innocent, eager joy of a child—he was ever careful to think of them, and remember them with some pretty trifle. He used to say, when any one spoke to him of it, "I think they would feel *so lonely* if they got no presents." As a natural consequence of this trait, he was very sensitive to neglect or slights from those he loved, and felt with exquisite keenness any unkind word or act.

And yet we have known him—such was the broad generosity of his spirit—to turn upon men who had abused and ill-treated him, and repay their abuse with favors and benefits. It seemed weakness to some, and doubtless so thought the very men thus favored; they could not attain unto it, it was too high for them. But now when he is gone we begin to see in the love that follows him how truly wise he was, and how, as he himself used to say, "Loving favor is better than silver or gold."

There was about him a certain delicacy of soul, a reserve that he never shook off even with his most intimate friends. Those who knew him well will remember how, on meeting after a separation, there was always a certain embarrassment, a timidity of soul, just like a bird looking askance and waiting trembling to enter into the old familiar intercourse. Uncertain whether his friend was still the same, and fearing to take liberties, he assumed a tentative position.

But enough of these memoirs. He was no great spirit,

his was but a humble position in the great army of teachers and authors; but he was a true-hearted, loving, trusting soul, whose sunshine and kindness lightened the path of many a weary toiler, and whose monument must be in the hearts of those that loved him.

T. B. STORK.

At the quarterly meeting of the Ministerial Union of Philadelphia, held on Monday, the 30th of March, Rev. Dr. Hotchkin announced the death of Dr. Stork, and Dr. Alfred Nevin moved that a committee be appointed to draw up a minute on his death. In accordance therewith, Alfred Nevin, D. D., E. H. Nevin, D. D., P. S. Henson, D. D., and Rev. T. M. Griffith were appointed said committee, who, after retiring, subsequently "reported resolutions expressing the regret of the Union at the untimely decease of a ministerial brother whose sincerity, fidelity and catholicity gave indubitable evidence of the genuineness of his piety, and greatly endeared him to his brethren in the ministry, and to all who came in contact with him; and tendering their heartfelt sympathies to the bereaved family." After appropriate remarks by Rev. J. Wheaton Smith, D. D., Dr. Crowell, and Revs. A. Cather and S. W. Thomas, the minute was unanimously adopted.

DEATH OF DR. STORK—OUR LAST CONVERSATION.

BY REV. JOS. H. BARCLAY.

From the Lutheran Observer of April 10th, 1874.

Death has again entered the circle of our ministry, and another dearly beloved of God has gone home. How rapidly the ranks are thinning out of the strong men of our Church! In such a little while, Hutter, Pohlman, Bachman and others have gone from us, and now to the list of our illustrious dead we must add one more—the noble-hearted, tender and gifted Stork. What a thrill it sends through the heart of the Church, that he who has profited so many by his preaching, his writings and his conversation, has left us, and we shall see him no more until we reach the great white throne!

Knowing Dr. Stork intimately for many years, having met him at home and in travel, we made it a special object to visit him only a few weeks since when in Philadelphia; and it was then we held the conversation we desire to relate here, as illustrating our brother's yearning after heaven, and one of the special premonitions he had of his approaching dissolution.

We had visited him on matters connected with the *Lutheran Monthly*, and through our brother's great kindness in subscribing for one of the memorial windows in our new church edifice in Baltimore, a subject was suggested for an article for the *Monthly*, "*How old art thou?*" which opened up the thought of growing old. Bro. Stork was very free and peculiarly tender that day upon heavenly things—the whole drift of thought and affection was upward. He was very weak, and his voice husky, and when we asked him of his own experience and feeling in growing old in God's service, and reminded him of the former days of health and vigor, he replied with that peculiar smile that so often played over his countenance, "I find that age comes unconsciously, and that with advancing years has come the grace to grow older willingly; it gets lighter, not heavier. I have scarcely been conscious of any change in that direction, of any regrets for the youth far back; but the really sad and most distressing aspect of the case to me, Bro. B., was the knowledge that through infirmities, not old age (remember, Dr. Stork was yet only on the edge of old age), I must quit preaching. I love to preach, and it seemed to me age was nothing, death nothing, in comparison with the saddening truth—I must preach no more. I could not for a time be reconciled, but I am now resigned to the will of God—only it seems to me I must be active."

We conversed on the little time really allowed us for the Master's work, and together we ran over the list of the active, influential pastors who were in their prime, and had a firm hold on the affections and admiration of the church only sixteen years ago, when the writer entered the ministry, and who had dropped, one by one, out of the active ranks, some of them to enter on their everlasting rest; and we were mutually surprised to see how few remained in the active work—when he added: "This conversation recalls to me the thoughts of a remarkable and to me premonitory dream I had only a few nights ago. I am not a believer in dreams, as a rule; but this was so real, so vivid, and developed to me such full ideas of old friends gone, and the heavenly recognition, that it has left a strong impression on my mind, and I have felt ever since that it has a connection with my own dissolution. You may not know that when living, Dr. Krauth, Sr., and myself were warm friends, and it was in this city that we frequently took long walks, often into the country, and we would talk of the work of life—its end, and the heavenly state and recognition; of how we should appear and know each other there. These conversations were profitable to me. He passed to his reward years ago. Well, a few nights ago he appeared to me while I was sleeping. I seemed awake, and I saw him in as real and tangible a form as I see you now. I knew he was a spirit, but the spirit appeared as the friend I knew in the days of his flesh. He looked as I saw him years ago in the vigor of life; his appearance, his manner, his voice, were precisely as when on earth. He came to me, and we renewed our old friendship. We took one of our old walks, and we resumed our conversation as those who have been parted only for a little while. He recalled the old impressions, and told me of his state, his experience, his consciousness, and how fully it corresponded with the views and impressions we held in the days of the flesh. And whilst we talked of the positiveness of this state, of the holy, comforting feeling of knowing each other in heaven, and renewing the old friendships of the glorified ones above, gone before, and how they recognized each other, he said to me on our return from our walk, as we were about parting like two friends who would meet the next day: 'You see how real it is; how like what we believed it long ago; how we shall know each other, and talk of the old ways, the old joys, as in the days of my flesh; how we can take up the threads of conversation laid down on earth, and resume it in glory. Be comforted. We shall soon meet again, and we shall know and love each other as of old. Farewell.' And so he vanished out of my sight, and I awoke feeling that death would only open the gates of glory. And so the end and dying has lost all its shadow and darkness, and I wait patiently."

So our conversation ended; but as we left Dr. Stork that day, so strong was the impression wrought by his words and manner, that we remarked to some of his old friends and former parishioners, "Our Brother Stork will hardly be long with us. He seems to realize an end fast approaching."

We had hoped to see him again in this world; but it is not so to be. Our noble, amiable, talented one has left us. Our gentle Philip Melanchthon is dust, and we wait patiently to meet him above, and to realize the truth of his own vision—we shall know each other there. Only a few short months ago we parted in a like manner from our dear Brother Hutter, when he too talked of, and awaited, and confidently expected his reward, without one doubt or sense of gloom. And so they pass from us and enter into rest, for "there remaineth a rest for the people of God." Sweet, indeed, must be the joy in the midst of sorrow to his loved ones, that husband and father has only gone to rest a little earlier in the day, and they shall meet him and know him in heaven. And may the lesson come to each one of us working in the Master's cause, "Work while it is called to-day."

REV. S. A. HOLMAN, D. D.,

Of Philadelphia, writes:

I had the pleasure of an intimate acquaintance with Dr. Theophilus Stork during the last six years of his life, and of his residence in this city. He possessed in an eminent degree "the wisdom that is from above; pure, peaceable, gentle, easy to be entreated, full of mercy and good fruits, without partiality, without hypocrisy." Not long before his death, some of the brethren were canvassing the characteristics of prominent men in the church, and whilst to some were conceded greater intellectual power and energy, it was admitted without dissent that none would be more highly exalted in the heavenly world than Dr. Stork. His spirit was of the type of the apostle John's. His preaching combined in a high degree the distinction which improves the mind, and the unction which touches the heart. His style was nervous and classical, and he was fond of illustrating truths by poetical quotations, which he selected with admirable judgment.

Dr. Stork was an early and steadfast friend of our Publication House, and aided it in its early struggles, more than once, in a substantial way. He originated *The Lutheran Home Monthly*, which, after his death, was merged into *The Augsburg Teacher*.

His life and labors are worthy of being embodied in a volume which shall transmit the memory of his virtues to posterity.

In Quarterly Review, January, 1875.
REV. DR. J. A. BROWN.

Having known Dr. Stork somewhat intimately for nearly a quarter of a century, and having been for a long time closely associated with him in labors, it may not be presumptuous for us to append a note to the sketch presented by Dr. Diehl, in this number of the *Review*. This is done not with any design or hope of improving what has been said, but simply to add our individual testimony to his talents and worth as a minister of Christ. Such a testimony, indeed, may not be necessary after the record of his life is given, but it affords us a melancholy pleasure to be allowed thus to express our appreciation of the character of our departed friend and brother. Dr. Stork possessed a heart in an unusual degree free from guile. He was naturally confiding, and hence more easily imposed on than many others of a more suspicious nature. His sympathies were tender and easily excited, and he trusted, at all times, more to his feelings than to his judgment. His errors, for he was prone like other men to err, were rather those of the head than of the heart. His talents and taste peculiarly fitted him for the pulpit. By nature and grace he was richly endowed to preach salvation to perishing sinners. He was not a man of patient, untiring study in one particular field, but loved to roam at large, admiring what was most attractive and beautiful in every department, and culling, wherever he could find them, the choicest flowers. Endowed with a quick and tender sensibility to the true, the beautiful and the good, his soul was readily fired by the grand themes of the gospel. He disliked all shams in religion and worship. He was deeply in earnest when dealing with divine things. We have heard him at synods, and on other public occasions, as well as in the ordinary ministrations of the sanctuary. Like all men of his temperament, his preaching was very unequal. To be truly eloquent, he needed to be aroused; and never was he more truly in his element or more deeply in earnest, than when holding up Christ as the Saviour of the lost. Though not of a strictly theological cast of mind, he delighted in the great doctrines of grace, and presented them with great unction and power. There was a fervor and a glow, at times, that thrilled the heart. He was emphatically a heart preacher. Of all our ministers whom we have heard, none ever impressed us as Dr. Stork did, in his most touching and impassioned appeals. We have heard more learned and more logical discourses than he preached, but none that were better adapted to move the heart, or to stir the very depths of the soul. If we should attempt to analyze his preaching and to say in what his power consisted, it would not be difficult to point out the more prominent elements; but there was a hidden fire, a mysterious magnetism, that must be felt to be appreciative. His eloquence was that of divine truth coming from a soul fired with the love of Christ, and intensely in earnest in the work of his Master. His poetic imagination, his tender sympathy, his earnest zeal, all contributed to give his utterances in the pulpit attractiveness and power. The eloquence was in the man and in his themes. The pulpit was his place of greatest strength. It was here that his influence was most felt. Whilst he will be loved and cherished as a friend and a Christian, it will be as an ambassador of Christ, as a preacher of the gospel, that he will be best known and longest remembered. As such this feeble tribute is offered by one who loved and admired him.

J. A. B.

TRIBUTES TO DR. STORK.

"*The memory of the just is blessed.*"—Most of our Lutheran contemporaries, both German and English, have noticed the death of Dr. Stork, and after detailing the principal events of his life, bear a uniform testimony to his Christian character and usefulness. We take pleasure in translating and publishing the following:

Dr. Krotel, in the *Lutherische Herold* of April 9th, bears the following testimony concerning Dr. Stork, as his successor at St. Mark's, Philadelphia:

"Dr. Stork was for many years one of the most beloved ministers of the Lutheran church, and by his lovely character had won many hearts. As we entered, in 1862, upon the discharge of our duties in St. Mark's congregation, organized by him, and which had also been served previously by Drs. C. A. Smith and C. P. Krauth, we had the opportunity of noticing the warm attachment which many still cherished toward him. We met him frequently and had the best opportunity of knowing him.

"Our friends know on which side the departed stood, in the struggle through which our church was called to pass during the last ten years, and we need not, therefore, dwell upon that point. Although we differed from him on various points, and sometimes came in collision with him, we, nevertheless, cheerfully bear this testimony, that he was most heartily devoted to the church of his fathers; that he sought her peace and prosperity, and that he clung, with a believing and child-like heart, to his Lord and Saviour. He always approached us in the most friendly manner, and after his recovery from his severe illness last year, he wrote us a charming letter, in which he expressed the earnest desire that all whom he had in any wise wounded, might forgive him as heartily as he forgave all who had trespassed against him. All of us have our weak side, and he was not an exception; but when we take a retrospect of his earthly career, we thank the Lord for the good which he has accomplished through his servant, and say of the departed, May his memory be blessed! The Lord comfort the faithful companion of his life, who was to him for many years an affectionate helpmeet, and impart grace to the sons to follow the example of their father."

The *Zeitschrift* of April 4th, says:

"He who has fallen asleep in Jesus was, indeed, by his training an American Lutheran, but he loved the church of his fathers and desired her welfare. He was endowed with beautiful spiritual gifts and a noble soul. He belonged to the good men in the domain of the General Synod, who rejoiced in the proposed Free Conference, and hoped to live to see it, but who have been called hence through death, before the time and place of its assembling had been determined. How many other leaders of the church may die before it transpires!"

The *Kirchenfreund* of April 9th presents the principal events of his life, and adds:

"We are again called upon to announce the death of one of the most prominent and honored members of the General Synod, Rev. Dr. Stork. Besides his successful pastoral labors, his various writings have caused him to become widely known and beloved, both in and beyond the bounds of the Lutheran church. He leaves a widow and three sons, with whom the Lutheran church mourns in him one of her ablest and best ministers."

The *Lutheran* appends the following to its notice of the obsequies of Dr. Stork:

"So ended the earthly career of an amiable and much loved minister of Christ. He had his weaknesses, like all the rest of us; let the recollection of them be buried with him. He had his worth and virtues; them let us cherish and imitate. Before the same Judge we must all soon appear, and in the one only Saviour can any of us hope for salvation. Precious in the sight of the Lord is the death of his saints."

RESOLUTIONS OF RESPECT.

At a joint meeting of the church council and the board of officers of St. Mark's Lutheran church, Philadelphia, Pa., held Tuesday evening, the 7th inst., a committee was appointed to prepare suitable resolutions of respect with reference to the death of Dr. Stork, the first pastor of said church, who reported as follows:

WHEREAS, It has pleased Almighty God to remove from the toils of earth to the joys of heaven, Rev. Theophilus Stork, D. D., the founder and first pastor of this congregation; therefore,

Resolved, That while we bow in humble submission to the will of Him who in His own good time calls His servants home to their reward, we testify to the zeal, ability and conscientiousness of our former beloved pastor, during all the period of his ministrations among us.

Resolved, That we tender the afflicted family our sincere sympathy in their great and sore bereavement, and commend them to Him who alone can give comfort and consolation in the hour of sorrow and sadness.
J. A. KUNKELMAN,
LEWIS L. HOUPT,
H. W. KNAUFF.

The *Harrisburg Telegraph* contains the following notice of this sad event:

"A telegram from F. V. Beisel, Esq., Philadelphia, to Rev. G. F. Stelling, announces the death of Rev. Theophilus Stork, D. D., in that city, at half past twelve o'clock last night. Dr. Stork was one of the noted divines of the Lutheran church. A most estimable man—a devout Christian—a successful preacher and pastor—a good writer and popular author, his death will occasion a profound sorrow thoughout the denomination to which he belonged."

We also find the following notice of Dr. Stork's death in the Baltimore *American:*

"Rev. Dr. Theophilus Stork died at his residence, in Philadelphia, Pa., on Saturday morning last, in the sixtieth year of his age. He ranked for many years as one of the most prominent of his denomination for culture, eloquence and pastoral success. His literary attainments were of the highest order, and few could equal him in pulpit services. He was the first pastor of the flourishing congregation of St. Mark's on Eutaw street, and was succeeded in that church by his son, the present pastor. Many friends in Baltimore cherish his memory most fondly, and will sympathize most heartily with his family in their bereavement. The pastor of St. Mark's was summoned by telegram on Friday, and arrived in time to see his honored father breathe his last. The announcement of his death was made by Rev. Dr. Morris, at St. Mark's, during the Sunday morning service, and produced a profound sensation, many tearful eyes giving expression to the heart-memories of their former pastor. In the afternoon, the intelligence was communicated to the Sunday-school, where many of those who entered the church during his pastorate are now active and efficient workers. Humanly speaking, the Church can ill afford to lose such a man."

TRIBUTES OF RESPECT.

PHILADELPHIA, May 2, 1874.

Mrs. Dr. Stork and Family; Esteemed friends: Permit me herewith to present you with the annexed extract from the minutes of proceedings of the last meeting (the only meeting since the death of your loved one), of the Board of Trustees of our church, and believe me, with warmest feelings of love and sympathy,

Yours very truly, W. J. MILLER.

WHEREAS: Since the last meeting of this Board, our former pastor and much beloved brother, Rev. Dr. Stork, has been called to his rest; and *Whereas,* duty and affection alike bid us to take suitable note of this sad event, *we therefore,* the official

Board of St. Matthew's Evangelical Lutheran Church of the city of Philadelphia, Pa., place this our action upon record.

Rev. Theophilus Stork, then of Winchester, Va., was unanimously called to the pastoral care of this church in the year A. D. 1841. He entered his new field of labor under many discouragements, occasioned by the divided and distracted condition of the congregation. By faithful labor and persevering prayer, however, a new era of progress was at once introduced. The list of members was rapidly increased, and precious seasons of revival were granted from the "presence of the Lord." As a preacher, Dr. Stork was eminently scriptural and impressive; as a pastor he was faithful and sympathizing; as a Christian he was earnest and exemplary. His guileless life and generous catholic spirit drew around him many strong and abiding friends. He was interested in all the prospects of his own church, and ever willing and ready to help in all general objects of Christian enterprise. He retained the pastoral charge of this congregation for nine years, and only resigned it to minister to the newly organized church of St. Mark's, which was composed of a colony from this church.

Having now passed away, we would remember his works with gratitude, and cite his devotion, zeal and fidelity to Christ as worthy of all commendation. We desire to record our conviction that his labors were in a marked degree owned of God, to this and to each of the congregations with which he was connected, and that in his death the Lutheran church has lost a bright and cherished ornament, and the church of Christ an able and distinguished defender.

Although he died before the infirmities of old age had come upon him, for "his eye was not dim, nor his natural force abated," yet could he with all propriety both say and write, as he did in the last known article from his pen, "I am now ready to be offered, and the time of my departure is at hand."

In view of this death, coming so quickly after that of his successor and intimate clerical friend, our late pastor, Rev. E. W. Hutter, D. D., we feel called upon, with chastened earnestness, to ponder anew the great fact that life is rapidly passing away, and that soon we too shall be called to render our account.

The example of our departed pastors is worthy our study and emulation, for we are commanded to "remember them which have spoken unto us the Word of God."

We extend to the sorrowing friends and relatives of our departed brother, the assurances of our sincerest sympathy and Christian condolence, rejoicing with them also in the worthy life and peaceful death of him we all so sincerely mourn.

Resolved, That this minute be communicated to the family of the deceased.

WM. J. MILLER, *Secretary*.

REV. CHARLES A. STORK, D. D.

CHAPTER I.

BIRTH AND PARENTAGE—JUVENILE CHARACTER—SCHOOL DAYS—LETTER OF HIS UNCLE JUDGE LYNCH—AT SCHOOL AT GETTYSBURG—AT HARTWICK—HARTWICK REMINISCENCES—LETTERS OF HIS PARENTS—HIS CONVERSION—REV. DR. HILLER—PROF. PITCHER—LETTERS FROM FRIENDS AND HIS PARENTS.

AS has been seen in the two preceding biographical sketches, both the grandfather and father of Charles A. Stork were Lutheran divines of eminent rank and wide-spread influence. Their names will be honored in the Lutheran Church for many years to come, and their highly-gifted and learned descendant will share with them their well-earned fame.

Charles was born on September 4, 1838, at the home of his maternal grandfather, William Lynch, Esq., near the village of Jefferson, Frederick county, Maryland. His father was Rev. Mr. Theophilus Stork, and his mother was Mary Jane Lynch Stork, daughter of the gentleman above named, and sister of the present Judge Lynch, of Frederick county. Mr. Stork was at this time pastor of the church at Winchester, Va. Three years after his birth, the child was taken to Philadelphia, where his father had accepted a call as pastor to St. Matthew's church. Five years after, in 1846, his mother died, near Germantown, and he and his younger brother William were left to the care of their bereaved father. Charles was now sent to a school kept by Rev. Lewis Eichelberger, in Winchester, Va., where, besides being taught the rudiments of education, he received some experimental instruction in the mysteries of the nursery which are not usually set down in the program of an academy. His juvenile indignation was often roused, because, with all his endearing caresses and soothing cradle-rockings, he could not quiet the clamors of his infantile charge. He has said, however, that he there laid a solid foundation for Latin.

The following interesting incident is mentioned by Dr. T. Stork in a letter to a friend in Winchester, dated February 19, 1844: "The children are all well and happy. Charles begins to read, and is of quite a serious turn of mind. Yesterday his mother was reading to him from the Bible, when he suddenly burst into tears and said, 'O mother, I am so wicked—how will I meet Jesus in judgment?' and then asked her to pray for him. And then Mary Jane and Charles and William knelt down in prayer together. It must have been quite an affecting scene. I was not present. Many of his summers during his boyhood were spent on the farm of his grandfather in Frederick county, where he continued to show an intense fondness for books, which was displayed from the time he had learned to read, and which ceased only with his death.

He seemed to take no delight in boyish sports, and was

consequently looked upon as morose and unsociable by his juvenile schoolmates. He would usually betake himself to some solitary place, the garret, the barn or a shady retreat in the woods, and there he would spend hours in reading books suitable to his capacity; but even as a boy his mental capacity was large, and books of an elevated character were thus read by him, and what he read he remembered. He was the most knowing lad within the acquaintance of many intelligent persons. In a letter from his stepmother, which will be inserted in its proper place, she says, "But, dear Charlie, how is it that you want 'The Arabian Nights?' I thought *you knew it by heart*—you have read it so often!" He was not over fourteen at that time, and the same might have been said of many other books in English literature—he knew them by heart, he had read them so often—and in many cases a single reading was sufficient to fasten every fact on his memory never to be erased.

The following letter from his uncle, Judge Lynch, comes in appropriately here:

FREDERICK, Md., March 14, 1855.

* * * * Charles, when a boy, spent much of his time in the summer season at my father's house. He was a quiet and studious lad; of a very sweet disposition, obedient and very respectful to his grandparents and his aunts, who had the care of him.

For one of his age, he was unusually fond of reading; I remember there were in the house old files of a paper, called, I think, *The New World*, full of interesting articles and stories of fiction. While the other children were at play, he would take these papers to a quiet room upstairs, lie flat upon his stomach on the floor, and read for hours at a time. He seemed to understand and remember what he read.

He never seemed fond of play. His brother Willie would often complain that Charlie was too lazy "to play with him and the negro boys on the farm."

When Charles was quite young, and before he went to Hartwick, I took him to a school in Winchester, Va., kept by Rev. Mr. Eichelberger. The only comment I ever heard him make upon the exercises of that school, was the complaint that, when not in the schoolroom, he was frequently required to "rock the baby," and when no one was present he would sometimes give the "baby" a slap. He was a remarkably good boy, especially kind and gentle towards the negro children on the farm, and was a great favorite with them all. And I think I might truly say of him, "And the child Samuel grew on, and was in favor both with the Lord and also with men."

As a man and a minister he was well known to you; and the Christian heroism with which he bore his long and painful sickness, we all remember.

TAKEN TO GETTYSBURG TO SCHOOL IN 1851.

At the age of 13, he was entered as a pupil in the preparatory school at Gettysburg, but he remained less than a year. He was sent there to prepare for admission into Pennsylvania College, but his father soon took him away, and he never afterwards patronized either the College or Seminary at that place.

The only information I could receive concerning Charles' career there, is furnished in the following letter from a respected layman, now living in Illinois:

Among the most cherished pictures of years gone by, which memory holds dear, is the bright cheery countenance and vigorous youthful form of a lovely lad with whom I lived in Pennsylvania College as room-mate about 6 weeks, near the close of a summer session, the summer (I think) of '51. We were associated in this relation, and for this brief time, by the absence from college of Seniors after their final examination. During this brief space of time, the only time we were destined to spend together on earth, I learned to love that youth as I have loved few beings on earth since. The brilliancy of his mind, the vivacity and sprightliness of his disposition, the patience, kindness and courtesy of his demeanor, are alike deeply engraven upon my memory and heart, and cherished among the choicest treasures of earlier associations.

In our eagerness to make time on those college stairways, we vied with each other, as students, in the number of steps one could distance at a single bound, whether we might be going up or down, and it so happened that Charles, in his eagerness to fly down stairs, sprained his ankle, which was the occasion of his confinement to our room a week or more, and of his going rather lame during a fortnight or so afterwards; and the way that child devoured books and reading matter while necessarily absent from recitation, was amazing to contemplate. A part of my time was pleasantly spent in waiting upon him, and in conveying food for mind and body to the youthful patient. But, though I rejoiced in the development of that youthful prodigy (for such I ever regarded him), and often eagerly hoped again to enjoy the sunshine of his magnetic personal presence, the fell destroyer intervened, and the pure spirit of my friend is basking in the glorious sunlight of His presence whom he delighted to honor upon earth. N. G. T.

I remember hearing Dr. Stork say that, during a long confinement, occasioned by a sprained foot, probably that alluded to above, he took lessons in Latin from one of our German ministers, who compelled him to read Horace over and over again until he got sick of him; but, said he, "when that teacher ceased giving me lessons, *I knew Latin!*"

I think that frequent repetition is the secret of successful teaching and learning.

TAKEN TO HARTWICK.

In 1852 he was taken with some other Philadelphia boys whose fathers were members of Dr. Stork's church, to Hartwick Seminary in New York, the classical department of which was at that time conducted by Rev. Dr. Miller.

I have been kindly furnished by some of his contemporaries at that place with some interesting reminiscences, which I shall here introduce, as well as some important family letters, all of which set forth the character of this most promising boy in a more impressive light than a mere narrative could do.

HARTWICK REMINISCENCES.

A fellow pupil of Charles A. Stork at Hartwick, thus writes: "When 'Charlie,' as we called him, delivered his maiden speech at the commencement exercises of the Seminary, Drs. Pohlman, Senderling, G. B. Miller, and many other prominent men, were present. Charlie performed his part so well that the boy gave promise of the coming great and good man. Dr. Stork, his father, at that time was in his prime, and his name and praise were in all the churches in York State. When the young orator had finished his address, there was a general and sincere applause, especially among the preachers and older persons in the crowd. Dr. Pohlman expressed the sentiment of all when he exclaimed in an audible whisper, 'This young Storkling will outwing the old Stork some day.' Charlie was a universal favorite during his school days at Hartwick."

LETTER FROM MRS. E. B. STORK TO CHARLES.

My Dearest Charles: Your prompt, ingenuous, and affectionate letter afforded me unmixed satisfaction; and in return we have all endeavored to please you by attending to your requests, which have been so modestly and sweetly presented. * * * Your dear father is as well pleased as I am with your affectionate letters, and you have given us good evidence that you are attending to the growth of the heart as well as to the expansion of your mind. This is as it should be, and we feel quite honored by your request for our photograph likenesses. * * * I have the books you wrote for. * * * My mother sends you . . for Christmas money, to which I add an equal amount, besides sending you lots of other good Christmas things, such as boys of your age like. * * * I also enclose a . . gold piece; do not spend it foolishly.

In another letter on family subjects, Mrs. Stork says in conclusion:

And now, my dearest child, lastly but not least among your list of duties, how is it with your soul?—are you living for eternity? Remember your responsibility even as a school boy, "Watch and pray." Cherish the sincerest love for your mother, and may the richest divine blessing be upon you, and may God's Spirit shield you from all evil.

FROM MRS. E. B. STORK TO CHARLES AT HARTWICK.

PHILADELPHIA, December 6th, 1853.

My Dear Charles: We will try to send you what you have already written for. But dear Charlie, how is it that you want the "Arabian Nights?" I thought you knew it by heart, you have read it so often. Do you love your precious Bible as much? How often do you read it? And do you remember *prayer?* Oh! my beloved child, these are the chief things to engage our earnest attention as travellers to *eternity.* Oh, do not trifle by the way, and perhaps lose your immortal soul, for a shadow, an empty dream. I do pray that you may be kept from bad books.

This is your great danger and temptation. Never take up a volume over which you cannot ask God's blessing. This is your only safeguard amidst the impure and infidel publications of the day. Shun the first thought of impurity and evil as you hope to be saved. "Blessed are the pure in heart, for they shall see God." "Evil communications corrupt good manners."

FROM MRS. E. B. STORK TO CHARLES.

PHILADELPHIA, Wednesday, Jan. 19th, 1853.

My Dear Charles: We are all of us delighted to find ourselves so affectionately remembered by you. I regret that you have been sick: perhaps you expose yourself too much to the cold; be careful, do not run into any danger upon the ice. You know you are rather heedless and incautious, and, my dear, you must *recollect* your *other* accidents as a check upon yourself. I desire that you should be strong-nerved and heroic, but the truly courageous are always prudent and self-possessed. Be, therefore, cheerful and active, but not venturesome. How did you get your skates? I am pleased that you have an opportunity of mixing in good and *educated female* society—it tends to refine the manners, and to remove the natural bashfulness and awkwardness of young boys and men. We enjoyed a most bountiful Christmas, and had a large number of good and serviceable gifts made to us by our friends. I was not well during the holidays. I have one request to prefer, which I trust you will not refuse or neglect, for the sake of one who *loves you;* it is that you will resolve, by the help of God, to bow your knees in prayer *every night and morning of this new year.* The Lord help you, my dear child, and enable you to *overcome all evil.*

Your affectionate   MOTHER.

FROM DR. T. STORK (*on the same sheet*).

Dear Charles: I am happy to hear you are so happy, and engaged so studiously in your duties. Nothing so cheers us as to hear of your doing well. The professors gave a very satisfactory account of all the Philadelphia boys. Try and always give us this satisfaction.

FROM THE PARENTS TO CHARLES AT HARTWICK SCHOOL.

PHILADELPHIA, February 3, 1853.

My Dearest Charles: You must not allow yourself even to imagine that I could forget you—no, indeed—you are ever on my heart, and in my prayers. And I would have made an endeavor to cheer you up ere this, if I could have known that you were ever a sufferer from heaviness of heart.

It must be terribly cold up there, and I am afraid your health may be impaired. How does it agree with your constitution? Are you warmly clad, and especially is your room kept comfortable, and are you well provided with bed covering? I am sorry that you had to shiver and shake so while writing your very interesting letter, and I should imagine that the intense cold weather would most effectually chase the blues from your soul.

We all laughed heartily over your description of a "Donation party," and your "rustic belle." What is she like, physically and mentally? And so your heart is not worth losing? Your father and I have set a much richer estimate upon your heart than you have, my boy. We think your capacities for loving are developing more and more, towards us, and we are delighted with your affection and ingenuous outgushings of youthful feeling.

I am pleased that you endeavor to make yourself agreeable to all around you, and that you are a favorite with Dr. Miller's family, and with your companions generally. Make a good use of your influence, and be ever high-minded and truthful. Be not too sensitive, and keep out of the way of tattlers and busybodies; these are the most dangerous kind of people, corrupting alike the heart and the mind. Be not afraid of men, but honor "God, who has power to cast both soul and body into hell."

I should like to hear Bulwer's history of a man who "died of a good heart," although this author is rather a questionable authority for anything, radically good. Suppose you write it out for us in your next letter. The terms "good" and "bad" depend very much upon the balance in which they are weighed.

I always weigh them in the balance of the sanctuary, and with reference to eternity. But if they are graded according to the world, and solely in reference to time—the same words will differ very widely in their meaning. Which of these scales do you use, when you prefer a good mind to a good heart? The Bible says, "The heart of the wise teacheth his tongue and addeth learning to his lips." It is pleasant to have a powerful intellect, and to exercise a mental force that shall be felt by all our compeers; but considering all things, I think I would rather solicit from high heaven a pure and holy heart; for my dear boy will find as great a difficulty in making (or in acquiring in the course of time) a good heart out of a bad one, as he would in making a powerful and good mind out of a weak and inferior one. Let no sophistry delude thee. "Every good gift, and every perfect gift is from above, and cometh down from the Father of light, with whom is no variableness, neither shadow of turning." And a "poor mind" could get wisdom also, if united to a right state of heart. "For if any man lack wisdom, let him ask of God, who giveth to all men liberally and upbraideth not." Thus you see, according to my scales, yours might not in the end prove to be a prudent and safe choice. I am not in the least surprised that you should be for a moment dazzled by its apparent desirableness. I wish you were among us again. I do not like this separation of children from the home circle. Willie will write to you soon: he wonders what makes you so gloomy. He says "He feels sad sometimes, but he don't know why," and he thinks you don't know the cause either. Your father says you are like him, that he used to feel like you, and often he would sit by himself, and weep bitterly; it may be constitutional, and you must not give way to a vague, melancholy feeling; try to regulate your feelings by reason, and conscience, and prayer. Seek to know the true cause, and then consolation will creep in, and gradually dissipate the gloom. Abbott says, "It is some secret, unacknowledged, discontent with ourselves which produces this uneasiness. It is unrepented sin weighing upon the conscience, and can only be permanently cured by the forgiveness of God, and His peace abiding in the soul."

If it is the movement of the Spirit of God upon your soul, strange as it may be to you, I must rejoice, and instead of praying that you may "regain your spirits," I must pray that you may be yet more unhappy in yourself, until you shall find peace in Jesus.

> "None but Jesus, none but Jesus,
> Can do helpless sinners good."
>
> "Cold as I feel this heart of mine, yet, since I feel it so—
> It gives some signs of life within, however low."

Can you sympathize with these lines? Do you pray morning and evening? You did not reply to my questions in my last letter. Will you be particular to reply to them in your next? Catherine sends her love, and now may the "Friend of Sinners" help you in your despondency, and give light to your darkness. He is ever near thee to cheer. Thus prays your affectionate mother, EMMA B. STORK.

Dear Charles: Mother has given you the best advice. I hope you will receive it and practice it, as it comes from one that loves you very dearly.

I used to feel very sad when at school away from home; it will gradually pass away. But, if you do not behave kindly to those around you, and thus excite their opposition, you must try to behave better. You never can expect to be happy unless you do right. And a powerful intellect without a good heart is an awful curse, instead of a blessing, "For what will it profit a man if he gain the whole world and lose his soul." You must not forget Eternity. Though you are young, you may die, and what would become of your soul if you do not seek forgiveness in the blood of Jesus? Give your heart to Christ, and then you will be happy. I am glad to hear of your progress in study. Think of our trip (next summer, if God spares us) to Niagara, and cheer up. May God help you, my dear Charles, and the greatest pleasure will be to hear that you strive to behave well and be good. Your affectionate father,

T. STORK.

FROM MRS. E. B. STORK TO CHARLES, AT HARTWICK.

PHILADELPHIA, March 29, 1853.

. . . . . . There is one alarming sign about your mental taste, which grieves and disturbs my heart : it is your fondness for *novels*, and that you should admire such writers as Bulwer, Byron, and others of like stamp. This occasions me much uneasiness, for I fear you may imbibe some of the pernicious principles which they insidiously inculcate. You well know they were men of immoral lives, and you would not dare to associate with such ; and yet you like to pore over their books without contamination of heart. My dear child, the Bible says, that no fountain can send forth, at the same time, both sweet and bitter waters, and "a bad tree cannot bring forth good fruit." I fear you are self-deceived in this matter ; be assured that this evil is no slight one against which I would guard you ; it may keep you out of the kingdom of heaven.

I will give you some safe rules, to which, as you value your immortal soul, I beseech you to give heed. They are given by Leigh Richmond to his children: "Characters are speedily discerned by their choice of books. Novels in prose I need not now forbid ; ignorant as you are of their bad tendency by experience, you, I am persuaded, trust me on that head, and you will never sacrifice time, attention or affection to them. But beware of novels in verse. Poets are more dangerous than prose writers when their principles are bad. Were Lord Byron no better poet than he is a man, he might have done little harm ; but when a bad man makes his good poetry the vehicle of his bad sentiments, he does mischief by wholesale."

The best rule with regard to books is this: " Books are good or bad in their effects as they make us relish the Word of God the more or less, after we have read them." Be cheerful, but not a giggler. Be serious, but not dull. Be communicative, but not forward. Be kind, but not servile. Remember, God's eye is in every place, and His ear in every company. Beware of levity and familiarity with young women ; a modest reserve is the only safe path. Grace is needful here—ask for it in prayer. Strive to maintain a praying mind through the day, not only at the usual stated periods, but everywhere, and at all times and in all companies. This is your best preservative against error, weakness; and always remember that you are in the midst of temptations, and never more so than when pleased with outward objects and intercourse. Pray and watch.

My dear Charles, I feel very serious. We have had a season of refreshing from the Great Head of the Church upon our Lutheran Zion. Your dear father has been greatly blessed in his labors, and on Easter Sunday he received by baptism and confirmation, and by profession and certificate, eighty-one persons into the church. It was a solemn occasion, and all our hearts were stirred—the church was crowded, and settees were placed in the aisles, and numbers could not get in in the morning. The Communion was in the evening. The Saviour seemed visibly present among us, and we trust it will be a day long to be remembered by us all. Oh! that you had been here to have partaken in the blessing; but our prayers are following you, and we trust the Lord will enable you to give yourself to Him in an everlasting covenant, and to be numbered among His saints.

FROM MRS. E. B. STORK, TO CHARLES, WHILE AT HARTWICK SEMINARY, AND WHEN HE WAS SIXTEEN YEARS OF AGE.

PHILADELPHIA, December 12, 1853.

My Dear Charles: I was glad to hear from you, as well as interested and amused with your letter. I am glad also that you are kept so busy with your studies. . . . . Your aunt, Sarah Lynch, mentions your having written to their family, and that your amusing style of writing afforded them much gratification. . . . . Your dear father is better, and his book (Children of the New Testament) will be out to-morrow, and I hope he will take a good rest in body and mind. . . . . I am sorry you will be disappointed in not keeping "Christmas at home" this year, but it will not be so cheerful a one to us, as there are so many of our friends sick and dying.

*   *   *   *   *   *   *   *

I have no remedy for failing spirits and dark, melancholy hours, but active exertion in some useful pursuit, and prayer and praise. "Is any one afflicted, let him pray; is any merry, let him sing psalms."

I trust that my dear boy, amid the preparation and bustle of this life, is not forgetting the "one thing needful."

* * * * * * * *

(To the above are appended a few lines from the father.)

I am now about as usual, but I sometimes think that my church (St. Mark's, Philadelphia) is too large for the strength of my throat. It is with great difficulty I can preach twice a day. Perhaps a different position would suit me better.

* * * * * * * *

HIS CONVERSION.

Reminiscence of Dr. C. A. Stork, by Dr. A. Hiller.

Dr. Stork came to Hartwick Seminary in the fall of '51 or the spring of '52, and remained here until the close of the summer term of 1854. He boarded in the family of Dr. Miller, and some of the Doctor's children who were home at the time, and were near young Stork's age, have pleasant memories of his school-boy days. He was quite young when his father brought him here, but soon became a great favorite. He was good company for those of his own age and even his elders, was full of wit and humor, and after study hours in the evening, he joined heartily in the sports of the youngsters at Dr. Miller's house, his favorite game being "*Consequences.*"

He was very fond of reading, and always had a book on hand which he managed to find time to read without neglecting his lessons, which he acquired very easily. In this way he gathered information rapidly, and used it to good advantage in his debates in the Philophronean Society, of which he soon became an active member. I well remember a very quaint and original composition he read on a public occasion while here, on the subject "*The Last Man,*" in which he very graphically portrayed the winding up of the world's history, as viewed from the stand-point of the last surviving inhabitant. About this time, when his active inquiring mind was beginning to assume freedom of thought and speculation that had no special regard to orthodoxy, in the good providence of God he was converted to Christ. I remember the circumstances very well. At that time it was Dr. Miller's custom to hold cottage prayer-meetings on Sabbath evening at the different houses in the neighborhood. At one of these meetings, at the house of Mr. D——, to the surprise of all present, Miss M—— became very deeply impressed, and with a good deal of emotion arose and asked for prayers. She was followed by her associate, Miss D——. This unexpected demonstration of the Spirit's presence, sensibly effected all in the room, not excepting young Stork. These two young ladies who arose for prayer were associates of his, with whom he was quite intimate, one being Dr. Miller's youngest daughter. My chum, Dr. Magee and I, that night when we returned from the meeting, on entering the Seminary campus, heard some one making a good deal of noise in the south wing of the building, and on listening we discovered that it was Charley Stork's voice. He had rushed out of the meeting ahead of us, and, as it afterwards proved, was making this demonstration with the view of throwing off his conviction. Dr. Miller, on discovering the presence of a special religious interest, appointed prayer-meeting for every evening during the ensuing week, and soon Charley became so burdened with a sense of personal guilt, that he went to Dr. Miller for advice. He gave up his studies, and I think, for a week, Dr. Miller talked and prayed with him and gave him suitable books to read. He came in our room, and Magee and I talked and prayed with him, and did what we could to lead him to the Saviour. For several days he thus continued an earnest, anxious inquirer, giving himself wholly to the question of his own personal salvation. It was during this time that the prayer-meeting was held at Squire D——'s, to which Bro. Magee refers in his reminiscence as published in the *Observer*. It was really after several days of patient, prayerful seeking, that Charley (as we all called him) found Jesus.

On the 24th of December, 1853, he was confirmed by Dr. Miller, and thus received as a member of the Hartwick Seminary Lutheran church. I don't think that Charley ever took a letter from this church; at least the records do not indicate it. The only note appended to his name is "*removed.*"

The Professors and Christian students who were here at that time greatly rejoiced when Charley Stork was converted to Christ, for we saw that he was a boy of unusual promise, and that if spared would be a *power* in the world, and we were anxious that that power should be devoted to the cause of truth and right and to the upbuilding of the church.

REMINISCENCES OF DR. STORK.

Dr. Irving Magee, of Rondout, N. Y., in a private letter written on learning of the death of Dr. Stork, gives the following pleasant reminiscences of him when they were boys together at college:

"Not only was Dr. Stork a *class*-mate in Williams, but we were *room*-mates and each other's most intimate friends all through. We spent three years together at Hartwick fitting for college. I was there his Bible-class teacher in the Sabbath-school, and most intimately associated with his conversion. It has always been, and more so now, a most precious thing to me, that he said to me some ten years ago about as follows: 'Do you know, Chum, that you said the words which, under God, brought about my conversion? You remember the cottage prayer-meetings at Hartwick. Well, after a meeting at Esquire D——'s, as we were coming out of the gate, you took my arm and walked down to the Seminary and talked to me about becoming a Christian. It impressed me very deeply. I went to my room and prayed, and date my conversion from that walk and conversation with you.'

"He had before mentioned a strange experience of that night. He felt very rebellious and resistant. He had been taught always to read his Bible and pray before retiring. He went to his room in a veritable tumult of feeling. He threw his hat in one corner and his coat in another, and paced the floor. He finally stopped in the middle of the room, took out a penny, put his feet apart, and bending forward and with a sort of reckless wildness unlike himself at any other time, said: 'Heads I read, tails I don't read'—and tossed the penny. It fell heads. It seemed as if God had spoken to him from the subdued manner in which he added: 'I took my Bible and read and prayed and gave myself to the Saviour.'

"He was always the same lovable fellow in college that he has always been since, and was a great favorite with every one. I think it will be pleasant for you to know that he was especially such with President Garfield, who was with us there. We were members of the same society, and were frequently in each other's rooms. Charley was one of the youngest and smallest boys in college. I have known Garfield to sit for long times with his arms about Charley in the most lovable and brotherly way. This fondness continued till he died. It is very pleasant to recall them both now.

"We were settled side by side, you know, too, in Baltimore, and our relations were the most intimate, loving and unbroken from first to last. I never loved any one more dearly, and he was right royally worthy of it."

LETTER FROM A FORMER HARTWICK STUDENT, AT PRESENT ITS PRINCIPAL.

When I came here a student twenty years ago, the traditions of "Charley Stork" were yet quite vivid. I remember the saying that was common, "that although Dr. Theophilus was an eminent divine, yet that the young Stork would fly higher than the old one." The habits of the student Stork must have been somewhat peculiar, as I have often heard that he was not very particular with his person or his clothing; indeed, it is said that Mrs. Miller had to take him in hand occasionally with regard to his toilet; and a lady speaking of him said, he invariably rolled up his pants when he was out, and left them rolled up wheresoever he was.

It is related of him and his three Philadelphia friends, that one Christmas they received a present of each a sled, and they were put up in the form of a box, and within were packed the various presents which parents and friends sent for their Christmas presents. Each of the boys had a special female friend, and it was the amusement of all on-lookers to see the boys draw their *girls* up and down street on their new sleds.

It is no doubt a most fortunate Providence that he was converted here just at the time he was. He is said to have had at that time a remarkably inquiring mind, and was never satisfied short of seeing the *reason* for things. This tendency, unbalanced by a religious conviction, was steadily leading him into a mild skepticism, and I have often heard it said that he would have made a "first-class infidel." It is, therefore, a very gratifying fact that his mind was turned to the truth, and he saved to the Church and the Gospel. J. P.

The following letter from a friend, although dated long after the occurrence of the events narrated in several of the preceding pages, yet will be adjudged not to be inappropriately placed here:

In 1873 Dr. Stork, jr., delivered a lecture to the Seminary students at Gettysburg—I think it was the Rice Lecture. Among other good points he made these: *Personal piety and personal character*, and in a discussion that arose among those present, he maintained, that in order to a successful ministry a man must have these two, *i. e.* there must be a Christian man back of all natural and acquired endowments, etc., and then related this: "The silent influence of two men of undoubted *Christian character* have had more to do in forming my character and the bent of my mental activity than all others combined, so far as I can judge. These two men were Rev. Dr. G. B. Miller, of Hartwick Seminary, of whose teaching I now remember nothing, for I was quite young then yet when he was my teacher, and the President of Williams College, from whose philosophy I dissent entirely; but their godly characters have gone with me a *silent, powerful influence through life.*" This made a deep impression on the students and all present. Dr. Stork made this statement with great earnest emphasis.

In the afternoon of that same day I called on Dr. Stork, and presented him a steel engraving of Rev. Dr. Miller, such as are found in a volume of Dr. Miller's sermons. Dr. Stork recognized his old teacher at a glance, and then repeated substantially the statement above given. I spent a pleasant hour with the Doctor in pleasant chat about Hartwick and its associations. Dr. Stork has left the Church just such a precious legacy—a *Christian character—consecrated manhood.*

C. W. E.

LETTER FROM MRS. E. B. STORK.

OCTOBER 31, 1854.

My Dear Charles: . . . . . . I do feel thankful that you know the power of Jesus' grace to sustain you, my dear child, in your conflicts. Drink deep draughts at this fountain to sustain you in this wilderness, for, oh! my child, you will need it in these latter days, when "iniquity abounds"—let not "your love grow cold," for "he only that endureth to the end shall be saved." I tremble for you, but I pray also, and an Almighty arm will sustain you, and give you the final victory. Persevere unto the end and thou shalt be saved. I rejoice that you can "delight thyself in the Lord (in the holy profession which you have chosen), and He will certainly give thee the desire of thine heart," and souls shall be thy hire and reward in the day of the Lord Jesus. . . . . . . I sigh for deliverance, and in some moments of "heaviness through manifold temptations," I could fain wish we were all safely landed upon the shores of the heavenly Canaan.

> "But present duty I'll fulfill,
> And patient wait my Master's will."
>
> "Though arduous the struggle, 't will cease before long,
> And then, oh! how pleasant the conqueror's song."

"Resist the devil, and he will flee from thee." Believe, only believe. "All things are possible to him that believeth."

FROM DR. T. STORK (*on same sheet*).

Dear Charles: . . . . . . I was delighted with your last letter. I trust, dear Charles, you will hold fast the profession of your faith, and let nothing move you. God has promised that His grace shall be sufficient. And that declaration of Christ concerning His love to His disciples—"As the Father hath loved me, so have I loved you." O, how precious is the love of Jesus ! We will pray for you, and if you look to Jesus you shall never fall.

LETTER FROM HIS FATHER.

My Dear Charles : I have been so much engrossed with various extra duties, such as delivering lectures before various institutes and societies, that I have neglected to write to you for some time. I am happy to hear, that although you have evil imaginings and inward trials, you are determined to persevere. If you had not trials and conflicts, your conversion would be suspicious. For the moment we decide for Christ, then will begin a warfare which will have to be waged with more or less severity through life. But he that endures to the end shall be saved. "Be thou faithful unto death," said Jesus, "and I will give thee a crown of life." He that is for you is greater than all that are against you. He will not suffer you to be tempted above what you are able to bear. Only look to Jesus, by faith and prayer. Hold fast the profession of your faith, for He is faithful that promised. You are never forgotten in our prayers.

* * * * * * * *

It will be necessary for you to to begin to think about when you expect to finish your collegiate studies. What do you think of Gettysburg now ? How would you like Williams College ? Or how would you like to graduate in the University here ? Then you could be at home. It is comparatively a matter of little importance about the institution in which a man graduates—for every man, after all, must make *himself*, if he is ever to be anything. Of course I mean under the blessing of God. Please let me know your feelings on these points. In regard to your studying for the ministry, you know my sentiments—you know that it would afford me the greatest satisfaction, and that no earthly honors in any sphere of human station would be as grateful to me as to see you a devoted and respectable and useful minister of Christ. But, then, you must be influenced not by any desire simply to gratify me, but you should feel constrained by a conviction of duty and a sincere desire to glorify God. If you sincerely seek to know the will of God, the path of duty will be made plain.

ANOTHER LETTER FROM HIS FATHER.

PHILADELPHIA, April 2. 1855.

My Dear Charles : . . . . . . I have seen from time to time notices of the religious interest at Williams College. I rejoice that so many of the young have consecrated themselves to Christ. God grant that many of them may devote themselves to the noble and Christ-like work of the ministry! I am glad, too, that *you* have shared in the *grace*, and that your soul has been refreshed and your faith strengthened. May you hold fast to the profession of your faith—steadfast to the end.

I hope you will make good use of your time, and prepare yourself well for a "workman that needeth not to be ashamed of his work." The older you grow the more will your judgment and conscience approve of the course you have adopted—the more glorious will appear the work of the ministry, and the more vivid your conscious unworthiness to partake in such a work—so Paul felt, you know.

I expect to return to my church in a few months, but I tremble, for of late I have had symptoms of my old disease. O how I wish you were through and could be associated with me; it would be a good school for you, and a great relief to me. Go on—perhaps I can, by God's blessing, hold on until you are ready to assist me.

LETTER FROM CHARLES AT WILLIAMS COLLEGE.

WILLIAMSTOWN, May 5, 1855.

Dear Mother : . . . . . . Our vacation commenced a day or two ago, and already time begins to hang heavy on my hands—somehow or other I feel very little inclination for study or heavy reading, and light reading don't suit my taste very well, so I hardly know what to do without my regular duties. I suppose my lassitude comes in a great measure from the fatigue of the mind after hard labor—for the last term is the hardest in the year, I believe, as we have very close examinations at the close —four of these examinations I think I can say I came through perfectly, the other two only tolerably. When I look back over the past winter I feel very much dissatisfied with what I have accomplished. I know I could have done more if I had tried, and though I am conscious that I have advanced in some degree, I feel that my time has not been improved as it should have been; yet I think it is not always good to look back so despondingly, for though the past may have been ill-spent, there is still a future to work in, and I do not know but that this feeling of time misspent urges us on to greater exertions. I know it does me, and I feel that by God's help I can and will do more. My health has been very good this winter, and I think my throat has been affected less than it has been for some winters before. I am afraid however, when I think of it, that it will interfere a great deal with my labors as a preacher.

FROM MRS. E. B. STORK TO CHARLES.

PHILADELPHIA, March 18, 1856.

. . . . . . Your dear father is better in health and spirits, and is entirely absorbed in his church and his Lord. He has the largest class of catechumens he has ever had, and many interesting inquirers among them. . . . . . . The Spirit of God seems evidently to be with us as a church, and we all feel this to be a solemn and important crisis. Our praying people have been for months past asking help of God. He has mercifully appeared for our encouragement. I wish you were here. I mourn your absence from our home circle, but all is well; if we are one in Christ, we can never be divided in heart communion. I should be comforted if you could find congenial spirits among your companions. I think I can fully sympathize with you, and I am happy in you as a child of God. I bless the Lord for leading you more and more out of yourself, and enabling you to give yourself more entirely to His service. It is a glorious cause, and your cross-badge will be your crown-circlet forever.

"Be of good courage, and He shall strengthen thine heart."

FROM MRS. E. B. STORK.

PHILADELPHIA, Sept. 25, 1856.

...... I am pleased that you cherish home recollections, and I think you would feel very happy among us now, when we have so many sources of internal enjoyment.......... Father is crushingly busy as usual, and almost ready for the publisher. His "Home Scenes" will appear at Christmas. Besides this, he has undertaken to prepare a juvenile book for the holidays, and he also writes for the *Home Journal*. He is quite too much occupied with pen and ink for his own comfort. . . .

. . . I want you to be frank about every thing which either pleases or pains you. You may ever command my sympathy, counsel and prayers. How is it about your sickness at Hartwick? Were you pained by old remembrances, or tried by the jeers or reproaches of the heedless and frivolous? I am glad that you feel as you do about your *life conflict to be a man*, and resolutely work out your probation. Every noble heart feels an earnest desire to acquit itself honorably, and to the satisfaction of friends. So be hopeful, my son, and the joy of the Lord will be your strength. I must leave a space for father.

FROM DR. T. STORK (*on the same sheet with the above*).

Your letter was very gratifying to us. We were glad to hear you had such a pleasant vacation, and that you were again entered upon a pleasant session.

I can appreciate your difficulties in regard to life. It is a serious thing to live. I have almost as much difficulty now as in the beginning, relative to the questions which now perplex your mind. It is perhaps best to feel diffident of ourselves, that we may be kept in constant and humble reliance upon God. You will thus learn to feel and say with Paul: "When I am weak, then am I strong." "Without me," says Christ, "ye can do nothing." But then there is another aspect of the subject: you ought not allow too much anxiety about the future to interfere with your present duty and enjoyment. "Sufficient unto the day is the evil thereof." Try to meet present duty and present obligation, and let the future be, as it is, with the Lord. The best way to meet the future is to fulfill the duties of the present; "As thy day, so shall thy strength be." If you are faithful you will never be tried above what you are able to bear. Only be faithful to Christ, and he will take care of all, and make you a blessing.

We are getting along very pleasantly. Our home is a sanctuary of innocent pleasure and holy worship. . . . .
I am very busy—two books to come out by Christmas. Do not trouble yourself about expense, provided you are reasonably economical. There is nothing I do with greater pleasure than helping you to your education and preparation for life. Only give me the satisfaction thus far granted in your character and deportment, and all will be well.

CHAPTER II.

DETERMINES TO STUDY FOR THE MINISTRY—JUVENILE INCIDENT—HOME LETTERS—WILLIAMS COLLEGE, 1859—CHARACTER AS STUDENT—COLLEGE LITERARY PERFORMANCES—HESITATES ABOUT THE MINISTRY—FINAL DECISION—H. M. ALDEN'S SKETCH—ANDOVER SEMINARY—CAMPING OUT—PRIVATE LETTER—DEPLORES THE CONDITION OF HIS EYES—HIS VIEWS ON RESPONSIBILITY—DEJECTION.

FROM MRS. E. B. STORK.

* * * I am glad, dear Charles, that you feel your own insufficiency for the momentous work to which you have devoted yourself. A minister of Jesus should in an especial manner be transferred into the image of his Lord. We are now reading the "*Mind of Jesus*," and I wish I could send you a copy of the work: at the conclusion of each meditation is repeated this motto: "Arm yourselves likewise with the same mind." It is a most edifying book.

In connection with the declared intention of Charles to become a minister may be stated the following little incident. When he was about fourteen years of age, his father once asked him what profession he would choose: he replied, "Father, I do not want to be a minister, for all good people die young." At a more mature age, he changed his mind.

FROM MRS. E. B. STORK.

My Dear Charles: We received your welcome letter, and I seize a moment to respond. Your dear father is too busy to write; he has just finished his proof-reading of "Home Scenes"—and is employed upon a Christmas book for children, "Childhood of

Jesus." I think they will be fine; "Work, work, work," father says;—he don't get time enough to sleep, and he designs some *one week*, to make a *reserve* to himself and sleep *it out* to his content and satisfaction. How do you think you will relish such a life of constant activities? Your friends will be glad to see you, and I hope you will in answer to our prayers be safely conducted home, and find it profitable to be among us again. I hope you are, with all your wisdom, wise concerning your habits and health—habit is second nature. How is it? Do you *obey* the laws of your outer man, as well as furnish and regulate the inward spirit? It is a very important duty—purity without and purity within—a clean and wholesome body invigorates and refines the soul. Use regular exercise in the open air, and renounce all stimulants, tobacco, coffee, novels and the like. "Purify the chambers of imagery," and be a Levite without blemish, or imperfection, or rebuke. "He that overcometh shall inherit all things." . . . . . . Our church is now very promising, and I hope spiritual blessings are in store for her; we have a female prayer-meeting at our house on Saturday afternoon, preparatory to the Sabbath, and it is a pleasant hour to meet with Christ and His people. Trusting to meet you soon in our *home* circle, I close. "May the Lord bless you, and keep you."

FROM MRS. E. B. STORK, PHILA., 1856.

Your dear father is better in health and spirits; he is wholly absorbed in his Church and with his Saviour. He has the largest class he has ever had, and many interesting cases, but yet there are many who harden themselves under all these privileges. The Spirit of God seems evidently with us as a church; we all feel this to be a solemn and important crisis. Our praying people have been for months past asking help of God, and He has mercifully appeared for our encouragement and reward. I wish you were here. I mourn your absent place from our home circle, but all is well—if we are one in Christ, we can never be divided in heart communion. I should be comforted if you could find congenial spirits and heart warmth among your companions. I think I can fully sympathize with you, and I am happy in you as a child of God. I bless the Lord for leading you more and more out of yourself, and enabling you to give up yourself more entirely to His service. It is a glorious cause, and your cross-badge will be your crown-circlet forever! "Be of good courage," and He shall strengthen thine heart.

FROM MRS. E. B. STORK, OCT. 24, 1856.

* * * * I am glad the time is so near which will bring you once again among us. I quite envy you the lovely mountain scenery which regales your eyes whichever way you look, with the diversified color of the herbage and other forests. I am gratified with the affectionate spirit which breathes through your letters, and also with the progress which they evidence in spiritual things. Doubtless, much of your depression is constitutional, but it belongs to all feeling hearts and earnest spirits, and it is, as you observe, a wholesome influence, if not excessive or morbid, to temper the innate vanity and levity of the youthful heart, and to produce a more thoughtful and humble character. . . . . . . Your dear father is much gratified with your conduct; it is a great privilege to have your parents' blessing and approval upon your opening years, and you well remember the promises to obedient sons, and you will be encouraged throughout your future life.

FROM MRS. E. B. STORK AT A LATER DATE.

"I should like your candid criticism upon my translations from Chateaubriand, which have appeared in the *Home Journal*. . . . . . . I am pleased that you cherish home recollections, and think you would feel very happy among us now we have so many sources of internal enjoyment. . . . . . . Your father is crushingly busy as usual, and his "Home Scenes" will come out this Christmas. Besides this, he has to prepare a juvenile work for the holidays. and writing for the *Home Journal*. He is quite too much occupied with pen and ink for his own comfort.

FROM THE SAME, DEC. 18, 1857.

* * * * I am rather disappointed about Mrs. ——.*

---

* A popular writer of those days.

What a life influence she might exert for her Saviour, over her own flesh and blood, and also over the young men around her; how powerful such a woman would be, if her heart carried her forward in this direction! What is fame to a mother's heart weeping over a Christless child? No, no! better one soul for Jesus than a world of empty plaudits. One might be tempted to envy the one, but the vain wish is silenced and reconciled by the other. It is also encouraging to a modest, retiring spirit, that there is not a universality of greatness in all departments, and that a limited circle may be the most useful as to the final issue, if faithfully filled up, and one is satisfied to work in patient continuance in well doing.

AT WILLIAMS COLLEGE, 1857.

Here, as at Hartwick—indeed, as at all the schools he ever attended—he was a universal favorite and maintained a high rank for talent and acquirements. At Williams, he was one of the youngest and smallest of the students, but he was equal to all and superior to many in the possession of brains, love of books and of study, and distinguished for uprightness of character and soundness of moral principles.

He there found as a student his old Hartwick friend, Irving Magee, who had such a decided influence upon him in determining his decision in favor of practical Christianity; he also became intimate with Horace Scudder, the popular author; Henry M. Alden, at present connected with the literary department of *Harper's Weekly;* and with James A. Garfield, late President of the United States.

Although he had taken an open and decided stand as a Christian, he sometimes hesitated as to which profession he should pursue for life, and in his youthful inexperience he at one time thought of studying law. But that idea was not cherished long, and just before he had finally made up his mind for the ministry, his father writes: "In regard to your studying for the ministry, you know my sentiments; you know it would afford me the greatest satisfaction, and that no earthly honors in any sphere of human action would be as grateful to me as to see you a respectable and useful minister of Christ. But then you must be influenced not by any desire simply to gratify me."

His father was gratified beyond expression at the final decision of his son, and already began to lay plans for their mutual work in the church field; and the delighted father lived to see his ardent hopes realized in having his gifted and highly educated son as his colleague and assistant in the church.

We have a picture of his college character presented by a fellow-student, Mr. Henry M. Alden, of *Harper's Weekly*, which was furnished as an introductory article to the "Selections" from the writings of Dr. C. A. Stork by his brother, Theophilus B. Stork, Esq. Mr. Alden and Charles were intimate friends, and among many other touching and fraternal observations, while speaking of his modesty and unostentatious disposition, he says:

"He probably never did anything in his whole life with the purpose of drawing attention to himself. He entered into no competition with his fellows. With unusual power of expression, both as a writer and as a speaker, he showed no desire for such expression. He had no outward eccentricity, and even his indifference to passing affairs was negative rather than positive, and escaped observation. He was reticent without shyness; and whatever may have been his inner life, he gave no outward sign of it.

"In all that makes up the visible exterior of a man, he was the same from the first to the last observation I had of him. When he entered college, he had in all these respects reached maturity, although he was almost the youngest of his class. . . Though not inviting notice, there were some peculiarities in his personal appearance that would arrest the attention of even a casual observer. His features—as large as those we notice in the portraits of Beethoven—clearly showed his Teutonic paternity; while his mobile mouth, his small hands—as delicate as a woman's—and the sensitiveness that interpenetrated his German phlegm, as clearly showed that his mother was of the finer southern type. His mood was that of habitual thoughtfulness, usually contemplative, but under excitement, lambent with fire and humor.

"His intellectual habits and tastes were, even at this early period, fully formed. He had read all the great books of our literature, and his literary taste was almost an instinct. He especially appreciated authors in whom humor was a prominent characteristic: but his taste was catholic, and he delighted in the keen humor of Thackeray as well as the broad caricature of Dickens. In history he read those works which interpreted the great drama of human progress, caring little for those which contained annals only. The early English poets were as familiar to him as the later.

"I approach with some difficulty the period of our nearer acquaintance. The memory of such a friendship is too sacred for expression, except in the lofty strains of a new 'In Memoriam.' It was the ideal friendship of my life, and its preciousness to me may be understood from the fact that at that time I had no other intimate friend. It was the characteristic of his generous nature that he sought to draw me out of the solitude in which I had immured myself. He had few intimate personal friends. Among them were James A. Garfield, of the class of '56, and Horace E. Scudder, of the class of '57. Garfield's graduation was near at hand. I remember his last evening at Williams, when a number of us joined hands with him on the college green and sang 'Auld Lang Syne.' Scudder was especially congenial to Stork, not only because of their intellectual sympathy, but because each of them had a pure, sweet and wholesome nature—the natural basis of a manly and lasting friendship.

"But one year of college life remained to Stork and myself, and we embraced every opportunity, such as friends always seek for intercourse, much of our time being spent in reading together our favorite authors. Of modern writers the poet Tennyson made the strongest impression on our minds. His thought—moulded after the antique, mediæval, or modern type—was at once poetic and interpretative. His wonderful rhythm and classic perfection of form gave æsthetic satisfaction, and we found in his poems sympathy with currents of modern thought into which we were drifting—especially that of "honest doubt." The studies of the senior year were largely of a speculative character, and, since these were pursued under the guidance of Dr. Mark Hopkins, it is needless to add that they developed independent thinking. But our talk was not wholly of books and metaphysics, and it is worthy of note here that Stork loved to talk about his home, and about the members of his family, always in terms of deepest affection. While then, and always, I was impressed by his sincerity, fidelity and earnestness, I could not but notice his disposition to indulge in playful humor. His dignity was natural, without any stiffness or self-consciousness. He was always companionable, and no classmate was ever more popular than he was.

"Among his writings at this time, I particularly remember an essay on Rhythm, which was published in the *Williams Quarterly*, and which displayed not only his extensive reading in English poetry, but also a critical ability of the highest order, because it was interpretative and sympathetic, as well as keen in analysis. But as a promise of his literary future, a brief essay entitled "Winter," written I believe while he was preparing for college at Hartwick Seminary, made a stronger and more lasting impression upon my mind. His winter landscape was associated with Shakespeare's *King Lear*. Nature was more to him than books, but its charms were, in his mind, inseparably connected with the creations of the master poets. He was himself a poet, having much of the virility and dramatic power that distinguish the works of Robert Browning; but he modestly regarded what he did in this field as studies made for his own satisfaction rather than as having any claim to public recognition.

"In his entire college career I can recall but a single instance of any public expression on his part. It was at a meeting of the faculty, students and friends of the college, in recognition of some important benefaction, and he had been chosen as a speaker to represent his class. He had written nothing for recitation; but, when he came to speak, it was evident that he had let his subject take full possession of his mind, and his address was natural in manner, thoughtful, eloquent and impressive.

AT ANDOVER.

"A few months after graduation we entered the Theological Seminary at Andover. He had reached the period when youth forecasts for itself a lofty career. It is not necessary here to indicate the plans we formed. Was there ever youthful aspiration that did not grandly shape the dream of the future—a dream never to be realized? The student lives in a world of his own—a world in which nothing seems impossible. He will probably do little of all that he then so vastly determines. He soon enters another world, in which duty takes the place of aspiration; and, if he follows this new guide, he finds later on that the work really undertaken and accomplished is, after all, greater than his early dream. Yet I am sure that neither of us ever afterwards regretted the studies in Greek literature, in the history of philosophy and the philosophy of history, that occupied us at the Seminary.

"If in connection with these studies, the spirit and active exercise of doubt were developed, they were naturally incident to the intellectual period upon which we had entered. All discords were afterward resolved. Until the component parts of the mind's object-glass are fitly joined together, there must be mental aberration. But those who read the "Selections" from his writings will find there no indication of such aberration. It will be clear to the reader, that whatever mental struggles he may have passed through, after the conflict his Saviour remained to him the one great real presence of his life."

His brother, in the brief sketch of Charles' life prefixed to the "Selections," gives the following incident as illustrating a strongly characteristic trait, his love and sensibility to natural beauty. It seems that during one of his vacations he tried the boyish adventure of camping out in the woods; but being, as he himself confesses, no great woodsman, he met with indifferent success. In a letter to his father, he says that he was wet to the skin with rain, he knew not how to cook the fish he had caught, and was very glad to return to civilization, scorched by fire, with bruised legs and blistered hands: "There is one lesson," he adds, "I learned, however, that was worth it all, and that is the grandeur and solemnity of solitude in the nights. I used to lie and listen to the lapping of the waters on the shores of the lakes, and the moaning of the wind in the forest, and look at the stars shining so silently and steadily, until I was really oppressed with the solemnity of the solitary night; . . . there are many things a man may learn from nature, if he will; . . . I get sometimes an overpowering sense of the careful working of God through all these vast scenes of nature. It seems like standing in His very presence, to watch the changes and all the movements of a strong summer day, for it sets before us His immediate workings for us and to us."

ANDOVER, August, 1858.

. . . . . . You speak of my early experience, mother, and ask for it; but I cannot remember my life so early as the age of four. My earliest connected recollections of life are of my school days in Winchester; before that I can recall only snatches and glimpses of days and weeks with no connection. But of my life in Winchester I can say, that it was neither happy in the spending nor profitable in the results. I missed very much the kindness and care of a mother, and all the genial influences of a home. I was thrown among boys of my own age when I was too young to learn anything from any life with them. When I needed all the restraining influences of parents, I was left too much to my own foolish guidance: and when I was too inexperienced to form any purpose of my own, I had none to direct me. . . . . To compensate for all these losses and injurious influences, all that I can now reckon up is a fine grounding in the rudiments of Latin. I cannot in a letter, mother, say all that I might about the comparative advantages of an academic or a home education in early life. The whole question, too, depends so much upon fortuitous circumstances that no direct answer can be given— such as the character of the person, the surroundings that he would have in his home life, etc.

But I can see no reason myself why a child should leave a home that is good, for a school, earlier than the age of eighteen. Before that age he will not have known nature enough to profit by a life among men, which, as I see the college life, is after all the greatest advantage it offers. Before that age he can learn all that is necessary at home, and before that age he should be surrounded with all the kindly and genial influences of home. But I think a college course indispensable to the educated man. He must at some time spend much time in study and thought alone; he must learn what his fellow-men are; he must live with them, dependent upon himself alone for his position and influence among them; and I know no better place for this than the college, with all its defects of incomplete courses of study and gathering of many bad men. But this is all rather premature for little Theo.: he has many years of happy childhood, that may be more to him in all his life than any college course. Let his life be pure and happy now, and he will not mar it much when he comes to be a man. And after all it comes to this—what will the person do himself? Will he be pure, and live a child of God, trusting in God as his Father, or will he not? And the responsibility of the issue of his life passes from us to himself. It often seems sad, even bitter, that the shaping of the life of some dear one rests not in our hands; but the responsibility of our own life is enough for each one of us. . . . . . . and *there*, in all the solemnity of life, each man for himself shaping a life that will either be a life with God, that is joy and peace to the man himself and a rich blessing to men, or a life apart from God, altogether vain and worthless, that brings to men the curse of vanity and sin, and is to him that lives it in the end only shame and unavailing remorse. . . . . . .

  Your affectionate son,   CHARLES STORK.

     ANDOVER SEMINARY, September 7, 1858.

 Dear Father: * * * My vacation too is almost spent; and I am heartily glad of it. You have no idea, father, how lonely, how tedious it has been for the last five weeks. All the walks about the town for three or four miles I have gone over again and again, till I became sick of the sight of the familiar objects. I tried camping out in the woods on the shores of a large pond—but both times I got wet through with rain, had to sleep in wet clothes and live on pork and crackers and the fish we caught, which after we caught we did not know how to cook. On this same expedition I bruised my legs and blistered my hands, and dried and blackened myself over the fire and in the sun till I was not fit to be seen. I think I shall not forego the comforts of civilized life very soon again for adventures in the woods. We just brought home this morning the last of our camp furniture, consisting of two blankets, a frying-pan, axe and hoe, and a sheet of canvass that served as the roof of our hut.

There is one thing I learned, however, that was worth it all, and that is the grandeur and solemnity of solitude in the night. I used to lie and listen to the lapping of the waters on the shores of the lake, and the moaning of the winds in the forest, and look at the stars shining so silently and steadily, till I was really oppressed with the solemnity of the solitary night. Ah! father, there are many things a man may learn from nature if he will— if he will be ready to see how God works in His wondrous ways. I get sometimes an overpowering sense of the careful and continued working of God through all these scenes of nature. It seems like standing in His very presence to watch the changes and all the movement of a full and strong summer day; for it sets before us His immediate workings for us and to us, appealing to us with all the perfection and glory of His works to be like Him in our life.

But, after all, one must have some human life and human sympathy, and plenty of it too. Byron and Moore had very narrow conceptions of the worth and power of human sympathy —when they talked about living alone with some *one* person— the family, not the man and wife alone—the community, the people. We must work for and with the many, and for my part I want to live with them too as much as I can. So here is another reason for being tired of vacation. I don't know anybody here, and I am almost alone; but when the students come back, and when I can get at my books again, I shall be satisfied —for my books are to me what men often fail to be, friends who have lived fine lives and with whom I have a common sympathy. You will know by this what books I am reading— the books of men that have lived fine lives either of thought or action. Homer and Plato I read last summer. I hope to do a great deal this winter; though it may be like all my years have been—at the opening full of rich promise and strong hope of good to myself, and through the purification and strengthening of myself, to men—and at the closing sad with the remembrance of little done and much lost.

The following letter is without date or place, but evidently written in New York to a *special* friend in Andover:

I suppose you think it a small thing to say "Good morning," but I know persons whose manner (and manner is the truest speech) in even that little thing was full of fine meaning. "Good morning" from them was a charming poem, or a snatch of welcome song; it meant: "Here we come to a new day of glorious life: we will live like men to-day, and sympathize in all that comes to us."

Want some news about myself? Would you like to know what time I get up? What I have for breakfast? How many miles I walk in a day? That's what most biographies are made of; the pious ones tell how many times the subject attended prayer-meeting, and what he said there. Adventures? We don't have any adventures in this part of the world except vulgar ones: for instance, the other day as I was crossing a street through a great crowd of people and carriages, a man made a snatch at my watch; fortunately the guard was strung so that I caught his arm before he broke it. I had some notion of handing him over to the police, but on second thought, as he was better dressed and infinitely more respectable in appearance than I, I was afraid the police might take me for the offender, so I let him go.

I am making the best of the city; but it is a horrid place. I would give all New York, its sights, luxuries, stores and galleries, for a quiet lane in Andover, or an evening on the back road to the Seminary, looking at the sunset.

A LETTER FROM CHARLES TO HIS FATHER.

ANDOVER, Oct. 23, 1858.

Dear Father: I am sorry to say that my eyes are worse. They seem to vacillate between health and disease. I have to write without looking at the paper, so you must make all allowance for straggling of lines, running together of words, and also for brevity. My health otherwise is in fine condition. I am strong and vigorous; and body and mind, in spite of my eyes, do a great deal of work. I am afraid I shall have to abandon all hope of using my eyes very much—all my cherished hopes of being a Christian scholar, as well as minister, are dying in me by inches. It is very hard to think it must be so, but, perhaps, it is for the better. I intend to preach without notes. I fear it will be hard work, but I must learn to do it. I shall have to hire some one to read to me what is absolutely necessary. The rest of my work I must do by mere dint of thinking and original creation. I do not despair at all of final success. This is the worst view of the case. I may recover my eyes, but I do not set my hopes on them. You see I face the evil as cheerfully as I can; but my courage is not always so good, I often despond and think I must be useless and worthless in the world.

It was about this time that he wrote the following letter, and it sounds strangely to hear a young man of twenty-one speak in this style of the weight of human responsibility; but he was a mature man long before many others older in years than he was, and of a sensibility the most delicate and refined. But, no doubt, his tendency to melancholy brought out these expressions, if they were not themselves that melancholy:

FEBRUARY 21, 1859.

But you have no idea how this longing for freedom from responsibility grows upon me. It tortures me beyond measure. Sometimes I feel as if I could be anything—a slave, a day laborer—to be rid of this ever-present sense of responsibility to men. My knowledge, my studies, all my long years of thought, only make my obligations the wider and the deeper; and yet the more I see of what is to be done, and what I can do, the more do I shrink from the work. I suppose I must show it in my manner. S— once said to me, "Stork, you will excuse my impertinence, but really, with all your learning and ability, I don't believe you will ever be anything in the world." I was, I confess, somewhat startled by this, for it seemed to confirm what I had already suspected in myself. But I don't think he was altogether right. Pleasant, indeed, would it be to live in a golden ease, and hard indeed does life look to me; and yet I shall work and never fear. This is weakness, you say. Yes, God knows I am weak enough, though not where men think me so; I am not weak to yield to temptation, but I am weak to shrink from the labor, even while I take it for my portion. I am so weak that I am miserable half the time from the struggle it costs me to hold to my purpose. I never would make a triumphant martyr; if I went to the stake it would be with bowed head and a desponding spirit; but I should go nevertheless.

CHAPTER III.

AT NEWBERRY, S. C.—SORE EYES—GOES TO BERLIN FOR TREATMENT—ST. JAMES' MISSION IN PHILADELPHIA—ASSISTANT TO HIS FATHER IN BALTIMORE—MODE OF PREACHING—LEARNS TO EXTEMPORIZE—CALL TO ST. MARK'S—LETTER FROM THE COUNCIL.—ACCEPTS AND HIS REPLY—HIS MARRIAGE—CALL TO PENNSYLVANIA COLLEGE AND SEMINARY — DECLINES — DESCRIPTIVE LETTER.

TO NEWBERRY, S. C., 1859.

CHARLES' father, as we have already seen, was offered the Presidency of a college recently established in Newberry, S. C., by our Synod of that State, which he accepted. In February, 1859, they arrived at that place, in company with Dr. Brown, the professor of theology. Charles was professor of Greek, and few young men of his age in the country were better fitted for that position. He had been a hard student of languages for years, and made himself familiar with them.

The civil war compelled the whole of the Northern professors to abandon their educational work at Newberry in less than a year, and they returned home. The eyes of Charles had been injured by hard study, and he was induced to go to Berlin to avail himself of the skill of the celebrated oculist, Dr. von Graefe. After six months' treatment, Charles was dismissed as cured, upon which he came back to the United States. Soon after his return he took charge for several months of St. James' Lutheran Mission in Philadelphia.

The following two letters describe his experience in Europe:

HAMBURG, March 5th, 1861.

My Dear R—: Well, I have made another journey and had another fit of sea sickness; and here I am, sitting in my room in the 3d etage (so they call the 3d story of a German hotel), with a German waiter talking to my traveling companion at a terrible rate. We were six hours crossing England, from Liverpool to Hull, through a most beautiful varied country—first was the low, flat country, looking like a garden, dotted with beautiful country seats, old farm-houses, and beautiful English villages; then comes the rough, hill country of Yorkshire (by the way, I passed within six miles of Haworth, the home of Charlotte Bronte). These wild hills and barren moors, you know, are the scene of her Shirley and her sister's Midfell Hall and Wuthering Heights: as we rushed through the passes and along the sides of the hills, I could almost fancy I saw Markham riding up to Mrs. Graham's house. You can imagine, how like a fairy dream everything seemed to me—the bleak moors with the quaint old English farm-houses on their borders, the jagged cliffs, the bleak uplands, the dark valleys, with the torrents rushing through them. I saw only one old castle, and that was a grand pile. I think that six hours' ride was the shortest, most crowded with intense feeling, I ever had. I didn't know I could be so affected—all it wanted for perfect happiness was you by my side to see with me and feel with me; but I associated you with everything I saw—each beautiful thing, every scene, suggested something to tell you; and tell you by word of mouth I must, for writing it is out of the question—one sees too much even to tell. Do you know I couldn't get Maggie on the Mill and the Floss out of my mind, all the time, especially after I had seen an old mill that would have answered exactly for Dorlcote Mill. By the way, I have heard some of the life of Miss Evans (George Eliot), which throws a new light, and one full of interest, on the subject we discussed so warmly. We got to Hull after dark and went to a veritable old English inn, where the landlady came out to the door to welcome us in, where we took supper in the travelers' room and breakfast in the commercial room, where we slept in a curtained bed and had to pay a sixpence to the Boots, where I went into the tap-room and called for a long pipe, such as Tony Weller used to smoke, and a tankard of ale such as Sam Weller used to drink, all to serve as an illustration with my next reading of Dickens with you. Hull is an old rambling town, running over with oranges as cheap as can be, and fish. Everything is old and dingy, and the streets are more crooked and narrow than those of Boston. I spent an hour in the old church, the largest but one in Great Britain, and over five hundred years old; it is full of curious and beautiful things, to say nothing of the fine Gothic architecture. It was the first genuine old Gothic church building I had ever seen, and yet somehow it seemed very familiar. I knew where everything was to be found, and recognized many things as old familiar friends. The choir were chanting when I went in, and the effect of the music (very fine music by the way), sounding through the old aisles, while the sun streamed through the great painted window in the east on to the memorial tablets with which the church is paved, was very strange. This realization of all I have thought and dreamt of, England and her memorial architecture, is a continual wonder to me—it seems a dream and no real thing. The church is about as large as half dozen of the Old South, with a vast vaulted roof of stone supported on colonnades of the slender groups of Gothic columns, such as you see in pictures of so many old churches. The floor is paved and the walls are completely covered with memorial tablets, some of the quaintest sort. In niches are stone effigies of life size, stretched at length with hands folded on their breasts. You cannot imagine what a sense of peaceful rest one breathes in from these calm stone statues that have lain so long with hands clasped in rest from all toil. I thought I would tell you of Hamburg while in the place, but I find I must wait till I get to Berlin.

BERLIN, March 6th, 1861.

Another German inn, with its discomforts, and not least the inability of the servants to talk anything but German (I have just succeeded by great exertion in getting a pen). Well, it's five o'clock in the afternoon (eleven in the morning with you), and I have trotted around the city till I am tired; but to begin where I left off—I was most gloriously sea-sick again between Hull and Hamburg; but the sight of land cures that. Hamburg is a dirty, crooked town, half old and half new. Some of the streets look like American streets, and some are so old that they have no sidewalks, only the street shelving from both sides to the gutter in the middle, and narrow at that, with each story reaching farther out than the one below it, till the tops of the houses nearly touch. But I am tired of writing descriptions. I must write of myself. I can tell you all when I get back, and I know you want to hear more of myself. I have seen Dr. Graefe, and he has put me into his infirmary, a large building that looks very much like a poor-house, where he keeps all his foreign patients. He visits us once a day. He has people here from every part of the world, and he effects the most wonderful cures—he has just cured a man from America who came to him perfectly blind. He is a tall, noble-looking man, of about thirty-three, nervous and restless; he rushes into my room, looks at my eyes a minute, asks me one or two questions, and then bolts out again. He never says much; he seems to gather all he wants to know of my case by looking at my eyes. His first prescription was a pair of spectacles. He hasn't told me yet what he thinks of my case, and all his patients tell me that he always discourages one at first; if there is the slightest chance that he cannot help you, he says he is afraid he can do nothing; but one thing is certain, acknowledged by all the oculists of England, Germany and France, that if Graefe cannot cure you, no one in this world can. He is one of the distinguished men of Berlin, his picture is in every paint-shop window, and everybody in the city knows him and talks about him. He has about one hundred patients in his infirmary; he has fifty students attending his clinical lecture; he operates every day

on about thirty people, and when I called on him to consult him his room was crowded. He speaks broken English in the most comical manner. Sometimes when he comes in, he says goodby instead of good morning; he tells me to be very *precocious*—meaning very *cautious*—and a hundred other things of the same sort. I told him about the hairs, but he says that's not the trouble. He makes me read with my spectacles an hour and a half a day, but he rather objects to my writing. . . . .
I am home-sick—it's a new thing for me, but so it is. When I get out of Graefe's hands I shall come home. Travelling is all very well, but if I have my books and friends at home, I can let slip Rome and Athens. There are finer things in this world than cathedrals and picture galleries, than the Rhine and Switzerland, and one's own home is better than all the rest of the earth. I want to see you very much.

Ever yours,   CHARLIE.

BERLIN, March 11, 1861.

My Dear R——. I wish you could see me in my little room in this eye-infirmary. It is a comfortable place, well furnished after the German fashion, but very dreary withal. Oh, I do get so terribly home-sick, and sick of myself and my eyes. Everybody I see have their eyes bandaged or sore; nothing is talked of but eyes, and in short, one would think the whole end of being was to cure one's eyes. They keep us on short allowance of food; for breakfast, absolutely nothing but two pieces of bread without butter and a cup of coffee; for supper, the same; and dinner, meat and potatoes, dessert, pastry, puddings, cake, pickles, preserves, are things unknown. I don't care for that, however. But the German beds—I don't know how they manage to live in the summer with them—the whole of the bedclothes consists of two large feather beds put into cases like two immense pillows, and between those you are expected to sleep—not a sheet nor blanket—isn't that pleasant?

The Doctor won't tell me anything about my case—he never tells any one, and I am sure I can't tell yet myself. I read with spectacles an hour or two a day, take pills, use ointment, saltwater baths, etc., etc. They are very easy about regimen; I can smoke, go to the opera, sit in the most brilliant light, and do what else I please.

March 12.

I went last night to hear Beethoven's "Fidelio;" the orchestra, though small for Germany (60 in number), was perfect—it is considered so even here. You know Beethoven's operas are all considered failures. Well, I understand now why as operas they certainly are very poor. The dramatic interest of "Fidelio" is very meagre. There is so little of passion and intensity in the movement that actually they have to drop the music sometimes and talk to keep up the interest. Beethoven could not write music for lovers to bill and coo in, and tyrants to bluster, and dying men to make pathetic speeches through—so all that is done by mere talk. But the music—I wish I could give you some idea of it. The overture was full of grand and strong passages that seemed to carry me as on the wings of the wind—it is unlike and yet very like Beethoven. So weird and wild was the whole that it seemed unfamiliar. The opera itself is made up of half a dozen grand connected pieces and four or five airs, the sweetest, most exquisite that one can conceive—you know what Beethoven can do in that way—they seemed almost to steal the very soul from one. I could almost fancy one might die of such music, as some faint from the exquisite fragrance of the tuberose. But what is the use of trying to describe it? I can only say that the effect of the whole opera on me was such that I went home completely exhausted; it seemed to take all my nervous energy from me, to listen to such music. They played the overture in "Leonore," another of Beethoven's operas, after the "Fidelio," but I was too tired to do it justice in the hearing; it was wonderful, bewildering, stormy, and yet full of sweetness —Beethoven all over—that's all I can say of it. I have heard "Martha," too, and at the cathedral on Sunday, Mendelssohn's Psalms. You see, I am living on music, and we can't do anything else in Berlin. There is a concert every afternoon of the very finest classical music, rendered by the best orchestra in the city, admission *six cents*. The operas of Mozart, Beethoven, Flotow, and Mendelssohn every evening, admission twenty cents. Positively the temptation is too great, one cannot resist it; but all the time I keep thinking how much better it would be if you could only hear it with me. It seems almost wrong, sometimes, to be enjoying so much away from you. Well, darling, I shall come back as soon as the Doctor cures my eyes. I don't care for Europe. I can travel in my library, by my own thoughts, to my heart's content, and I will gladly give all the operas and concerts of Germany to be back in the old familiar room, listening to you while you render our favorite music.

Music is very cheap here. I can buy all Beethoven's sonatas for two dollars and a half, all of Mozart's for a dollar, and they throw in as a premium a portrait of each. I got a beautiful Parian bust of Beethoven the other day for you. I keep it on the table before me, and the more I see it the better I like it. It is a noble head.

March 22.

A long stop, but I must write when I can. The Doctor changes my spectacles every once in a while, and then I have to wait two or three days for the new ones to be made. How are my eyes? Well, I don't know. I am reading three or four hours a day, with as little pain as I ever had under Dr. D—— when I read not a bit. Dr. von Graefe tells me I must read till the pain is so great that I cannot read any longer. And I have not got to that point yet. He is going to set me reading by candle-light to-morrow evening, half an hour an evening. I am almost afraid to try it, but he says I must, and there is no disputing with *him*—one must do as he says or leave.

I have the oddest pair of spectacles now, they are called prismatico-convex glasses. The glass is on one edge thicker than a half dollar and slants off to the opposite side to the thickness of a five-cent piece. They are so big and heavy that they have made the bridge of my nose sore with carrying them. The Doctor has tried to explain their use, but as his English is poor and my German worse, I can make nothing out of it. Graefe tells me that the eye itself and the nerve are perfectly good, but the muscles by which the eyes are held fixed and moved to and fro in reading, have been strained by excessive use. He intends to restore their tone by the use of these peculiar spectacles. He says he shall dismiss me when I can read eight hours a day. When that will be, if ever, I don't know. He won't tell me, nor promise me anything. He is an odd man with his patients; he always discourages them as much as he can. You can have no idea how much he is beloved. The children hang round him like a father, as he is as gentle with them as a woman. The poor fellow is worked to death. Just think of his visiting four hundred patients every day. He came into my room a few minutes ago looking all fagged, and he told me he could not attend to me to-day, that he was too tired. He sees me every day for a minute, and examines my eyes with the microscope minutely every five days.

TO BALTIMORE, 1861.

His father had been called to be pastor of the new congregation styled St. Mark's in Baltimore, of which a full history has been given in his biography. At his desire, Charles was called to be his father's assistant. Not being the responsible pastor of the church, he did not at first mingle freely with the members, and only discharged such pastoral duties as the chief pastor required from him. He was backward and retiring, and did not consider it his duty to seek the acquaintance of the people, and hence for several years he was not personally known to many of the people; but he was universally admired as a young man of fine talents, extensive acquirements, and of brilliant promise. He did not associate intimately with any of the Baltimore clergy at that early day; but subsequently, when he became full pastor, his whole manner changed, and several ministers of other churches and he became intimate friends. They were

New Englanders, with whom he seemed to have more sympathy than with others.

At that time, he was a close reader of his sermons. He was a fair reader, still much of their force was weakened by his style of delivery. He lacked in fervor, and had imbibed the New England ideas of preaching, which did not suit his congregation in Baltimore; and yet a New Englander who heard him one Sunday morning, and the pulpit of the church of which he was a member being vacant at the time, remarked to a friend after church, "That is positively the kind of man we need in our church! and I'll inquire whether he cannot be got!" But it was not only the mode of young Stork's delivery that roused the admiration of this stranger, but it was the mature thought, the exquisite taste, the sound argument and striking illustrations of the young preacher.

The people endured the reading of his sermons, for his father had practised it in the same pulpit several years before him, but the preacher himself began to ask whether after all he should not lay aside his manuscript and talk instead of read to the people. He had never practised extemporaneous speaking, and he said it was difficult to learn. He was encouraged to persevere, and by continuous effort he in less than a year acquired a faculty of uttering unwritten thoughts in the choicest and most forcible language. He never hesitated for a word and never repeated one for want of another, but words flowed smoothly and fluently from his eloquent lips. All this was owing to his unsurpassed mental vigor, his indomitable perseverance, and the broad extent of his knowledge.

And yet with this wonderful facility of utterance, he sometimes would not risk the exercise of it, but preferred to read a sermon, which thus lost much of its power. I remember once at a Synodical meeting he closely read a sermon before a plain country congregation, when I knew he might have thrilled his hearers with his off-hand impressive style of speech, and presented the truth with much more effect.

CALL TO ST. MARK'S.

Letter of the Council of St. Mark's to C. A. Stork:

BALTIMORE, June 21, 1865.

Dear Sir: It gives me pleasure to inform you that at a meeting of the church council of St. Mark's, it was unanimously resolved to extend to you a call to the pastorship, which will become vacant on the 1st of July next. This action is based upon an election held on the 14th and 16th instant, when you were the unanimous choice for that position of all those who voted.

The constitution of the church requires that two-thirds of all the electors shall be necessary to elect a pastor, but I congratulate you upon the fact that more than three-fourths of the electors have thus expressed a desire that you should succeed to the office of pastor, and of those who have not voted—a number of whom are out of the city—it is not known that a single member is opposed to your succeeding to that position.

Such unanimity of feeling among the members of the church upon such an important question, leads us to believe that under the blessing of God, and the earnest prayers of the congregation, your ministry among us, in the event of your acceptance of the call, will be eminently successful.

The history of the church is well known to you; at our first election for pastor in the fall of 1860, the same unanimity of feeling existed, and the church has been most signally blessed of God, both in its spiritual and its temporal affairs, under the ministry of him who has so endeared himself in the hearts, and whose memory will be cherished by the members of St. Mark's, but who is now about to leave us; and this, too, was commenced at a time when all around was dark and gloomy by reason of the rebellion which was about bursting upon our land, and when many churches of our city were very much crippled in their operations thereby.

But now that God has granted victory to our country, and the glad tidings of peace are again heard in the land, may we not reasonably hope that as you have so acceptably filled the office of assistant pastor for the past three years, a favoring Providence will grant that under your ministry the future history of the church will be as glorious as in the past?

This call was accepted on June 23, 1865, in the following letter:

BALTIMORE, June 23.

Your communication informing me of the action of the congretional meeting of St. Mark's, resulting in my election, and extending to me a call to the pastorship now vacant, has been received.

It gives me sincere pleasure to respond to a call made with such unanimity of feeling and choice on the part of the congregation as intimated in your letter. Our relations hitherto have been of the most pleasant and, I trust, not unprofitable character. In signifying my acceptance of the call to the pastorship of St. Mark's, I can only express my hope that the same harmony and mutual love, that under the blessing of God have characterized our past intercourse, may continue in the new relation of pastor and people that we shall now assume.

I propose to enter upon my duties on the first of July. Praying that the blessing of God and the grace of Christ may cheer and sustain us in the work that is before us as a church, and that we may faithfully occupy our place in the vineyard of our common Lord, with many thanks for your kind consideration of myself,

I remain yours in Christ, C. A. STORK.

He was now master of the church himself, and for a number of years he maintained the character of an able preacher, a diligent student and successful pastor. He was a most conscientious and sympathizing shepherd of his flock, and although not addicted to paying mere social visits and spending his time in unprofitable talk, yet he was ever ready at the call of the sick or needy, and was a most affectionate comforter of the bereaved.

HIS MARRIAGE.

Soon after his settlement in Baltimore, he married Miss Maria H. Ellis, of Andover, Massachusetts. Two of the children died young, and two, a son and daughter, with the mother, still survive. After her husband's death, Mrs. Stork retired to Andover, where she still lives.

CALLS TO PENNSYLVANIA COLLEGE AND TO THE THEOLOGICAL SEMINARY AT GETTYSBURG.

In 1866 he was elected to the Graeff Professorship of English Language and Literature in Pennsylvania College, which he declined, and in 1868 he was chosen to a Professorship in the Seminary, the result of which is set forth in the following letters.

TO HIS FATHER.

BALTIMORE, Oct. 29th, 1867.

Dear Father: . . . . . We are purposing to celebrate the Jubilee year here in as good style as possible. We will publish tracts, raise subscriptions, and try to awaken the church.

I had been somewhat cast down of late. My church has seemed so dead, and I have been so sluggish myself; but the cloud is beginning to break away. I hope we shall do better.

I have cast the burden of this work on God, and now I trouble myself less about results.

It seems to me the longer I live the harder, more perplexed, life becomes. My ministry grows heavier; more anxieties, cares, disappointments, fall upon me. I feel like saying with Paul, "Who is sufficient for these things?" Perhaps I have not been working right. My watch-word has been, I fear, "duty" rather than "love." I have begun to pray for more love, that all my nature and life may be love to God in a Saviour. I cannot keep up much longer under the *duty* pressure: I must have something higher, and stronger, and warmer. I feel like crying all the time "Lead me to the rock that is higher than I." Indeed, I have felt that there must new light and life come into my soul, or I must give up my ministry. I could not live doing my work in a perfunctory, professional way. I must love it more, love it for Christ's sake more, or lay it down. I must realize that to live is Christ, or I feel as if I must die.

Indeed, father, I have been going through deep water of late; the floods have gone over my head. But I do not despair. I think I see the source of all my trouble. It has been self-sufficiency. I have felt too strong. I have been leaning upon my gifts of mind and conscience. I have been more of a philosopher than a Christian. I have come to the convalescent period. I think I have made the total consecration of myself. I have, I hope, brought the last reserve and laid it down; but I am very weak —when I pray, after I come from my closet, my soul burns, but the flame is feeble, it is soon quenched again. I must be ever new-consecrating myself. Pray for me, and come and see me.

CHARLES A. STORK.

Dr. Stork's letter declining an election to the Professorship of New Testament Exegesis and Church History in the Theological Seminary at Gettysburg:

BALTIMORE, 76 N. Paca St., Oct. 6, 1868.

Rev. W. M. Baum, D. D.—Dear Bro.: I should have written you before, but pressing business has made it almost impossible to write at such leisure as I wished.

I gave the considerations urged by the Committee careful thought, and left myself to such new impressions as your representations and those of Dr. Hay and Dr. Brown made ; and with the best light from reason and prayer, I cannot see my way clear to do otherwise than decline.

The necessities of Gettysburg are important, but I cannot feel them so great as to call for my presence. This point I fully set forth in my letter to Dr. Brown. As far as the leadings of Providence are concerned, I feel only led to stay where I am. I feel a repugnance to the Professor's sphere : nay I feel more, a dread of it. I know, and on this point I only can be a competent judge, that I should be doing violence to the whole bent of my nature to lapse into the mere speculative thinker and teacher.

I am deeply touched by Dr. Hay's kind offer of the pastorate of the church in Gettysburg, but that would be no such sphere as I need. I have often felt that I must be an active minister of the gospel for my own sake—that in some sense I must preach and be a pastor to save my own soul.

I am sorry to disappoint any expectations your kind brethren may have had concerning me. I feel all your kindness; indeed, one strong element of bias in considering the whole matter has been an earnest desire to please and satisfy those whom I so much respect and love. But, at last, in the final decision, I felt constrained to put both the brethren of the Board and the brethren here in Maryland and Baltimore wholly out of sight, and decide without regard to the feelings or judgment of any one—simply on what I with the light God would give me could see to be my simple duty. I have decided. I have done to the best of my ability. I certainly may be mistaken, but I see no other way. Do not think more hardly of me and my decision because they may be adverse to your wishes. With the highest regard for your faithfulness and frankness in all matters, I remain your brother, CHARLES A. STORK.

In illustration of a passage of this letter, the insertion of an extract from a letter of Dr. Hay to me, is proper at this place. He had the above letter of resignation beforehim when he wrote his letter :

"Dr. Stork's allusion to my offer of the pastorship of Christ's church in Gettysburg, as an inducement for him to accept the Professorship, reminds me of a similar offer I made to him when we as a College Board elected him to the Graeff Professorship of English Language and Literature some years ago. Dr. Sadtler and I were sent to Baltimore to urge his acceptance of the call, where we had a long interview with him. When he hesitated, and said that he would enjoy that sort of literary work, but feared to devote himself to it lest his own spiritual life should suffer, and that he needed the stimulus of the pulpit and pastoral work for his own sake, I then offered him the College and Seminary pulpit, for I had not very long before that reluctantly consented to take it, when Dr. Baugher insisted on giving it up, and none of the others would take it. I took it for the time being, and would gladly have turned it over to him, and I am sure the people would have sanctioned the arrangement. But he could not be prevailed upon to accept the position. You see from this letter that I renewed the offer when he was elected to a Seminary Professorship, and that he appreciated my feeling in the matter."

I here insert several extracts from his letters to Mrs. Stork, during his presence at the meeting of the Synod of Maryland at Emmittsburg in October, 1870. They were dashed off in his rapid manner of writing, but they show his exquisite love of nature and his admiration of its beauties. Well might Mr. Alden say, "Nature was more to him than books, but its charms were, in his mind, inseparably connected with the creations of the master poets." He was himself a poet:

Dear R. : We have got to Monday morning, and Synod is still under way, full of business, and adjournment yet far off. I have just come into Synod, leaving the beautiful morning with reluctance to shut myself up in the church. It would be hard to make you understand how beautiful the country about this village is—a broad rolling plain, verdant, heavily wooded and yet soft and tender, sweeping to the foot of a range of mountains that are not lofty and abrupt enough to be grand, but yet are enough to give the softness of the landscape dignity and something of strength. Yesterday was one of those lovely Sundays that seem to come down out of heaven—the air so soft and balmy, the sunshine so mellow and golden, the light haze on the hills and woods not enough to obscure, but only lending a tenderer, remoter atmosphere to all the scene. I got through breakfast and my preparation for service by half past eight in the morning, and then strolled out into the country to the top of a long, sloping hill, through a quiet winding lane that stole away from the town into the heart of the woods and hills. The hill gave me a pleasant outlook over the whole country almost. Oh, it was too sweet to leave! I don't know which was the better, the morning view or one I had in the afternoon about 4 o'clock from a little valley, where a brook came bubbling down and wound away into the silent fields.

* * * * * * * * *

This morning I got up at 6½ a. m., and took a walk into the country on another road, that faced the range of the mountains. I stood and looked at them again in the morning light, for they change with all the hours of the day. There was one long broad slope to the right of the range that rose very gradually from the valley—its long, retreating swell was cleared of the forest, and farm after farm could be traced by the eye in their various colored fields stretching up and up, until on the edge of the cleared land—in a hollow, that seemed narrow enough for a man to stride across—a white farm-house, with gardens and orchards, peeped out. Beyond and above rose the thick woods away to the bristling top. To the left swept up a still taller peak, abrupt, steep, covered with woods from bottom to top. I thought I could look on all day. If you will go into the study, and look at that picture of mountains over the mantel-piece, you will get something like an idea of what I see; imagine that to be real, and fuller of trees, and you have it. I wish you could be with me to enjoy all these things.

* * * * * * * * *

EMMTITSBURG, MD., Oct. 8th, 1870.

Dear R.: I have had no time to write in Synod to-day, and indeed I have very little time to-night. It is 6½ p. m., and I have to go to church to make a speech pretty soon; still I must give you a few lines.

It has been a lovely day. Such serene airs, mellow sunlight, and the beautiful, unchanging mountains lying so silent, and yet as if they had so much to tell—how wonderful they are! I was sitting down on the slope of the hill below the church in the afternoon, not a soul near, in all the stillness and soft beauty of the autumn sunlight. I drank it in, and got better and softer. We have had stormy times in Synod, and I have had to play a conspicuous part, and it had made me irritated and unrestful; but the beautiful still afternoon soothed it all away. I grudged to go back to the church, and lose all the tranquil life of the open country-side. I walked up through the old grave-yard that lies round the church, and read some of the inscriptions on the tomb-stones, and listened to the tune that rolled out of the open window and mingled with the soft sighings of the wind in the willow trees over the graves. It was very solemn, and it was a good place to muse, and wander up and down.

But I had to go in. I heard a good preparatory sermon, and then we had rather a rough session of Synod.

My health has been better; my rest and diet has helped me. I am getting quite tired, however, for the calls of business are incessant. The strain, too, on our temper is very hard. I am afraid it would spoil me to stay in such scenes long. I have to pray a great deal to keep straight.

* * * * * * * * *

Your affectionate husband, CHAS. A. STORK.

CHAPTER IV.

1874—1881.

SECOND VISIT TO EUROPE—SYMPTOMS OF DISEASE—COMPELLED TO LAY ASIDE WORK—DEGREE OF D. D.—LECTURER ON HISTORY—LETTER FROM CHESTER, ENGLAND—ITINERARY—RETURN—WORK AT ST. MARK'S—MINISTERIAL STANDING—CONTINUOUS SORE THROAT—DESPONDING LETTERS—REGAINS HOPE ONLY TO BE BLASTED—SUCCESS AS A PASTOR—HIS FATHER'S SERMONS—CHURCH AFFAIRS AND WORK.

AS early as 1870, evidences of failing health began to be developed, but such was his indomitable energy that he continued to study and preach without interruption for several months, until he was compelled to lay aside his work for a while almost entirely. He, however, recovered from this attack and resumed his pastoral labors in the autumn. He was obliged to be exceedingly cautious, for the least exposure or unusual fatigue would betray suspicious symptoms. He was constantly on his guard, and this necessary vigilance was of itself depressing and had an unfavorable influence upon his delicate sensibility.

But in 1874, there was such a manifest development of pulmonary disease that he was advised to give up all work and to spend the winter abroad, and he chose Egypt for the place of his retreat. On September 30, 1874, he sailed for Europe, accompanied by his younger half brother, Theophilus B. Stork, of Philadelphia.

The following letter to Mrs. Stork is appropriate here. Let the reader remember that this and all others of his letters occurring in this sketch were not intended for the public eye but those to his family are the mere natural out-gushings of fond affection written for them alone, and the others are mostly on business relating to the seminary and church. Dr. Stork never had time to write letters of mere friendship after he entered upon his life work.

Before I introduce the letter, this is the proper time to state that in June of this summer, 1874, the honorary degree of Doctor of Divinity was conferred on him by Pennsylvania College, Gettysburg, and never was the distinction bestowed upon a man more eminently entitled to it.

The previous winter, he delivered a course of lectures on History to the students of the Theological Seminary. This did not require a constant residence at Gettysburg, but he went up from Baltimore, remained four or five days, then returned so as to be in his pulpit on Sunday, and this was kept up for several weeks.

LETTER FROM C. A. STORK TO HIS WIFE.

QUEEN HOTEL, CHESTER, Eng., Oct. 11, 1874.

Dear R——. I am someway into England already, you see. We landed in Liverpool, Saturday, October 10th, at 10 a. m., after a run of 9 days and 17 hours, a short trip. We had the gale we met to thank for that; it was a fierce storm, but as it came from the west it helped us on our way. It was so tempestuous on this coast that none of the steamers left Liverpool for New York on Thursday. We had a nerve-shaking time.

We went ashore in a pelting rain. A long drive of four miles to the hotel which opens right into the great North Western Railway station. Theo. and I got a room, cleaned ourselves up after the abominations of the voyage, and then sallied out into Liverpool in the fog and rain to get some money and do some shopping. We neither of us knew anything of the city, a place as big as three of Boston, but somehow one gets an instinct of cities, so we got through in good time, strolled through a market-full of the richest flowers and the cheapest fruit on our way back, and by rushing things, got off to Chester by 3½ in the afternoon. The clouds cleared away, and after a rushing ride of 50 minutes we glided into Chester in a glorious sunset. We strolled about the town till dark in the midst of a great horse fair; the place is full of farmers. jockeys, Welsh horses and men, and the most cunning, meek little Welsh ponies, about the size of a good-sized calf.

We are stopping at a comfortable, yes, even elegant English hotel. Everything is heavy and cumbrous compared with our American hotel equipments, but all is rich and unspeakably clean and comfortable. Perhaps this is enhanced by contrast with the horrors of the ocean voyage. Such great, soft beds, such heavy carpets, snowy linen—the name of the hotel is not only on all the china and silver, and steel, but even woven into the table linen, stamped on the knives. Did I not sleep well last night?

This morning I was awakened by a multitude of sparrows chirping at my window. The sun rose clear and warm. I hurried out and took a walk of an hour before breakfast. I strolled through a beautiful park, saw the ruin of an old abbey, now restored to St. John the Baptist church, built 1067. I dropped in at the Cathedral on my way back to early morning service, and got back to find Theo. just sitting down to breakfast. We attended service at the Cathedral at 11 o'clock. I will not attempt to describe the Cathedral ; it is too big and rambling, with cloister enclosing a green lovely bit of sward, and all manner of curious and beautiful things. But the Cathedral service was something marvellous. From 50 to 100 choristers, with no end of singing. All the "Amens" are sung ; all the Psalms are sung instead of read—in fact, they sing everything they can. I would have hardly been surprised if the preacher had sung his sermon—he came as near to it as he could in a sort of stammering recitative; but it was a good, wholesome, kindly sermon, and the preacher was a lovely old man. I got a pleasant bow from him as I strolled through the Cathedral after service. But the music—well, it is simply wonderful; the soprano voices of the boys were so heavenly clear and pure; such tenors, and a great rolling bass—I don't mean one man, for each part was carried by 15 or 20. It was the perfection of church music. How I wished for you to be beside me. But the setting of it all: that great, arched ceiling; those columns and arches stretching away in the distance; the wonderful glory of the vast stained windows; the vestments, the rich throng of clergy in parti-colored vestments—and then through a great row of high windows far up in the vaulted ceiling, streamed in right in the midst of one of the anthems a full burst of sunlight. Well, it was all very fine, beautiful, inspiring; but do you know I did not feel half so religious as in the evening, when I went to a Methodist church and heard them sing, and joined with them, in "Not all the blood of beasts," etc. The Cathedral service was over two hours long—so Theo. and I refreshed ourselves with a stroll round the ramparts. You know Chester is an old Roman city, and it still has its wall about it entire, two miles long. We walked round the whole city, seeing the most ancient and curious sights; looking into people's back-yards and down into their kitchens, with a fine view into garrets and down chimneys. Such a quaint, queer, racy old place as this is, such picturesque views, and strange old houses all jumbled up without place or order, I cannot describe.

To-morrow we hope to get to Hereford on our way to Devonshire. It is too cold and wet for Wales—so we have given that up. My health is very good; I am drinking quantities of milk—I think it agrees with me. I took cold on the steamer; but that is wearing away.

Ah, R——, do you think all these fine things make me glad to be here? I tell you I would, if only my health would permit, choose without a moment's hesitation to be back at work—I am home-sick: that is, I have a steady longing to be back with you all. I want quiet. I would give all these strange and really beautiful experiences for my old study, and the old dining-room, you and the others with us. Sometimes I think it will never be: but that is wrong. "Your Father knoweth that ye have need of all these things." I hope I am growing more submissive and content with His ways. But I do hate travel; though I will get the most I can out of it. Love to all.

Your affectionate husband,   C. A. STORK.

It is to be regretted that more letters describing his foreign tour could not be procured. I here place a meagre itinerary furnished by one of the parties, which will still be read with interest by many of his friends:

September 30th, 1874. Left New York in Cunard steamship *Algeria*.

October 10th. Arrived in Liverpool; experienced gale off Irish Coast.

October 11th. Chester; attended service in Cathedral, it being Sunday.

October 12th to 31st. Hereford; fine Norman cathedral. We wandered southward, visiting Ross, Tintern Abbey, Raglan Castle, and then crossed the Bristol channel to Bristol, then to Wells, with its fine cathedral, and then to Exeter, the capital of the West. From Exeter we went to Bideford on the North coast of Devon, Clevelly, Ilfracombe, Plymouth, and finally to Torquay, a fashionable watering place on the South coast, where we spent two weeks.

November. We went up to London, and thence almost direct to Cannes, in the south of France, breaking the journey at Paris, Lyons and Marseilles—Dr. Stork not feeling strong enough to go through without stopping. We arrived at Cannes Wednesday, November 11th, 1874. As December approached it began to grow cold.

December 11th. We left for Genoa, there to take ship to Egypt.

We sailed December 15th in the Italian steamer, but we had hardly got outside the harbor when she broke down, and we had to put back to anchor. The next day we crossed to Venice, and took the Peninsular and Oriental Company's steamer *Venetia* for Alexandria, where we arrived on Christmas eve.

From December 27th, 1874, to February 17th, 1875, we spent quietly in Cairo, walking, or riding on queer little donkeys, about the city and its vicinity.

We left Alexandria for Malta in the steamer *Bavarian*, being the only passengers, and arrived at Malta February 24th, 1875.

From Malta, March 3d, 1875, we steamed to the ancient Syracuse in Sicily, about twelve hours' trip. By rail we skirted the eastern coast of Sicily by Catania to Messina, thence to Palermo by steamer, the railway going no farther.

From Palermo we steamed north to Naples; and, after numerous excursions in the neighborhood, we reached Rome on Easter eve, March 27th, 1875.

April 30th. From Rome we went, by way of Orvieto and Sienna, to Florence, stopping a day in each of the first two cities. From Florence to Bologna, then to Venice, and then to Milan, Turin, Geneva, via Mont Cenis, spending a week at Villeneuve, on Lac Leman; then to Paris, visiting Chartres cathedral, Dover, taking a glance at Canterbury cathedral, then to London, May 31st, 1874.

While staying in London we ran down to Brighton, and across by Plymouth to the Isle of Wight, then back by Winchester; and finally we went north, taking on our way to Liverpool the three great cathedrals of Peterboro, Lincoln, and York, reaching Liverpool about middle of June. Thence we sailed in steamship *Parthia* to Boston.

He returned from this tour, which extended east as far as Egypt, where, as has been said, he spent the winter much benefited, and resumed his work in St. Mark's with bouyant expectations of long years of uninterrupted activity. He labored with an energy which too severely strained his strength, and for several years he vacillated between hope and fear, apparent vigor and very decided debility; and it was during this period that he wrote and preached those beautiful sermons in the "Selections," entitled "The Fellowship of Christ's Sufferings," "True Christian Patience," and others of a like character. He was not a constant sufferer; frequently he seemed perfectly well, and at such times his anxious friends would be buoyed up with hope; but, perhaps, the next Sunday would show the unwelcome reality that his throat was seriously affected, for his voice would be hoarse, his breathing labored, and his cough painful. The slightest effort seemed to exhaust him, and he was liable to take cold in an atmosphere which was bracing to persons in good health. His hearers deeply sympathized with him in his infirmities, and listened to his preaching with the utmost apprehension. They admired the zealous spirit in the man which impelled him to preach when he perhaps should have been in bed, or at least at home in his quiet study. But amid all his constrained exertions to speak distinctly, with which the hoarseness of his voice often interfered, there was no deterioration of mental vigor. His genius sparkled with the same brilliancy, and flashes of light still burst forth from his eyes. His language was as rich as in his palmiest days, and the most striking illustrations flowed forth abundantly from his fervid imagination.

There never was a pastor who was more highly esteemed by his people. They besought him to cease his efforts, or preach but rarely. Occasionally he would be compelled to yield, and for weeks his voice would not be heard in the pulpit, and he would go on short journeys; but he was uneasy and dejected, for this compulsory silence, with cessation from study, was exceedingly irksome to him. How could a man of his active mind endure such privations with any degree of composure?

Early in 1877 he writes:

> I have been suffering from my throat ever since I was in Philadelphia. You will remember I had a cough then. Well, it got worse, and I have not preached for a month till last Sunday. I tried one sermon then; but it threw me back. The doctor says it will be a tedious affair. Possibly I may be laid up for the summer. I have no pain, but only a loss of voice. My cough, which was quite bad, is nearly all gone; now I must wait for strength to come back. . . . . . But the long continuance of the weakness is beginning to make me feel a little depressed. I suppose I am to struggle as did father—now able to preach, and then laid up. But the doctor tells me it is nothing; if only we could fully trust the doctors . . . . . . We shall have a pleasant and profitable summer; that is, if we do not get too much depressed about my throat. I know we ought to be cheerful, and take gladly anything God sends, but a weight of melancholy seems to press on me sometimes, and though I am not rebellious, I do feel sad.
>
> Perhaps God means us to be sad. It may be good for us to be made to feel weak and dependent. I am sure I inherit from father something of a tendency to be melancholy at times.*

A few months later he writes more cheerfully: "I am feeling very strong and able to work; I rejoice in the strength and want to use it for the best while I have it, knowing that when the days of weakness come, as they must come to all, then God will give me just as perfect

---

* "Light on the Pilgrim's Way," p. 22.

peace and satisfaction in weakness, as I have now in strength."

He had by this time secured an influential reputation in our church. He was known to be one of our most thorough scholars and most impressive preachers, and his writings in the reviews and church papers were universally admired, and yet no man was ever less ambitious than he of gaining the applause of men and less sensitive to praise. But it was not only in the literary and theological departments of his profession that he became conspicuous, but in many of the active operations of the church he felt the liveliest interest. The mission work seemed to be his favorite, and his earnest sympathy for this cause easily led his brethren to the conclusion of electing him to the responsible position of President of the Board of Foreign Missions. This office he filled with great credit to himself and advantage to the Society.

He raised more money in his own church for the various religious societies of the church and benevolent objects in general than three or four other congregations together, and it was all owing to the perfect system he adopted and the industry and energy which he infused into the young persons appointed as collectors of these funds. Everything was admirably arranged and the whole machinery worked without friction or delay. And this, for the most part, is the secret of success in raising funds for missionary and other purposes. Many a minister complains of failures, when the fault is in himself and not in his people. He follows no system, nor rules, nor order; every thing is done in confusion, or is entrusted to incompetent hands; no pains are taken to render the people intelligent on the subject, and no wonder that failure and mortification ensue.

BALTIMORE, March, 1878.

* * * * You know we Americans are always overworking ourselves. It is a tremendously busy age; we forget what Christ said to the disciples: "Come ye apart and rest awhile." We think nothing will go unless we are always pushing. I am learning how to rest. Some days, I just throw myself down and lie on the lounge and play with our boy, or read a novel all day, as if there was nothing else in the world to do, and then the next day, I am fresh again. Sometimes I think our feverish activity is not so much from ardent consecration as from a lack of faith in the vast unseen power of God moving on the world.

ON THE PUBLICATION OF HIS FATHER'S SERMONS, TO HIS BROTHER.

BALTIMORE, 1876.

My dear T——. I am glad for the advanced condition of the "Sermons." Some one asked me last night when they would be out; an expression of interest called out, I suspect, by my article on father's texts. As for the covers, I am satisfied to leave that to you and S——; something modest and yet rich, and with a touch of individuality, so that the book is not lost and indistinguishable among the mob of such publications.

Your description of the attractive quality of father's sermons reminded me of one of Beecher's sayings of popular preaching— "People like to hear preaching that shows them their own thoughts idealized, so they can say, 'I knew I was right; but now I see I was *gloriously* right;'"—that is the substance of it. But I fancy there were some things father said, that many of his hearers honored with a vigorous dissent. I know he used sometimes to have the comforting testimony of opposition and irritation aroused by his preaching. But on the whole, however, what you say is a very just criticism.

Did I ever tell you of a scene in my church one Sunday night, *apropos* of the above? I was preaching on Lot's choice of Sodom for a home and its disastrous outcome, as showing the peril of worldly association and the mischief a man makes for himself by putting wealth and ease first in his scheme of life. At the close, after deploring Lot's miserable failure in fortune and life as the legitimate result of his mercenary choice—I said: "Who would make Lot's choice, and take Lot's end?" And at this point, a young man who had been twisting and showing his dissatisfaction for some time, rose up and cried out—"*Here's one that goes for Lot,*" and picked up his hat, rushed down the aisle and slammed the door after him, with all the signs of being in a great rage. I thought at first he was drunk. But those sitting by told me he was not, but had been waxing uncomfortable all through the latter half of the sermon. Odd, wasn't it?

How charming the coming of spring has been this year. I was out in the country a day or two ago; it was cool and fresh, and the foliage and grass green of that brilliant tint that looks as if the fields and groves were just about breaking into a smile. Do you know I was reminded of Devonshire and the green hills there; but we only have that soft, deep touch on our verdure for a week of May and then it is gone. We have such a fierce, brassy summer. But as I looked from the crest of a hill across a rolling country of fields and woods I thought that for a short time, at least, we need not go away from home to find beautiful nature.

TO HIS STEP-MOTHER.

BALTIMORE, February 3, 1876.

Dear Mother: . . . . I have been troubled a good deal with my church. Whilst I was away some difficulties arose . . . . . . and I as pastor cannot escape being involved in them. Disputes and disagreements are bad enough anywhere, but in the Church of Christ they are a double grief. I feel as though my hands were tied. When I get up to preach it seems all in vain; and it is hard even to pray. One man has left the church, but the matter is not settled yet. But I think I see the way clear to an adjustment. I do not want to trouble you with these things—only I know you will sympathize. Father had the same distresses, and I think they bore more heavily on him than on me.

I feel so strong and well that I easily throw the matter off; only I do grieve for the church. Of course such things retard the progress of the Gospel. The Spirit flies from strife.

Still we prosper. The church is in good condition. This will pass over.

Very pleasant things come in to refresh and cheer, too. The other day an elderly lady from Boston, a friend of R.'s, who is spending the winter in Baltimore, applied for some religious books to read: among others, I gave her father's "Afternon;" and she came back delighted with it. She said it seemed just written for her, and wanted more of his books. I gave her "The Unseen World;" and then she asked if he had no sermons. Willie gave a copy of "Afternoon" to his partner, Mr. Wright, who you know is in consumption; and he said it had done him a great deal of good. Here are two, who never knew father at all, edified and helped by his words. I was worried and dejected when this lady came to speak of the delight father's book had given her, and I cannot tell you how the little incident cheered and refreshed me. It made me think of the words, "He being dead, yet speaketh."

I have been trying to stir up our Conference to do something special for the debt of our Foreign Mission Board. It is a shame that we should be so supine here at home, when our missionaries are really harassed in their work by money cares. I see by the *Observer* what you have done for them. You have your reward. I only hope others may be stirred up.

BALTIMORE, July 14, 1877.

Dear Mother: The cold I had when I was last in Philadelphia increased afterwards, and I was laid off from preaching for nearly six weeks. I was afraid it was something serious. My voice was very weak. But now that is all past. I am preaching again, once a day, and my throat is rapidly regaining its usual vigor.

One thing that helped me to get well sooner was a press of

business in church matters that gave me no time to think about my condition.

You know, I suppose, that a change has been made in the Board of Missions. Most of the old Board have been removed, and the new body is composed of ministers and laymen in Baltimore and Washington. This was that the members might be all in the same neighborhood, to facilitate conference and the dispatch of business. I have been appointed President of the Board in place of Dr. Albert, and new men fill the other offices.

This makes quite a clean sweep. I knew nothing of it till it was all done. I should have opposed the change had I known it in time. For one thing, I hardly feel able for the responsibility and additional labor it imposes on me. I am not strong, and what strength I have I think I could use for the church in a more private station, to greater advantage. A great deal of planning, correspondence and general direction comes necessarily upon me. My doctor opposed my assuming the position, but I consented to try it for three months. I have got things pretty well into shape for the rest of the summer, and now I think of taking some rest. I went to Gettysburg to deliver an address to the young men at Commencement; I had also a good deal of work in the Board of the Seminary of which I am a director, so I came home quite tired, but I am rested now, and feel ready for fresh labor. The older I get the more I feel the force of Christ's words: "The night cometh in which no man can work;" and the more peace and joy I have in serving Him and my fellow-men. It is a great blessedness to feel that I can do something to be helpful to men, to know the sympathy of seeking goodness for myself and for others, and to be a colaborer with God. I am not restless, nor feverish; but while I work more, I have a great inward calm. I am subject occasionally to fits of melancholy, like father; but these I think are only the reaction from work. And most of the time I can say "great is their peace who wait on Thee."

* * * * * * * * *

TO HIS STEP-MOTHER.

BALTIMORE, December, 1877.

My work is prospering measurably. I believe I am one who is destined never to have any great success, nor any *great* failure. I jog along the foot-path way. I can't say but that I would like to have something more stirring and marked, a great crowd to preach to, many and striking conversions—large achievements. But if I am to do ordinary work in a quiet way I hope to be satisfied. I was much struck lately by a remark made in the *Spectator*, *apropos* of the life of a good man who, with many opportunities and some fine gifts, yet failed of his chief project for doing good, and passed away impressed by the thought that he had achieved very little. His character, however, was greatly chastened and ripened as he grew old, and the reviewer says his friends at last recognized in his life "that the highest end of existence is neither to shine nor to achieve, but to do the Divine will." That, after all, is the deepest truth; we fall back on that, when all else fails; that we cannot be disappointed of—being one with Christ in accepting and accomplishing God's will.

There have been a good many deaths in my church this fall. And the hard times press everybody. They have been rather dark days—not to me personally, but in the sympathies called forth for others. I have been trying to help a good many; and, to tell the truth, I have been imposed upon by some plausible rogues. I have been a little mortified to find how much I have lacked the "wisdom of the serpent." You will say that is no fault; but I think it is. It is our duty to get wisdom, to learn, to know how to help men without being imposed on. Well, I have learned something.

My foreign mission debt effort is almost finished. We have raised the $7,000 within a few hundreds—only seven more shares are needed, and I have do doubt those will be in after a few days. It has been right hard work, but it has done the churches good; they are somewhat surprised and greatly encouraged to see what they could do. It is not much, indeed; but it is a step in advance.

I am down for a paper on "Liturgies" at the Diet to be held in Dr. Baum's church, December 27th. So you may look for me about that time. I hope we may get some food out of this meeting. We come together not to dispute and legislate, but to confer together as brethren on great points of church life. I could have wished that the subject had taken a more practical turn, but I had no choice in that.

* * * * * * * * *

LETTER TO HIS STEP-MOTHER.

BALTIMORE, March 27, 1878.

. . . . My eyes are getting better. I use them two hours a day now, and that suffices for the present. My enforced rest was good for me. I went out to visit my people, and had plenty of time to sit in my chair by the fire and think. Meditation I find quite as profitable as study. It is good to be pulled up in the midst of active labors and be compelled to stop and think on one's ways. I find when I am well, and have nothing to hinder my activity, I get going too fast—I become absorbed in what I am doing, and lose myself. Then comes a spell that throws me back on myself—as the old devout writers say, I *re-collect* myself; I find where I am; I see what a poor thing one's best work is. I get time to settle, and that is a good thing, for there is no doubt one's heart and life get turbid by too much business here and there. In this way I get a fresh hold on reality, on God, and then I am off again. So I do not feel it lost time when I cannot study or write. It is so good to be fallen for a time; to be perfectly passive, and find how God works on us when we can do nothing.

The trouble with this age, religiously, as well as in other things, is its intense activity outwardly; it has no time to think —to be still before God, and recognize how vast is that power that is working in us and through us. Our intense practicability and hurrying to and fro stir up a cloud of dust that hides God from us.

* * * * * * * * *

BALTIMORE, February 11, 1879.

Dear Mother: I have been intending to write for some days; but every day seems full to the brim. I am glad you get any comfort or cheer out of my letters. I know I ought to write oftener; but I never yet have got over the miserable fault of procrastination in letter-writing.

Since the first of the year I have been very busy with a series of meetings in my church. We began the year by observing the Week of Prayer in union with all the churches, and a good week it was for us—it gave us a start. Then we had meetings in our own church without intermission night after night. We are now in the fifth week. And what has come of it? Well, the church has been much quickened, a few of careless young people have been brought back, and there have been a few conversions. But the work thus far has been chiefly in the church itself. You know it must begin there; and my church needed it. We have had a great deal of what I call "dead-wood"—mere nominal professors, who come in and go out, and are very respectable, but have no real life. They have been a burden on me and a hindrance to the real work of the church, and now I think the rubbish is getting on fire.

I have had some very interesting experience in watching the flush of life come into souls—these torpid souls. I never tire of the wonder there is in a soul that begins to come to itself, and opens its eyes on the spiritual world. The wonder, the vision that comes to them then, of a new existence that was before unseen—they are a miracle.

I have done all the work myself, preaching every night. I have held out wonderfully well, for preaching, it comes very easy. You know I seldom write, but make a few notes, and then dash on.

My congregations have doubled in size, and strangers are coming in. But I do not expect to go on much longer There is such a thing as an excess of religious meetings, and I am not going to have my people strained unreasonably.

I have been quite intimately associated with Mr. Moody in his work here. He is a rough man, with no education outside of the Bible, but there is a great charm about him. His humility, frankness, sweetness of temper, and downright sincerity, make him very attractive. I took his place one night at his request; he was taken sick, and asked me to preach for him. I had a great church packed with people.

* * * * * * * * *

TO HIS STEP-MOTHER.

BALTIMORE, September, 1879.

. . . . . . I am busy just now, in addition to my other work, in reviewing Dr. Sprecher's new book on theology. It is a huge work (500 octavo pages) of very tough and profound writing, and it is quite a task to go through with it faithfully. It will be a credit to our Lutheran church, and though very philosophical, is very full of the Spirit of the Gospel. I have found it quite stirring. But you will see my review of it in the *Observer* and in the *Quarterly*.

I have been reading a very tender and deeply spiritual book this summer, "*The Letters of Thomas Erskine.*" He was a very deep and earnest Christian of Scotland, a friend of Dr. Chalmers. His presentation of Christian truth struck me as very rich and sweet. You may have noticed a story I quoted from him in a piece in the *Observer* of last week. He specially dwells on the thought of our fellowship in the sufferings of Christ; and that the Christian is not complete in Christ until not only he has received Christ crucified for him, but is also crucified with Him. That I think is a very deep, and though at first-sight a repelling, yet when we experience it, a very precious truth of our holy faith. To die to self, to be baptized in suffering, to receive the strokes of God, and so to rise in Christ, and to be one with Him —that to me of late is growing more and more a rich part of the faith.

* * * * * * * * *

TO HIS BROTHER, T. B. STORK.

BALTIMORE, October 8, 1879.

. . . . . . I can imagine how happy you must be in your home. The touch of the earth—one's own bit of mother-earth—

gives a flavor to life that is unique; it is the homely flavor that gives to all the rest of life's finer experience the sense of reality, of being solidly based, and not a mere dream. I never had a bit of ground myself, and have always lived in houses that were mine only by a fiction. I am like Abram, who lived in tents, and had not a foot of ground in the land promised him. But I enjoy the earth-love by proxy. I have had so many friends that were rooted in their own soil, and by a sympathetic transfer I tested their experience.

One of the drawbacks to a minister's life is, that he never takes root ; that is, he of course does fasten to the place of his labor by many very tender and pleasant ties, but they are only rootlets after all—he never can let himself strike down, so to speak, a tap-root, and be anchored for life. In some sort of sense he is always feeling that his field is the world.

I have just had under consideration a proposal to go to San Francisco; there were many reasons to urge my going, but I finally settled to decline, because of the danger my throat would be in from that raw climate. And now I am thinking of a call to another far-away city. Probably I shall not go, but the mere openness a minister must feel to these calls hither and thither, all give him the sense of a rover. I read last night a beautiful prayer of an old German which ends thus, and somehow it seems to voice my feeling—"*Adde animum imperterritum, ut ex hac vita tanquam ex hospitio, non tanquam ex domo, Te jubente, placide discedam.*"

But I enter into your feeling about your spot of earth ; it is natural, healthy, and one of God's very best gifts to us here. I am glad to see a man settled on his own turf; and when I walk about with a friend over his place, that home-feeling seems to me to be one of the sweetest senses that this old earth of ours can afford.

*   *   *   *   *   *   *   *   *

BALTIMORE, Sept. 28, 1880.

Dear Mother: Thanks for you for the recipe for a throat-gargle ; I should think it would be good. My voice is something better, and I think on the whole I am improving; but it is slow work.

I found my church in good condition. The people received me cordially, and I set to work with good heart. I am only preaching once on Sunday for the present, till my voice improves.

We have been quite busy in Foreign Mission matters, getting a missionary to take Mr. Rowe's place in India. We think we have a man, one who will make a most excellent missionary. But Mr. Rowe will tell you all about this when he sees you. He expects to be in Philadelphia at the end of this week, when he will call upon you, and explain all India matters.

* * * * * * * * *

BALTIMORE, April, 1880.

. . . . The older I get the more I feel that there, after all, is our strength. I used to think when I was beginning my ministry that I was strong and able to do great things, but every year I am less and less self-confident; I think sometimes I am growing timid; but I trust a great deal more in God, and I go to Him more.

I am trying just now to patch myself up; I have been going through a siege at the dentist's, and I go every morning to a new physician who promises to cure my throat. He has already done me good, and I think I am in a fair way to get rid of the soreness and hoarseness; but the process by syringing the throat is very disagreeable and even painful. What an amount of patching and mending these poor bodies of ours require!

* * * * * * * * *

My church goes along in a steady way, though I have been much depressed of late to see how little good, in comparison with what I hoped to do, I am effecting. I measure my pastoral success by what father used to do, and I see how far short I come of what he was able to do, and I feel cast down. Sometimes I think I inherit more of his melancholy and timidity than of his effective gifts. I feel sad and unable to do any work from an influx of unreasonable despondency, and it is only by prayer and active exertion that I succeed at all in shutting it off. I look back over my life, and it seems sometimes as if I had done nothing at all, that I have been only an unfaithful and wasteful servant. I am afraid I have been naturally very proud and self-sufficient, and it has required a great deal of humbling and painful experience to bring me to a true and real sense of just what I am. I have no complaint to make of God or any one, but it does make me sad to think I have come to be over forty and have made so little real spiritual progress. People look to me for counsel and inspiration and guidance, and I often feel as if I was unfit to guide or inspire any one; I need to be counseled and led myself. Well, God has told us to come to Him and be counseled and inspired by Him; and all I can do is just to throw myself on Him, and beg Him to have patience with me and give me greater measure of grace, and to fit me yet for better service.

I did not mean to write in such a doleful strain, but somehow it has come of itself. There are so few to whom I can speak the deeper troubles of my soul; so few who are like-minded, and can understand what one means by feeling empty and poor in spirit. Sometimes I think the only blessing I can fully claim is that first one, *"Blessed are the poor in spirit,"* for I am feeling of late very poor in spirit.

* * * * * * * * *

Dear Mother: The last few days have made us feel as though summer were almost over; there is a feeling of autumn in the air. How swiftly the seasons and years flee away! I am sorry the summer rest has not done for me what I had hoped it would. I kept getting steadily worse till the middle of August; then things seemed to take a turn upward, and I have been slowly improving. I am under the treatment of a physician who has been quite successful in throat diseases. He promises me that I shall be fit for work by November or, at the latest, December. But till then he forbids me to preach or lecture even in the class-room. I shall make arrangements to be relieved of work till the middle of November. Then I hope to go on—this is the hopeful view. Of course there is another side; I may go back again. I think my throat is a good deal like father's, and I suppose at last it will carry me off. But whatever comes, it is all right. I am ready to go on and work, and I hope I am ready to lay down work if the Master says so, and go hence. I do think these sufferings of the body, telling us how weak we are, how frail the thread that holds us here, help to make us sit light to the world, and to give up what we naturally cling to.

. . . . . . The Seminary is thoroughly repaired, the painting done well, and everything, thanks to you, looks well, fresh, clean and strong.

* * * * * * * * *

You will see in the September number of the *Missionary Journal*, that I have taken your remarks in your last letter as the text of an editorial on "Our Hindrances." I, with you, grieve at the slowness of God's people to answer to the cry to come to the help of the Lord; but yet there are gleams of brightness; there are the faithful ones and the Lord reigneth.

* * * * * * * * *

LETTER FROM C. A. STORK.

BALTIMORE, March, 1880.

Dear Mother: I am, indeed, hard at work, doing what I can, and having to refuse to do a great deal more. I have had a cold in my system for the last few months that has exhausted me a good deal. This new *Missionary Journal*, too, takes a great deal of time and thought. So I should be glad to rest after Easter.

. . . . . . As to going to Atlantic City, I do not know; I do love the sea, and it rests me. Will Theo. go? But that can be disposed of after I get to Germantown. I have some thoughts of going on to New York for a few days; but I have fixed on nothing. . . . . . . It is a great pity Mr. Rowe must return from India, but I suppose there is no help for it. We are looking about for some one to take his place: it is hard to find one who is strong enough in body, able enough in mind, and at the same time fervent enough in spirit to be sent out as a missionary. We had one young man in mind who was fully qualified, and full of zeal to go but the Doctor said no he would not be able to stand the climate for six months. So him we had to give up.

As to the Madras Scholarship, I think it would be best to defer acting in that matter till we see Mr. Rowe. The Board have been discussing the expediency of postponing the erection of the boys' boarding school of which Mr. Uhl wrote, and for which you gave the $300, and putting up first a school and room for the Zenana work among the women, which has opened a new field for our mission. Of course that will be just as you say. If you prefer the boys' boarding school, as you proposed, that will go on; but if you would wish to have the Zenana school for the caste girls and women, you could transfer the money to that purpose. We have already sent the money out to India with instructions to build the boys' school; but, perhaps, it would be better to let that wait, and hasten on with the Zenana school building. It will be just as you wish.

And now about scholarships in our institution for the grandchildren. Many thanks, dear mother, for your kind forethought: as you suggested, *education* is the best thing we can give to those that are to come after us. As to scholarships for the girls in our female seminaries, there are no provisions of that sort made in female schools. That arrangement is only found in our colleges. For the boys a scholarship can easily be had in the college at Gettysburg. What the cost would be, and the details, I do not exactly know. I will inquire and find out all about it; and then we will discuss the matter when I see you after Easter.

Dr. Brown's sad condition has put everything in such an uncertain state at the Seminary, that we all feel unsettled as to what is to come out of it in our educational work. You know the probabilities are that his mind will never be fit for much again. They have already asked me to take the *Review*. I would like to do it; but I cannot take any more such loads. I promised to do what I could to help them; but the control and headship of so grave a responsibility I felt constrained to decline.

My people are fearing they may want to call me to Gettysburg to teach there. I trouble myself not at all about it; all these things are in the future, out of my reach, and I feel that I have no right to be taking serious thought about such a far-off morrow. If God wants me to go, He will let me know in due time. In the meanwhile I live on from day to day, not forecasting the future, but doing the work of the present.

BALTIMORE, 72 N. Paca St., Oct. 21, 1880.

...... You will notice by the *Observer* that our Mission Boards have requested the churches to observe Reformation Day, October 31, as a special day of prayer for missions. I expect to preach on the mission work on that day, and to have a prayer-meeting in that interest.

My throat is slowly gaining strength. I spoke last Sunday twice without any serious difficulty. It seems to me Doctor Da Costa's treatment has done more for me than anything else I have had. My voice is gradually growing stronger, and gives promise of complete restoration. I feel thankful to God for this among so many other and greater mercies. I have some notion of running over to Philadelphia to see Doctor Da Costa some time before Christmas.

My general health is good; and I feel encouraged in my work. We are all settled down at home once more. Ritie and the children are in excellent health, and everything moves on in quiet and comfort.

We are thinking of celebrating the 20th anniversary of the establishment of St. Mark's in the early part of November. We expect to have a Sunday-school celebration on Sunday, November 14, and a church anniversary address and social gathering during the week preceding. In twenty years God has blessed the church very greatly, and made it the means of blessing to the community here, and to our Lutheran church generally. So we wish to celebrate what the Lord has done for us. I wish you could be here to join us, in the memory, among other things, of father and his work here.

* * * * * * * *

We are just getting through with the distraction of our great Sequi-Centennial Baltimore celebration. It has been a week of excitement and show; the city has been crowded; all business suspended, and church work crowded out; and all has been gaiety and sight-seeing. I confess for one I have had enough and long for quiet. The splendor and shows of the world one soon sickens of: they are not satisfying.

*	*	*	*	*	*	*	*

CHAPTER V.

ELECTION TO GETTYSBURG—POSITION—DEVOTEDNESS TO HIS WORK—HESITATION IN DECIDING—REASONS FOR ACCEPTING—LETTERS TO FORMER STUDENTS—WISE COUNSELS—LETTERS.

THE evidences of increasing infirmity and of inability to preach were alarmingly plain. There was a vacancy in the Theological Faculty, occasioned by the lamented death of the Rev. Dr. Brown, and all eyes were turned to Dr. Stork as his successor; and yet the question was, could he lecture five or six times a week when he could not preach? He was willing to make the trial, and succeeded well for some months. He gave a course of lectures on Didactic Theology characterized by his intellectual power, his profound yet distinct thinking, and thorough aquaintance with the subjects treated. His style of lecturing was pleasing, and his pupils are enthusiastic in their praises of him as a teacher. The man who was not profited by Dr. Stork's instruction must have been incapable of appreciating every thing intellectually refined and elegant. Although he had himself sat at the feet of the theological Gamaliels at Andover, yet he did not copy their style or mode of teaching, and pursued methods of his own. As in all other things, he never followed the ways of any master. He struck out in independent paths, and came to conclusions as the result of his own reflection and researches.

It was a sore trial to leave St. Mark's. For twenty years he had served that people faithfully, and though sickness more than once interrupted his work for a season, the mutual attachment was strong, and the parting was painful.

He greatly enjoyed his work as a professor and also occasionally preached in the churches of the town and elsewhere. His home was delightful, and a generous hospitality was dispensed to his friends.

After the lapse of a year, he writes: "I am glad my first year's work is nearly over. It ends June 25th. It has been quite hard for me, making lectures on new subjects. I have been kept too close in my study. But the summer vacation will mend that: and next year I shall not be pressed so hard.

"I hope I am doing good here, but I find in doing work for the Lord, as in all the Christian life, we must walk by faith, not by sight. We cannot see always that we are really accomplishing anything. The only way I find is to live day by day, being sure that the Lord has given us a certain work to do, and then doing it, even though we cannot see the fruit. I preached yesterday on Mary's words at the feast of Cana, 'Whatsoever he saith unto you, do it.' How simple and beautiful that rule is—to take our work from His lips, our particular work, whatever it is—and then faithfully and loyally to do it just because He says it.*

---

* Light on the Pilgrim's Way, p. 26.

LETTERS TO HIS STEP-MOTHER.

BALTIMORE, July 7, 1881.

I write to you at once on making my decision about Gettysburg. I have just written to the Board of Directors accepting the call. I shall be with my church here till October 1, when I go to Gettysburg to begin work in the Seminary.

I need not tell you that it has been hard to decide. I love the pastoral office; I love my work and people. I dislike the business of teaching. . . . . . . I do not believe I shall enjoy my new duties and responsibilities as I have those here; in all respects it looks forbidding and dreary to me.

Why then, you will ask—why go? To that my dear mother, there is but one answer: I have come to a deep conviction that God says to me—go. I have pondered and prayed; for a long time I have foreseen what was coming, and I have tried to see the whole situation; and then I prayed over it continually. And the longer I dwelt on it, the more I seemed shut up to this one path. And now how could I say no? All my wishes bid me to refuse, and I go with only one reason for going—that God would have me go.

It seems as I look around that there is none else to go. The whole church fixes on me. Again and again I have put it away, and still the call returns. And so I feel like a soldier who is sent out on a hard campaign—every consideration of personal comfort and peace urges him to stay at home; but his duty sends him out.

One of the things that have helped to embarrass me is the reduction of my income involved. I will receive at Gettysburg about $400 less a year than I do here. And it does pain me a little to think of the pinching process as applied to my wife and family. For myself I do not care; I can live plainer; but I hate to have to put them on short allowance. . . . . . . Another thing is the change of social relations. We have been a family beloved and kindly cared for; but now we go out to be pretty much alone. . . . . . . All these things are against me; but we have counted the cost, and are content.

Do not think we are complaining. We are satisfied to go where God sends : but I wanted to tell you just how we felt, and give you an insight into our experience. These are things we do not speak to outsiders ; but you ought to know all about us in so great a change.

GETTYSBURG, 1882.

. . . . . My health is very good. The throat is quite well again. I preached yesterday with good, strong voice, and had no trouble. . . . . It has been quite hard on me preparing lectures on a new subject. I have been kept too close in my study. But the summer vacation will mend that, and next year I shall not be pressed so hard. I hope I am doing good here ; but I find, in doing work for the Lord, as in all Christian life, we must walk by faith and not by sight. We cannot see always that we are really accomplishing anything. The only way is to live day by day, being sure that the Lord has given me a certain work to do, and then doing it, though we cannot see the fruits. . . . . I preached yesterday on Mary's words at the feast of Cana, "Whatsoever He saith unto you, do it." How simple and beautiful that rule is : to take our work from His lips, our particular work whatever it is, and then faithfully and loyally to do it, just because He says it."

GETTYSBURG, January, 1882.

. . . . I have been unusually busy. I have been off to preach every Sunday since Christmas, at various places, and once at St. Mark's, Baltimore. The people received me very cordially indeed ; in fact, I think they are more anxious to hear me than they ever were when I was pastor. I enjoyed preaching to them very much : one person came and said it seemed as if every word went right to their souls. . . . . . . We are all uncommonly well. Gettysburg is a great place for health. I have no more headache, and have lost the old tired feeling I used to have. The children are pictures of rosy, happy health. So you see we have great blessings of our Father, for which we cannot praise Him enough.

*　　*　　*　　*　　　　*　　*　　*

GETTYSBURG, Feb. 1, 1882.

Dear Mother : Your kind gift of the furnishing of a room will be received very gratefully by all of us who have charge of the Seminary. It came just in the right time. A new student entered this Christmas, and we had only a half-furnished room left to give him. He said he was used to roughing it, and did not mind ; but the other students had to lend him things from their rooms to furnish him out. Now we can give him a room comfortably and fully fitted up.

Your condition that the room shall not be defiled with tobacco we can very readily comply with, for one of the rules of the Seminary is, that no smoking is allowed in any of the rooms or halls of the building ; and all students are required to be cleanly in their habits—no spitting about, etc.

Our students are generally a good class of young men, of good habits. Some are devoted Christians, already fitted for a good work ; others are careless and untrained yet ; but we are trying to teach them what a Christian gentleman should be. . . . .

. . . . . The snow-storm was a beautiful sight—all day it came drifting down, and we watched it across the wide landscape—so pure, and gentle and soft it came, it was like a visitant from heaven. You know snow seems so different in the city, where it gets dirty as soon as it falls.

We had a good day on Sunday—Day of Prayer for Colleges. I addressed the young men in the college in the morning, and then in the evening I spoke again at the union meeting in church in town. One feels very much drawn out to these young men, who are so soon to be called to the place of trust—oh ! that they were all Christ's men.

* * * * * * * * *

LETTER TO REV. DR. BORN, SELINSGROVE, WHO AS TREASURER OF SYNOD HAD SENT A CONTRIBUTION TO THE CONTINGENT FUND OF OUR SEMINARY.

My Dear Brother Born : Many thanks for your remittance. I enclose a receipt for the amount. It was very welcome, for we have had extra repairs, and our funds were running sadly short.

I do not think our contingent fund has yielded this year very much more than you have received. You are to be congratulated on having such warm and helpful friends. I am glad to hear you have been so relieved.

We have yet a month of work, and the heaviest end of the log comes now. We shall send out eight young men this year. The most of them have their fields of labor in view; and, as with you, there is always a demand for more preachers than we can furnish. I do not think that all our two Institutions can send out will more than meet the demand.

I hope you may be prospered more and more. There is no reason why the two schools should not do their work in harmony and brotherly love. The field is bigger than we can fill, let us do our best.

It would be pleasant to meet and have free talk over our common work. I hope I may see you soon.

I have been suffering a good deal with my throat this spring, and have been unable to preach much. Happily I can lecture without inconvenience. Still trouble in the throat always makes us feel depressed, and mine has been weighing on me.

Yours truly, C. A. Stork.

Gettysburg, Pa., May 25th, 1882.

I here insert a few letters to several of his students, which show his kindness and his tender interest in their welfare and their work:

Gettysburg, February, 1883.

Dear Friend: Your letter gives me great pleasure. We had all been wondering what you were doing, and how life seemed to you now that you had struck out into the wide ocean for yourself, and your account of your place and work was very gratifying.

I am glad that you are engaging so heartily in work, and I trust you are beginning to find compensation for your labor in the work itself. As I read your letter it recalled all my own early experience in a half-mission church, with a handful of workers, many of them not of a high grade of intelligence or social influence, with all sorts of labor, worries and discouragements upon me—and yet it was a very blessed life. As I look back I seem to myself never to have rightly appreciated the privilege given me to be a worker with God upon men. Now that I am cut off so much from activity, I see that the trials, perplexities and interests that once appeared quite burdensome, were a real gift of God.

I have passed through a winter of great deal of physical weakness; my throat has been very troublesome, and is at present quite sore. I have not been able to do more than half my work, and now the doctor has ordered me to milder air. [This order was afterwards recalled.—J. G. M.]

* * * * * * * * *

I am sorry not to have been able to write more for the *Observer*, but my illness has made it hard for me to write. When I get away I will try to do more. . . . . . . I would suggest that you try to get your people to do something for missions. If possible, organize in the Sunday-school a band or society for foreign missions. It will help the church, and be a blessing to the young.

BALTIMORE, March 30, 1883.

. . . . . . I shall probably be here till the latter part of April, when I hope to be able to return to Gettysburg. The summer I hope to spend in the White Mountains, and altogether my expectation is to be able for work in the fall, though at one time it seemed as if I must give up all hope of resuming my work in the Seminary.

* * * * * * * * *

I shall always maintain that no work gives such a pure pleasure as that of the pastor. I have tried a variety of things, but nothing equals the experience I had when in the vigorous performance of my duty as preacher and pastor.

You have taken a good step in organizing your missionary society in connection with the school. It will be a school of Christian training to the young, to yourself, and a blessing to the church. I shall take what you say about it to make a note for the *Missionary Journal.* * * * * *

I understand how it is that the water sometimes runs low, or that the fountain of knowledge is occasionally exhausted. A permanent and full supply comes only from continuous and extensive reading, together with meditation. My experience is that everything turns to material for preaching when a man is bent on his work. I used to get sermons, or matter for them, illustrations, etc., from novels, daily news, and all kinds of study; but there are special books which stimulate sermonizing, just as certain kinds of food go to milk in animals. Such books as Farrar's Life of Christ, his work on St. Paul; Geikie's Life and Work of Jesus; Conybeare and Howson's Life and Epistles of Paul, I have found very fruitful; sermons too of the suggestive order, as those of Moseley, Brooks, Maclaren of Manchester, England, Bushnell, and the like.

* * * * * * * * *

You must find time to study and read. The secret of the drying up we see in the lives of some very good ministers, is the failure to feed their minds with new thought by study and reading. A library into which there go no new books is one from which come out sermons with no fresh thoughts.

JULY 7, 1883.

I wish I could give a better account of my health. I have been slowly improving . . . . but the improvement is very slow, and with many discouraging relapses; but God has given me twenty years of activity in his service—now, if he calls me to suffer and wait, I am satisfied.

The physicians have forbidden me to lecture or use my voice at all next winter. The Board have given me furlough for a year, in which time I hope to regain my usual strength.

JULY, 1883.

I regret to hear you had so many things to embarrass and annoy you in your work; but it is often so in the beginning. What you say of the discouragements that meet you reminds me of my early experience in the ministry; often I felt as if I could not bear the burden much longer. But God held me up and led me on, and the lions I found in the way were chained. Perhaps you do not see such fruit of your labor as you could wish. You seem to toil long, and sometimes achieve nothing. Well, you must have faith in God, and hold on. We are often building better than we know, and the accomplished result comes at last when we least expect it.

You must remember, too, that God has you in training; you are learning how to endure hardship as a good soldier of Jesus Christ, and you are being made capable of greater work by your hard experience now. An old minister told me once when in my youth I was depressed by having so little success, that I was having as much success as God saw was good for me to have.

I wish I could help you; but though you have a sea of trouble to struggle through now, I know it will come out well with you.

. . . . Your account of the state of things where you are at work is encouraging. You have a good opening, a field for work, the sense that you have been sent of God to this work; your weapons are newly sharpened and burnished—and now what more can a man want?

I hope you are enjoying your work. You ought to. I say this with something of a sorrowful recollection of how little I myself enjoyed the first year of my ministry. I worked against the grain for some years, feeling that I was called of God, that there was nothing else for me to do in the world, and trying with all my might to do my work in the best way, and yet conscious that I was not hitting the nail on the head at all. At last I worked out into the clear, and then the ministry was a continual field of delight. Perhaps my long apprenticeship when I fumbled about and botched everything, was one reason why I learned to preach as well as I did; above all, perhaps, it was what trained me to be a teacher of other preachers. There is no bungling that I cannot sympathize with, having been such a bungler myself.

I follow with deep interest and sympathy you young brethren who have gone forth. I shall count your success as a part of my reward. Nothing could give me more pleasure than such kind words as yours, with respect to the help I have been permitted to be to you. The whole business of religion, with all its necessary parts of theology, creeds, etc., is to me so vital a thing that I cannot bear to treat it in a merely scholastic way. It is a reality, or it is nothing.

GETTYSBURG, January 10, 1883.

Your letter gave me much pleasure. I rejoice with you in the fruits of your work. It makes me glad to hear that you are really feeling the reality of the work, ... and I can understand the sense of humbling that comes with the answer of your labor. There is a humility that springs out of success as well as from failure. We wonder who we are, that such fruit should come from our tilling.

As to difficulties, I am afraid that the trouble is not one to be cured by more light.

Let us look at the three first cases you mention. The one who is trying to make himself better—the one who has doubts about inspiration—and the one who thinks Christ only a man. All are unconsciously hiding themselves behind false defences. The real difficulty is not what they aver, but an indisposition of the will to obey and submit. They flatter themselves, probably, that if these particular objections were removed they would be ready to be Christians—but that is a delusion. The way to deal with them is to demolish the objections, and then show them that with the objections removed, they are still unwilling. Often these are the hardest to convince. I would urge on them that the trouble is "they *will* not," and point out to them Christ's way of clearing up doubts, that he that does the will of God shall know of the doctrine—that obedience is the way to knowledge in religious things, and not knowledge the way to obedience.

As to the fourth question about the heathen, I should say, "What is that to thee?" Every such case must be decided on its own merits. If the woman lived up to her light she is acquitted; but who can tell what light she had, and if she followed it? None but the omniscient God. Hence the absolute need of an individual judgment by the omniscient Son of God who is also the sympathetic son of man. It comes at last to this: Should not the judge of all the earth do right? Yes certainly he will, but what is right in one individual case depends on the circumstances of the case. One woman may be doing right to give her child to death according to her light, and the next be doing wrong; but who shall weigh all the life with its modifying circumstances but the Omniscient, All-loving? In any case we have nothing to do with it, and the question if seriously urged evidences a deep frivolity and spiritual impudence. The only answer is Christ's to Peter, "What is that to thee? follow thou me." * * * * *

After giving his young friend direction how to act in a church case of no general interest, Dr. Stork proceeds:

I see you have difficulties, and I do not wonder that they annoy you. Often we fret under these perplexing affairs. We want to finish up as we go, to leave no unravelled skeins behind us; but a part of our trial is that we must leave much unfinished, wrongs unrighted, errors uncorrected, deluded souls going deeper into the dark. It is one of the terrible burdens of life that nothing is perfect; so much is irremediable.

My refuge has been to take it all to God. I do my best, and then I can leave it to Him. I am willing to be accounted inconsistent, to have failed, to leave knots and tangles behind me unsolved, if I can only keep close to my Master and do faithfully my best to get things straight and make men right. How much He had to leave behind; how many sighs He heaved over the stubborn, the stupid, the incorrigible, whom even He could not reach. We must leave our unfinished or marred work behind and press on—there is much to do—we shall not get through work until life ends.

EXTRACTS FROM OCCASIONAL LETTERS.
TO DR. HAY.

BALTIMORE, 1883.

I am glad to be able to say that the improvement in my throat still continues. I am desirous of going back to Gettysburg . .

but the doctor still detains me. If I continue to improve steadily through April, I hope to be at home in May.

Miss Boggs arrived in this city from England last Wednesday. She is in better health than when she left India, though still weak.

* * * * * * * * *

I wish I could furnish you with some good subjects for theses. I will venture a few :

The three stages of missionary work : 1. Breaking the ground. 2. The coöperative stage. 3. The stage of self-support and independence.

The relation of the Renaissance to the Reformation.

Reformers before the Reformation.

The modern doctrine of Christian perfection.

Jewish and heathen conceptions of a future state.

Fenelon as a devotional writer.

The place of Origen in theolgy.

The duration of the state of probation.

The relation of bishop, presbyter, and deacon in the primitive church.—This is treated by Hatch in his Bampton Lectures.

Original sin as a mysterious truth.

The theology of Chemnitz.

The place of the Lutheran Church in the religious life of America.

The use of unfermented wine in the Eucharist.

TO DR. HAY.

BALTIMORE, April 21, 1883.

I am glad to say that I am greatly improved, and growing in strength every day. I can talk without difficulty, but the doctor does not weary in urging upon me that I am not to use my throat in the way of any effort this spring or summer. It is a hard precept when one feels so well, but I am preparing myself to obey . . . . . . I expect to be in Gettysburg by May 15th, so that I can superintend matters during your absence (at the General Synod).

TO HIS MOTHER.

GETTYSBURG, May, 1883.

Dear Mother : I have settled down again at Gettysburg. The doctor thought the fresh, pure air here would be better for me than the close atmosphere of the city, even though I might not have so much of his treatment. . . . . . . My throat improves slowly, but very slowly. I am having a thorough lesson in patience. I think sometimes I have had enough, but the Master says, "No, you must go over the old lesson again." I have been wondering how those who have no assured trust that God does all well, and that he steers the ship, can keep from falling into despair.

You will be gratified to see that all the missionary enterprises of the Church have been advancing in a very encouraging way. The income of the Foreign Board for the last two years ($50,000) is greater by $15,000 than in any preceding two years of our history. I do think there is an awakening of the Church to the call of God.

* * * * * * * * *

The season though late is wonderfully beautiful here. I never saw Gettysburg looking so lovely. We have been having a succession of the most charming days, when everything in earth and sky seemed perfect. As I walked through the fields I could only praise God for the view He gave of His wonderful beauty —all the beauty and purity seemed a reflection of His own exceeding loveliness and perfection. I think sometimes we do not dwell enough on the beauty and sweetness of what He does give us, and let our hearts go out in praise and delight in Him, the infinitely beautiful and good. We have so much sorrow and pain, and we see so much that is dark and sinful, that often we let the shadow of these miserable things come over what does reveal the beauty and goodness of God's works. I reproach myself often, since my weakness and sickness have been so heavy on me, that I do not praise God more for the sunshine He pours so abundantly on me in it all.

I wish you could be here to enjoy the season with us. The

roses are blooming generously this morning, and all the fields are spread out green and fresh and inviting.

* * * * * * * * *

TO THE BOARD OF DIRECTORS OF THE THEOLOGICAL SEMINARY OF THE GENERAL SYNOD.

Brethren: It is proper that I should ask the attention of the Board to some matters respecting my official relation to them.

It is known to all that for the last few months of the scholastic year I was unable from illness to attend to my duties in the Seminary. These duties were assumed by Professors Hay and Wolf, imposing on them much additional labor. For this labor it seems just that they should be compensated. If the Board is able to make such compensation it would be gratifying to them and myself. If no provision can be made otherwise, I shall deem it incumbent on myself to provide such compensation.

It is also due to the Board that they should be informed of my physical inability to undertake any duties involving the use of my throat next autumn and winter.

My physicians, skillful specialists of Baltimore and Philadelphia, have warned me, while I may in all probability recover the use of my voice by prolonged rest, that any use of my throat next autumn and winter will be in the highest degree hazardous, and have absolutely forbidden it.

It is absolutely necessary, therefore, that I rest for the greater part of the next year. In view of these circumstances I have to propose to the Board that exemption from duty be granted me for so much of the next year as may be necessary to my restoration to health. Also that arrangements be made with the rest of the faculty or others to take my work, the compensation for that work to be provided for out of my salary.

This, or some such arrangement, I should prefer. But I am aware that it may not be the course most conducive to the welfare of the Institution. If it should seem desirable to fill the place permanently at once, I would therefore cheerfully tender my resignation as Professor of Didactic Theology, feeling it to be but just and right that my own preference should not stand for a moment in the way of the best interests of the Seminary.

CHAS. A. STORK,
Prof. of Didactic Theology and Homiletics.

Gettysburg, June 26, 1883.

TO DR. HAY.

ANDOVER, July 23, 1883.

...... I have had a painful attack of sciatica since coming here; it is, however, yielding to treatment. My throat is better...... I had purposed going off to the mountains or the sea shore, but the sciatica has kept me home. I shall not leave Andover till I am much better. The doctor tells me that all these attacks of neuralgia, sciatica, and the like, are due to the general debility of my system. I am glad, however, that the throat seems no worse.

Dr. Park (of Andover Seminary) met me the other day, and bewailed the sad condition of orthodoxy in the Seminary here. He thinks Dorner is to be blamed for the lapse from the faith of the younger Congregational ministers. He asked my opinion of Dorner, and also that I would give him reviews of Dorner in the German theological journals.

CHAPTER VI.

LEAVES GETTYSBURG—GERMAN HOSPITAL—SURGICAL OPERATION—SUFFERING—LETTERS.

BUT, to the profound grief of all his friends, the students and directors of the Seminary and of the Church, he was compelled to abandon his work altogether, and after most acceptably serving the Seminary for about two years, he left Gettysburg—never to return. He repaired to Baltimore, where he passed the winter under medical treatment. The subsequent summer he spent in Andover, Mass., and went to Philadelphia in September, intending to sojourn during the winter at Lakewood, N. J. On arriving in Philadelphia, however, dangerous symptoms developed themselves, and his physician directed his removal to the Pennsylvania Hospital, where a surgeon could be within immediate call at all times. He remained there but a few weeks, and was then removed to the German Hospital, where he was subjected to the severe operation of tracheotomy, by which his larynx was severed, and a silver tube inserted, to enable him to breathe. He was in this critical and painful condition for more than two months, with varying indications of improvement and relapse. Although his body gradually became weaker, his mind was bright and active, and he occupied himself with reading, and also with writing to some extent within a few days of his death.

During this period of suffering and anxiety, his letters are not despondent, although full of the tenderest emotion. In one he says, "I feel in myself a greater desire to communicate good—a greater richness of thought and experience to communicate—and then to lie still, to be shut up in silence, is a hard trial. But God knows best. When I feel restive, impatient, weary, despondent, I just fold my hands and say over those words of Jesus, 'Thy will be done,' till I feel how blessed that will is, and all the waves of strife in me go down, and a heavenly peace comes in. I was reading yesterday the words of Adolph Monod, repeated so often in the last months of his life, when he was suffering so much, 'The crucified life is the blessed life.'"

Again he writes, "My throat improves slowly, but very slowly. I am having a thorough lesson in patience. I think sometimes I have had enough, but the Master says, 'No, you must go over the old lesson again.' * * * * I reproach myself often, since my weakness and sickness have been so heavy upon me, that I do not praise God more for the sunshine he pours so abundantly on me in it all."*

TO DR. HAY.

ANDOVER, August 7, 1883.

. . . . . . As to myself, I am not getting on as fast as I could wish. My general health improves slowly, but the throat makes little progress. It is a discouraging business, but I try to make the best of it.

*   *   *   *   *   *   *   *   *

I shall probably remain here until the cold weather sets in;

---

*Light on the Pilgrim's Way, page 27.

then I must seek a warmer climate, but where to go I am in doubt. On the whole, California seems to promise the best, but I dread the long journey, so I put off the decision until the time of departure comes.

ANDOVER, Aug. 25, 1883.

My Dear Dr. Hay: I have just received a copy of a Washington paper giving an account of the Farewell Missionary Meeting. I am glad to see you were able to be there. It must have been a very interesting occasion. But what a muss the reporters make of it ! I see they make Unangst say there are 250,000,000 people in India, about three times as many as there really are, and that they (our missionaries) have divided these into 120 congregations, that is, over 2,000,000 to a congregation ; thus it might be seen how universal was their field. And yet we go on believing the papers.

The weather has been delightful, and I think I have been improving somewhat. My general health is good, and the throat seems less inflamed and irritable.

I am still thinking of California, though I dread the distance. I have got over all my desire to travel ; all the scenery and novelty of new lands would not tempt me a hundred miles from home. But health makes a man put up with all sorts of things.

TO DR. HAY.

ANDOVER, Sept. 4, 1883.

. . . . I had a letter from Dr. Radebaugh, which rather discouraged me from going to California. He is very full and careful in his statement, but I gathered that, on the whole, the good to be derived was very doubtful in my case. Some are benefited and some are not. I am beginning to incline towards Nassau, in the West Indies.

* * * * * * * * *

TO DR. HAY.

ANDOVER, Sept. 15, 1883.

. . . . . I am not so well as I was. My throat has given me a good deal of trouble. It is slow business, and nothing will help but patient waiting.

* * * * * * * * *

LAKEWOOD, OCEAN CO., N. J., Sept. 29, 1883.

Dear Brother Hay: I am sorry I cannot be at Synod; but the doctor (Cohen, of Philadelphia) wants me steadily under his treatment. Besides, the excitement and fatigue of Synod would be too much for me.

I found I was not improving in Andover, so I came on here last Monday, and put myself under Cohen's treatment. Cohen is a celebrated throat expert of Philadelphia; he promises to get me all right, and has sent me to this place, a resort for throat and lung cases, in the pine woods of New Jersey. I have not much hope that it will do any good; but, as you remarked once, a man will try everything and anything for a chance of health. I have not much pain, and I am pretty strong, but I suffer from great shortness of breath and a wearying cough.

* * * * * * * * *

Do not think I am melancholy. I think I have learned, or am learning, in whatsoever state I am therewith to be content. Of course pain and weakness are not pleasant companions, and I often groan under them, but I think I have an inward peace that bears me up. As God takes our pleasant things away, He gives us what is better, His peace. One thing long sickness and weakness does for us, it takes us down into the valley of humility, and it does this so gently that we are not mortified or covered with shame, but only made to feel what we truly are, our weakness and emptiness, and the great, blessed fullness and richness of God.

But I don't know why I am preaching to you, unless it is that you are a very dear and intimate friend, and I speak right out to you what is uppermost in my mind.

Many thanks for your last kind and genial letter. I hope all is well with you and yours. Remember me to the brethren. When you get that check cashed I wish you would ask if Mr. I. A. H. Becker is in town, and if he is going away. He is in the firm of Gitting & Co.

Yours fraternally, C. A. STORK.

TO DR. HAY.

GERMAN HOSPITAL, PHILA., Oct. 6, 1883.

...... I am something better (*i. e.* than for a few days past). I am still in bed. Dr. Cohen talks of operating on my throat—tracheotomy.

* * * * * * * * *

LETTER TO A FRIEND.

PHILADELPHIA, October, 1883.

My Dear —— —— : Your letter was a very pleasant surprise. It is doubly pleasant in the dark day to be reminded that we are loved, and that we have done something for others that still abides as a blessing. For, indeed, as I have been lying here helpless, suffering—absorbed in the hottest pain—it has seemed as though all my first life had shriveled up, and nothing was left of it but a blank memory. It has seemed to me as though I had done so little, and was nothing. Well, the last is true enough; we ever feel nothing in the grasp of pain and long weakness.

I have been trying all through to seem brave and cheerful, but I can hardly say that I have been really so. "No affliction for the present is joyous," and when God chastens us, there is no escaping the pain; He does not mean that we should. I have been greatly tried in my patience, and sometimes the waves and billows have gone over my soul, and seemed to doom it. But God has kept me. . . . . . Everybody has been very kind, and I am humbled to receive so many expressions of love. Surely God has given me many warm friends.

..... I do rejoice in your sympathy and kindness. It is something to know that God has permitted me to be of real service to one of His children.

Yours truly, C. A. STORK.

TO DR. HAY.

GERMAN HOSPITAL, PHILA., October 18, 1883.

..... I am slowly getting better, though still weak. The great relief is to my breathing. I was slowly suffocating.

Now, I eat well, grow stronger, walk about a little, and suffer only from sleeplessness which is due to the irritation of the wound. My many friends have been very kind, and God has indeed been good to me. I rejoice to hear of the prosperity of the Seminary.

I thought I could stand a good deal, but that operation was very severe. Twenty-five minutes under the knife with no anæsthetic tries one's nerves—and then the coughing and eating with that wound filled with a silver tube, I have just braced myself for a week to endure. But the worst is over. Now I have little pain. * * * * * *

TO DOCTOR HAY.

GERMAN HOSPITAL, November 3, 1883.

. . . . I am still in the hospital. I get up about 10 a. m., and stay up till bed-time. I walk or ride out a little and try to pass away the time as best I can; but as I can neither write nor study much, I am often quite weary, especially towards the end of the afternoon. I grow tired, and the whole system becomes irritated; my cough increases and I have no rest till sleep comes late in the night.

The Doctor thinks I improve slowly, but I cannot feel any great progress. The wound has healed well, but the old cough is very irritating, and I cannot talk above a whisper. I do not see where the end will be. . . . . . . I rest upon God day by day, and He gives me grace to go through each day, but none to spare.

Dr. Mann called on me yesterday: he was very kind. Also Dr. Conrad, who gave me a glowing account of his doings in the Luther celebration, and of his visit next week to Chicago, also of what he is writing. . . . . . . Whilst he sat before me gesticulating and full of excitement, I thought, if I could have a little of that superabundant energy! * * * *

GERMAN HOSPITAL, November 27, 1883.

Dear Doctor Hay: I am rejoiced to hear that all goes on so well on the hill. A new spirit for missions seems to be kindled in the students. I hope it may not be confined to the few who think of going to foreign lands, but that the leaven may leaven the whole lump.

Is it not a little singular that, while we feel the deepest interest in the heathen in their own lands, yet when they come here we begin to be suspicious of them? Here is this Armenian ;* if we had letters of him or from him in his own land, we should feel drawn to him ; but now he is here, and we really come in contact with him, we are shy of him. The fact is, the vice of deceit and dishonesty is so deeply ingrained into the minds of men that it seems almost impossible to root it out, and so when we fairly meet one of these men, we feel we must be on our guard. I do not for my part much believe in these converted heathens coming to America to get an education. Their place is at home, among their own people, doing what they can to make Christ known. We do not send the Gospel to Asia to have the Asiatics come over to America to learn our ways and get half Americanized, and so unfitted for work in Asia. The work of Christ is not to make Hindoos and Turks into Americans, but to leaven their style of civilization with Christianity. So I am shy of all those converts who want to be converted not only from heathenism but also from their nationality, and become a sort of mongrel Americo-Oriental. Let every man abide in his lot where God hath called him. I am afraid I shall have less patience with the Armenian than you.

I have seen of the celebration at Hartwick in the papers. It must have been a very stirring occasion. What a great waking among the churches this Luther year has occasioned. I have not been able to take part in any of these great celebrations, but I have looked on with the deepest interest.

My health does not improve much. I am still weak, and the throat is very sore and feeble. I think my Doctor gets discouraged at times ; but we hope for the best. I suffer no great pain ; but weakness is often worse than pain, and my irritation from the throat is very exhausting. I am learning some new and deep lessons in this school of suffering.

Yours truly, C. A. STORK.

---

* An Armenian had come to Gettysburg Seminary to study theology, but I believe he intended to return to his own country.—J. G. M.

GERMAN HOSPITAL, December, 1883.

My Dear Brother H.: It was a good long letter you sent me, and I am really ashamed to send such a scrap in return. Your picture of me as being overrun with letters of condolence and sympathy was a little overdrawn. I have a great many friends and many expressions of their regret and remembrance, but they have not overburdened me with letters.

Yours was a very cheering and pleasant letter. It did me good. As for my health, it does not improve as I had hoped. I drag out weary days and long though not uncomfortable nights. What a trying thing it is to look day after day for health, and not see it come any nearer! But I try to bear up patiently. My great trouble is shortness of breath arising from weakness. And for weakness you know it is hard to find a remedy.

Of the great Luther meeting in Baltimore I read several accounts in newspapers and letters. You surely had a grand festival. It has been a great Luther year, only I fear the people will get surfeited with him and wish to hear no more of him.

I spend my time reading, and writing a little, though of this last the Doctor will not allow much. I do not study, I am too weak for that, but I read all the light and easy matter I can get. Still even of reading I do very little. I sleep a good deal, but my rest is much broken and I have to take two hours to get one hour of solid rest. But I think when you are sick you do not care for occupation. I know I sit and half dream, half think, for hours. I seem so unlike my old self—then I was always working at something, now I only want to be quiet and let my mind wander over the thoughts of all God has done for me and is doing in His kingdom. Sometimes he sends me very precious and delightful thoughts. Like David, I commune with Him in my thoughts in the night-watches. My bed is now my closet, my Mount Tabor where I pray and renew my strength.

Mrs. Stork keeps well and strong. She is a great cheer and comfort to me, as well as a most tender and efficient nurse. I have my friends here in Philadelphia who are kind and attentive. They call on me and give me the news and cheer me up.

The children are under good care, and are well and happy.

So you see I have nothing to worry me, nothing outside of this miserable broken body. I only wish I could forget it, be more strong to disregard it; but there, I cannot, it will drag me down.

Yours truly, C. A. STORK.

LETTER FROM A FRIEND.

I happened to be in Philadelphia only a few days after the operation had been performed upon his windpipe. I went to the German Hospital and asked permission to see him. The attendant physicians below told me how remarkably well the Doctor endured the operation, refusing an anæsthetic, and yet never wincing under the operation. They said he showed more will-power than any patient that ever came under their treatment. Shortly after this I was taken up stairs and admitted to the sick man's chamber. I found him sitting on a large armchair by an open window. He greeted me with a pleasant smile, and a cordial shake by the hand. After an interchange of a few words, I remarked that I was surprised to learn how wonderfully well he endured the severe operation. He looked at me thoughtfully and seriously, and then lifting up his right arm, and with a serene smile on his face, his eyes beaming with love, he pointed with his forefinger heavenward; thus indicating the source of his strength and endurance. If I were an artist, I should aim to paint that scene; it is a precious and abiding picture on my mind and heart.

CHAPTER VII.

DEATH—FUNERAL SERVICES—ADDRESSES—DR. HAY, DR. BUTLER, DR. CONRAD—VARIOUS RELIGIOUS PAPERS—EULOGIES—COMMEMORATIVE RESOLUTIONS—SEMINARY—THEOLOGICAL FACULTY—CHURCH BOARDS—DR. MARK HOPKINS—DR. MAGEE—PRESIDENT GARFIELD—DR. VALENTINE—DR. WOLF—DR. BARCLAY—HIS FUGITIVE WRITINGS—TRIBUTES FROM STUDENTS.

REV. CHARLES A. STORK, D. D., died on Monday morning, December 17, 1883. For a good portion of the following account of the funeral services, I am indebted to the *Lutheran Observer.*

THE OBSEQUIES OF DOCTOR STORK.

The funeral services of the late Dr. Charles A. Stork, of the Theological Seminary at Gettysburg, took place on Thursday afternoon, December 20, 1883, at St. Matthew's church, Broad and Mt. Vernon streets, Rev. Dr. W. M. Baum, pastor, who conducted the services of the sad occasion. Rev. Dr. J. G. Morris, of Baltimore, read the Scripture lessons; Rev. Charles S. Albert, of Baltimore, offered prayer, and Charles Wesley's hymn—"Jesus, lover of my soul"—was sung by the congregation.

Dr. Baum then made in substance the following remarks:

The services of this sad occasion have been arranged with as little show or ostentation as possible. Studied eulogy, however deserved, will not be attempted. His life was the best eulogy possible. *As* he lived *so* he died, rendering loving service to his Lord and Master, working with his vigorous pen, when his feeble voice could no longer be heard. It is a circumstance that deserves mention that in this particular his end was similar to that of his father—their last articles appearing after death. His father's was on St. Paul's declaration: "I am now ready to be offered, and the time of my departure is at hand"—and how soon he departed! The last article of the son was "The Secret of Christmas," *To come near and see Jesus.* How perfectly now he understands that secret! Fable tells us that the dying notes of the swan are the sweetest: *faith* more truly thus works its grand consummation. How he served the Lord Jesus by serving the church, as pastor, as teacher, as theological professor, as member of Church Boards of Education and Missions, others will attest. He was ever diligently occupied and rendered useful service. Into his short life how much was crowded—not years but deeds are the true measure of life. Among the truths illustrated by his life are *the value and beauty of personal godliness.* There is a divine and a human aspect to our religious life. It is not always harmoniously developed, but here it was: grace, education and self-culture developed a lovely character—firm, yet not severe; loving, yet not weak; tender in all relations, yet justifying no wrong; fulfilling all the obligations of human life. There was no seeking, scheming, planning, in seeking a field for work. He was content with what was, and accepted God's ordering. With capacity for the highest, he despised not the lowest. In that lay the secret of his contentment and usefulness.

Rev. Dr. C. A. Hay, senior member of the Theological Faculty at Gettysburg, then uttered the following touching words:

Alas for thee, my brother! No; not for thee, but for us who have lost thee! Thy troubles are over—ours is the sorrow now. And it is no common sorrow.

My dear friends, *we* it is who need consolation in this hour of sad bereavement. We keenly feel our loss; but we know that we shall feel it all the more when we come to realize it better, as we go to our homes and resume our daily duties and miss that genial face and gentle voice, and patient, quiet spirit, that had won its way to our hearts.

We stand perplexed and confounded in the presence of such a dispensation of Providence. The early removal of one so highly gifted and so admirably fitted for the discharge of the responsible duties to which the Church had summoned him, startles us and tries our faith. We need to pray for a spirit of submission, and for an unwavering confidence in the wisdom and kindness of all our Heavenly Father's ways. His ways are not as ours, nor His thoughts as ours.

O what the pulpit of our church has lost in the death of this dear brother! How fresh, how stimulating and suggestive were his expositions of divine truth? How eagerly his hearers hung upon his earnest and impressive appeals! We do not wonder that under such ministrations his church steadily and rapidly advanced in all that constitutes true growth in action, intelligent and efficient piety.

His brief career in the Theological Seminary proved him none the less fitted for the professor's chair than for the pulpit. Entering with enthusiasm upon his work in that sphere, with a profound estimate of its great responsibility and grand opportunities, he devoted himself to it with characteristic zeal and energy, quickly imparting to his pupils a measure of the same ardor and keen relish for its sublime themes, and urging them on to independent research in that field. Men love to follow such a leader. They catch his spirit and are borne forward under its influence. No wonder that all connected with our institution bitterly bewail his loss.

And the affectionate family circle! Nearer still to you, dear friends, comes this sad and sudden blow. Hoping to the last that the insidious disease, that had so long interfered with his pulpit and class-room duties, would yield to skillful treatment, and that his weakened constitution could be restored to its wonted vigor, you have after all been called upon to bid him farewell for a season. Dear friends, it is only for a little while.

That voice is not silenced forever. Those rigid features will yet again be wreathed in smiles, the smiles of heavenly recognition. "Be not afraid, only believe."

Farewell, my brother, till we meet again!

Toplady's hymn—"Rock of Ages, cleft for me"—was sung, after which Rev. Dr. J. G. Butler, of Washington, who was associated with Dr. Stork in the Board of Foreign Missions for a number of years, bore his testimony to the high character and unselfish devotion which he had always manifested in the work of his Master. Among other things, he said:

I shall probably never forget that sweet, guileless, peaceful smile that lighted up this face now quiet in death, when a few weeks since, after a word of prayer at the bedside of our dear brother, I said good-bye. The legend says that when our Lord was bearing his own cross to Calvary, a Jewish maiden, touched with sympathy, wiped the sweat from his brow with a napkin, and that he left the impress of his face upon that napkin. This service to-day marks the earthly end of one of our Lord's burden-bearers, upon whom Christ has left His image.

"Burdens when they weigh severely,
Stamp the Saviour's image clearly
On the heart of all His friends."

The smile that beautified this face was the product of years of labor and suffering for Christ. From a child he had loved the Saviour, and that which beautified his character was Christ in him, the hope of glory. The pen of inspiration writes, Moses, the servant of the Lord, and Paul, the servant of Jesus Christ. To-day we write, Charles, the servant of God, as expressing the fullness of our dear brother's character and life. His lips and his heart, now silent, would rebuke eulogy to-day. He would write himself a sinner saved by grace. And yet, associated with him as I have been, intimately, during all his ministry, loving him as few men can be loved, for his unselfish goodness, whilst my heart is stunned by this providence, I am glad to mingle in this love-service. He rests, whilst we are yet among the burden-bearers, with the responsibilities of Christian ministries upon us. This well-rounded life, though it add another broken column, is full of inspiration to those who remain. How mysterious the providence! "I was dumb; I opened not my mouth; because Thou didst it." Brethren, God reigns. Clouds and darkness are around about Him. Justice and judgment are the habitation of His throne. Even so, Father, for so it seemed good in thy sight.

Called by the church to the high position of training young men for the ministry, because of his preëminent fitness, upon whom shall his mantle fall? It was not simply knowledge and intellectual culture that qualified him to mould the future teachers and pastors of the church. These are important, but it is the man behind the teacher and preacher that gives power to his life. This man of God, imbued with the humanity and meekness and gentleness and self-sacrifice of the Gospel, gave inspiration to every man who sat at his feet. The need of the pulpit to-day and every day is men fully imbued with the Spirit of Christ, and wholly consecrated to the work of saving men. For that he lived.

Though full of sorrow to-day, we will not say, Alas! my brother! Shall we not rather say, See how the Saviour saved him! Behold what the Saviour made him! How boundless the possibilities now that Jesus has taken him to Himself! The savor of this young life yet gives inspiration. How the people love him—the people whom he served so faithfully for years! And the young men who sat at his feet, and all of us who went about with him, lo! these many years, as together we labored in the great harvest! With us he yet remains. He still lives among us, though now he sits, as he has ever sat, but now nearer the Saviour's feet, an apt learner in the school of the Great Teacher, Himself the Truth. On this earth-side we commingle our tenderest sympathy with this deeply-stricken household. But we will not forget that death has given release from a suffering body, and introduced the ransomed spirit into the

11*

fullness of the joy of our Lord. Here we know in part; there we shall know even as also we are known. In every relation of life, domestic, social, ecclesiastical, we shall miss him; but where the faded flower shall freshen, where God wipes all tears and where they die no more, we shall be with him soon. Farewell, my brother!

Dr. F. W. Conrad next presented a sketch of the life and character of the departed. The benediction was pronounced by Rev. Henry Baker, of Altoona, and the congregation and friends present were invited to take a last look at the face of the departed, whose remains were placed in a casket before the pulpit. All availed themselves of this sad opportunity. His remains were taken to Andover, Mass., for interment with the kindred of his wife.

Among the clergymen present at the funeral, besides those already mentioned, were Rev. Dr. M. W. Hamma, and Revs. George Scholl and J. A. Clutz, of Baltimore; Rev. Dr. L. E. Albert, of Germantown; Rev. W. H. Steck, of Ardmore; Rev. M. Sheeleigh, of Whitemarsh; Rev. J. H. Harpster, of Trenton, N. J.; President Julius D. Dreher, of Roanoke College, Virginia; and Revs. S. A. Holman, E. Huber, J. H. Menges, J. K. Plitt, S. Laird, S. A. K. Francis, and Dr. Henry E. Jacobs, of Philadelphia. Besides the clergymen from Baltimore already mentioned, there were also present some twenty lay members of St. Mark's church of that city, which he served as pastor for so many years.

"The memory of the just is blessed."

TESTIMONIAL OF THE THEOLOGICAL FACULTY.

DEATH OF REV. C. A. STORK.

The news of this sad event reached Gettysburg at an early hour on the 18th inst. The exercises of the Theological Seminary were at once suspended, and the Faculty convened and took the following action:

WHEREAS, Our Heavenly Father has been pleased to end the protracted sufferings of our dear brother and colleague, Rev. Charles A. Stork, D. D., by a peaceful death; therefore

Resolved, That it becomes us, who were so intimately associated with him in official and social intercourse, devoutly to acknowledge our gratitude to God for the privilege we have enjoyed in communion with one so learned, genial and loving, and to put upon record our deep sense of the loss we have sustained by his death.

Resolved, That we sincerely deplore the loss inflicted, by his death, upon our institution, which had learned to prize the labors of one with a mind so cultivated and a heart so pure, with such a peculiar aptness to teach and power to arouse in others an ardor and enthusiasm in the pursuit of knowledge, and to win their confidence and affection.

Resolved, That we sincerely share in the profound sorrow that will be felt throughout the Church in being deprived of the labors of one so well qualified to serve all her interests in the pulpit, in the professor's chair, and in the religious press.

Resolved, That we express our hearty condolence with his bereaved family in the desolation which this mysterious dispensation of Providence has brought upon them, and with earnest prayer we commend them to the grace of Him who is the Father of the fatherless and the Husband of the widow.

The Faculty and students assembled in the Missionary Hall at 11 o'clock, and appropriate religious services were held. By a rising vote, the above resolutions were silently and solemnly endorsed by all present, amid deep feeling.

Ever since the disease under which our dear brother was laboring assumed a seriously threatening form, the most lively sympathy was felt and manifested for him by all the inmates of the Seminary. He had greatly endeared himself to the hearts of all; and the knowledge of his severe and protracted sufferings cast a shade of sadness over our daily life. We recently learned that he was longing to be released, and our grief at the news of his decease is assuaged by the assurance that he has passed from a scene of sorrow and pain to a blissful home of unmingled and endless joy. H.

Gettysburg, December 18, 1883.

TESTIMONIAL FROM ST. MARK'S.

The council of St. Mark's English Evangelical Lutheran church, of Baltimore, has learned with deep sorrow of the death of Rev. Charles A. Stork, D. D., and desiring to record its appreciation of our late pastor, adopts the following:

Resolved, That we are mindful of his work and labor of love for us, as individuals and as a congregation, and that we recognize evidence of his profound Christian teachings in the godly lives of many who, through him, were brought to know the love of God in Christ.

Resolved, That, in remembrance of his long and faithful service among us as pastor, we do set apart Sunday, December 30th, as a day for special memorial services.

Resolved, That we express our deep sympathy with his family, and ask for them the benediction "of God, even our Father, which has loved us and given us everlasting consolation and good hope through grace."

EULOGIES ON DR. STORK.

The *Workman* of January 3, 1885, says:

The year of 1883 began darkly with the death of Rev. Dr. Krauth, of the Philadelphia Seminary, and it was closed with the death of Rev. Stork, of the Seminary in Gettysburg. The son of the Rev. Dr. Theophilus Stork became the successor of his father as pastor of St. Mark's church, Baltimore, and for sixteen years gave to it the rich fruitage of his studies, travels, and various attainments. Called in 1881 to fill the vacant professorship of Didactic Theology in the Gettysburg Seminary, he entered upon a new life of study and toil, and labored assiduously with the happiest results. But the embarrassment and depression of a most distressing affection of the throat was upon him, and his labors and services were sadly interrupted by this insidious disease. At last, on December 17th after a surgical operation, his strength constantly growing weaker, he calmly fell asleep in Christ and in peace.

* * * * * * * * *

Dr. Stork, like many other thoughtful men in this transition period, was drawing nearer and nearer to its faith, and coming more and more into loving sympathy with its inner life. In this respect, also, the loss of one so sincere and devout is all the greater to the Seminary and the ingenuous youth who gather in its halls. But the truth lives, though its confessors and teachers pass away.

* * * * * * * * *

Dr. Mark Hopkins, President of Williams College, thus speaks of Dr. Stork in a letter to the editor of the *Lutheran Observer:*

My remembrance of Dr. Stork as a student is distinct. He was a student of books, industrious and faithful, but not merely that—he was naturally, and from the first, an original investigator. He did not reject authority, but made the conclusions of others his own only as he saw their ground. This placed him in the first rank among students in my studies, and I was not surprised at the eminence he attained and was attaining. His character, while at college, was unexceptionable.

The editor then continues: "The exhibit of character given by Dr. Hopkins of Garfield and Stork as students, proves that the diligence, perseverance and fidelity of the student determine the activity, success and usefulness of the man. The following incidents show the intimacy, devotion and Christian character, which distinguished Garfield and Stork as college-mates, friends and brothers beloved in the Lord.

"Dr. Irving Magee, a college-mate of Dr. Stork, told our readers at the time of his death, that Garfield was in the habit of sitting for hours at the side of Stork, with his arms about his neck. After General Garfield became a member of Congress, Dr. Stork paid him his first visit, which he described, at an interview with Dr. Magee at the house of a friend in Baltimore, as follows:

"By the way, Magee, you remember 'Gar.' I was in Washington the other day, and determined to go up to the Capitol to see him. I sent my card in to him by a page, and in a moment he came out, picked me right up in his arms and embraced me, he was so glad to see me.

"Towards the close of General Garfield's career in the House of Representatives, to whose leadership he had risen, Dr. Stork visited him at his house, where they spent the evening together in conversation on old scenes and friends. As it had been their habit to pray with each other, at the close of each day in their rooms, Garfield proposed to Stork that, before separating, they should unite in prayer as they were wont to do in their college days at Williams, whereupon they knelt down and prayed with one accord to that God to whose service they had devoted their lives in the days of their youth, and invoked His guidance and blessing upon the work in which each was engaged. And while General Garfield was inaugurated President of the United States on the 4th of March, 1881, Dr. Stork was inaugurated as Professor of Theology and Chairman of the Faculty in the Theological Seminary at Gettysburg, in September of the same year.

"On Easter Monday, 1881, we called at the White House, and were presented by Dr. Butler to the President. In passing through Baltimore, Dr. Stork requested us to present his congratulations, and to say that as soon as the press was over, he would pay him a visit. The President in reply said that he recollected Dr. Stork very well, and that he would be happy to see him at any time, and requested us to present his acknowledgments. But before this contemplated visit was paid, the President was shot, and they never met again since they prayed together at the interview described above. They parted on earth at the throne of grace, and they have doubtless met each other again in heaven, according to the Word of God, around the throne of glory."

COPY OF RESOLUTIONS ON THE DEATH OF DR. STORK, FROM REPORT OF BOARD OF FOREIGN MISSIONS TO GENERAL SYNOD.

1. *Resolved*, That in the death of our sainted brother, Rev. Dr. Charles A. Stork, our Board has lost a zealous member, a wise counsellor, and a most efficient presiding officer; the foreign mission cause has lost one of its warmest friends and most able

pounders and advocates ; and the Church has lost one of her most gifted and cultured ministers, a scholar at once profound and clear, a theologian who was at once liberal and yet loyal to the standards of the Church, a teacher who could not only impart instruction to his pupils, but also inspire them with the love of the truth, and a preacher of rare spiritual insight and power, and who was able, beyond most men, to rightly divide the word of truth.

2. *Resolved*, That we bow in humble and trustful submission to the divine will, as revealed in this sore bereavement, knowing that God's ways are always wise and good, and assured that our loss is our brother's gain.

3. *Resolved*, That we will ever cherish the memory of our departed brother's virtues and graces as a most precious legacy and will seek to emulate his noble disposition, his deep and earnest piety, his broad catholicity of spirit, his generous interest in every good cause, his thorough consecration of heart and life, and his untiring activity in the Master's service, believing that we will thus most honor him and best glorify God.

4. *Resolved*, That as a testimony of our esteem for the deceased these resolutions be adopted by a rising vote, and that a copy of the same be spread upon the minutes of the General Synod.

FROM REV. DR. CONRAD, OF THE LUTHERAN OBSERVER.

Dr. Stork was endowed with rare natural talents, and received a thorough literary and theological education. His thirst for knowledge impelled him to make full proof of his ministry by reading and diligence in study. Giving special attention to exegesis and theology, he did not, however, limit his researches to their respective boundaries, but extended his inquiries to other departments of knowledge. He kept pace with the progress of science, was well read in history and general literature, was a master in Greek, and well versed in philosophy. His mind was one of peculiar mould, and his gifts distinguished by great excellencies. He had clear apprehensions of truth, and a remarkable facility, terseness, simplicity and beauty of expression. He was also gifted with a profound spiritual insight into the mind of the Spirit as expressed in the Scriptures, and had the happy faculty of bringing out the hidden meaning of the Word by apt and striking illustrations. He was also possessed of fine literary taste, a good memory, and great fluency of speech. These varied attainments he exhibited both in his writings and in his sermons in the pulpit.

As a writer, Dr. Stork was distinguished by his purity of style, richness of illustration, and spiritual unction. His articles published in the *Observer* and the *Quarterly Review* have placed him in the front rank of our literary men. As a preacher, he brought out of the Scriptures "things old," clothed them in new forms of expression, and invested them with peculiar freshness and force. Thoroughly acquainted with his people, he discussed subjects adapted to their wants, and kept back nothing that was profitable unto them. While he made careful preparation, he did not read his discourses, but delivered them in a clear style and in an easy and natural manner.

In person Dr. Stork was of medium height, and of a phlegmatic temperament, easy and natural in his manner, and undemonstrative in his bearing. While he was reserved and unobtrusive in society, he was, nevertheless, a genial and pleasant companion. In his intercourse with his brethren he was modest, kind and considerate. In his pastoral relations he was peculiarly happy. He moved among his parishioners as a spiritual father, intimate friend and wise counsellor, and was cherished by them with peculiar tenderness and affection. His devoted piety, pastoral fidelity and pulpit ability, were demonstrated in the numerical increase, the spiritual progress, and the Christian liberality and activity of St. Mark's church, to which he ministered for nearly twenty years. Its members are his epistles, who "remember the words which he spake unto them while he was yet with them," and will cherish his memory in their heart of hearts to the last day of their lives. But his influence was not confined to his own congregation. He took a lively interest in every good work in the city. As a member of the Board of Foreign Missions, and more recently as its president and the editor of the foreign department of the *Missionary Journal*, he rendered valuable service, and exerted an extensive influence.

As a professor, Dr. Stork's labors were of short duration; the intervention of war compelled him to vacate the chair of Greek at Newberry, and the inroads of disease cut short his theological labors in the Seminary. His instructions in both institutions were, nevertheless, sufficient to establish his theological ability and aptness to teach, and to give the assurance that, if he had been permitted to continue at his post, his success in the professor's chair would have equaled that which he achieved in the pulpit.

God's dealings with our theological seminaries in the East are strikingly significant, and call for serious reflection. Just four years ago, Dr. J. A. Brown, the predecessor of Dr. Stork in the Seminary at Gettysburg, was made speechless by a stroke of aphasia, and a little less than two years ago he was laid to rest at Lancaster, in his native county. A short time before, Dr. C. F. Schaeffer, Professor in the Philadelphia Seminary, was called from his labors on earth; and less than a year ago, Dr. C. P. Krauth, Professor of Theology in the same institution, was stricken down in the zenith of his intellectual powers. And scarce a year had passed after Dr. Stork commenced this theological work at Gettysburg, when he was disabled by disease, and now the church is called on to mourn his departure from earth. But one of these distinguished theologians had reached the period allotted to man; three of them died in the midst of their labors, and in the very prime of life. In view of these inscrutable providences of God, we are constrained to exclaim: "How unsearchable are His judgments, and His ways past finding out!"

Our relations with Dr. Stork were of the most intimate character. Our intimacy began more than twenty years ago and continued until the day of his death. Our association with his father, as associate editor of the *Observer*, both in Baltimore and Philadelphia, brought us frequently together, and gave us opportunity of knowing him well, and constantly strengthened our esteem and affection for him. We felt towards him more like a father, and mourn him, as far as that is possible, not only as a brother beloved, but also as a son. We regarded him personally as one of the excellent of the earth; intellectually, as an original thinker, an accomplished scholar and polished writer; and ecclesiastically, as one of the most effective preachers and ablest theologians in the Lutheran church of this country. If to any one can be justly applied the inspiring declaration of the prophet Daniel, it can be to him: "They that be wise shall shine as the brightness of the firmament; and they that turn many to righteousness, as the stars forever and ever."

DR. STORK AS A THEOLOGIAN, BY REV. DR. VALENTINE.

THEOLOGICAL SEMINARY,
GETTYSBURG, PA., April 30, 1885.

Rev. J. G. M.—Dear Doctor: You have asked me for a word concerning Dr. Stork as a theologian. I comply with your request the more willingly because of the possibility that his other intellectual and spiritual excellencies may draw away attention unfairly from what is due him in this relation. Undoubtedly his fine intellectuality, general culture, and Christian consecration and earnestness, formed his most noticeable features as he was recognized when living and is now remembered by the Church. It was by these that he attracted the Church's attention, and won the wide admiration and love with which he is regarded. Most of the productions of his facile pen, whether in *The Lutheran Quarterly* or elsewhere, dealt with the living questions in the speculative and practical inquiry of the day. Few men were more thoroughly abreast with the knowledge and thought of the times, or more competent to give a discriminating judgment as to their bearings. His discriminating clearness, the subtlety of his analytic power, the freshness of his way of presenting and illustrating truth, all brightened by the play of a rich but delicate imagination, made all his discussions delightful and instructive to intelligent and cultured readers. But those who best knew Dr. Stork, knew that his theological attainments were of high order. It would have been almost impossible for one gifted as he was, with such varied knowledge in history, literature and metaphysics, and so keenly interested in all the highest truth that has been engaging Christian thinkers, to fail to do fair and thorough work in distinctly theological study. But his theological habit was not that which often assumes to make the theologian. His Christian spirit was too living and earnest to be satisfied to reduce theology to the technicalities that are learned by rote and perpetuated by authority out of the scholasticisms of the past. He was, indeed, well versed in the history of doctrines, and in the theological discussions through which the doctrines have been shaped in dogmatics. But his earnest spirit was more concerned with the substance of truth than with its forms. To him theology was much more than the simple mastery of the dogmatician's definitions and formalæ and rounded system, put into the mind by a sort of mechanical transfer, and coldly kept in the memory. To him it was the living knowledge of God—not wanting, indeed, in systematic accuracy, but fused by the fervor of his soul into the practical aims of redemption and life. With all his intellectuality he illustrated the old maxim : *Pectus facit theologum.*

Though so full of the earnest living present, Dr. Stork was by no means disposed to break with the past, as so many do, or to vaunt the knowledge of this age, as if the theology of earlier centuries were of little or no account. He was at once conservative and progressive ; and few men recognized more fully than he how firmly and grandly all the great doctrines of God and redemption, as formulated in the orthodox faith of the Church, have stood all ordeals, and are but growing stronger in their victories. Those who remember his essay on Liturgical Forms in Worship, at the Lutheran Diet in 1877, will need no other evidence of his strong grasp upon the principle of the continuity of theology and church-life. He showed in theology the same intellectual characteristics which marked him in the other relations—wide range of view and observation, cautious and subtle analysis, and sound discrimination. This close analytic discrimination is well illustrated in his review of Newman on Justification.

Our interest in Dr. Stork as a theologian is mainly concerned with relation to Lutheran theology. His reception of theological training in a non-Lutheran institution did not alienate his love from his Church or her theology. There was a natural affinity between his deep pietistic temper and the theology of his Church. Both the thoroughness of his intellectual habit and the helping influence of his practical ministry, led him into strong attachment to the system of truth found in her communion. Those who recall his discussion, some years ago, of the subject of ministers changing their ecclesiastical relations, will have no doubt of the strength with which his convictions had made the Lutheran system of theology his own. And while he troubled himself comparatively little with the dry and rigid definitions and old phrases of the scholastic dogmaticians, his theology laid hold of all they sought after. It was one feature of the service he was rendering in the Seminary, that instead of fixing, by mechanical drill, the old technicalities in the minds of the students, he was translating the Lutheran theology, in its profoundest essence and life, into the forms of thought and speech of the living present.

Yours most fraternally, M. VALENTINE.

TRIBUTE BY REV. DR. WOLF, OF GETTYSBURG.

A SANCTIFIED SOUL.

That Dr. Stork was a man of extraordinary excellence was never questioned by any one who was intimately associated with him in life. His supereminence was so patent that it never awakened the envy of those who stood nearest to him. You might long to reach the sunlit altitude in which his lofty spirit was calmly moving, but you could not expect soon to rise to such a height, much less think of dragging him down to the common level by base disparagement.

It was especially a pure, exalted and fervent spirituality that distinguished this dear brother. He was a holy man. His life was hid with Christ in God. I never sustained close personal relations to any one else who to my mind possessed so large a measure of the spirit of Christ, and so near an approximation to Him.

* * * * * * * * *

His society was sure to be an inspiration to one's heart, just as it proved a never-failing stimulant to one's mind. My greatest regret on leaving the pastorate in Baltimore, was the consciousness of what I was losing in separating from one whose intense spiritual influence I had so often felt. When at a later period I was again to have the privilege of being daily associated with him in the Theological Seminary, I welcomed him particularly in view of the godly aroma which his presence here would be sure to diffuse. To be an hour with him was to be carried away from sensuous and sordid objects, and to be lifted to the enjoyment of divine and eternal things. In an experience of twenty years of intimate friendship I never detected in him a selfish thought, or had the faintest reason to suspect an unworthy aim, an interested motive, or a vindictive feeling. He never sought his own, never seemed to have a thought of himself, of his superior gifts, or of any personal advantage. He never manifested a spark of what is called ambition. Honor, popularity, crowds, were nothing to him. He was a stranger, apparently, to the peculiar temptations of the ministry. He was an Israelite in whom there was no guile.

It was the divine power in his soul that made him the model of a successful pastor. Nature had not endowed him with those peculiar social qualities which prove so helpful in pastoral ministrations among all classes, but he had the wisdom from above which inspires men with tact and adaptation ; he bore his people priest-like upon his heart, as every one felt on hearing him offer his inimitable prayers; and his conscience withal gave him the courage both to tell every man his whole duty, and to minister to every needy soul, even at the risk of fatal contagion.

It was largely the riches of his spiritual resources that left him without a peer in the Lutheran pulpit. In his preaching he knew nothing but Jesus and Him crucified. Though he had enjoyed a wider and perhaps a deeper range of reading than any of us, his pulpit was too sacred to be converted into a show-window for the display of his learning. The effect of all his striking illustrations, his brilliant thought and tender pathos, was to make his audience see "Jesus only." Who that listened to his sermons on "Christ died for our sins according to the scriptures," " I beheld, and lo, in the midst of the throne . . . stood a lamb as it had been slain," "Show us the Father," "Lead me to the rock that is higher than I," could fail to have his heart fired with the love of Jesus, and to feel strengthened with might in the inner man? When, occasionally, in Baltimore, the opportunity was given me of hearing other men preach, I would sometimes go to hear Dr. G's eloquence, Dr. J's originality, or Dr. M's metaphysics; but when I craved spiritual nourishment I always went to St. Mark's, and invariably found a gospel feast. I do not, indeed, recollect having ever gone elsewhere when I had the privilege of hearing Dr. Stork.

From his abiding devotion to his Lord sprung also his inflexible loyalty to the Lutheran church. Having grown up at a period when secession from his mother church had become a fashion, and having received his entire classical and theological training in New England, it would have been little short of a miracle for him to have felt any special attachment to a denomination which to the eye of sense at that time presented such an uninviting contrast to the dominant churches of the country. I knew Dr. Stork when he would have sacrificed no doctrinal conviction, no affection, and no taste, in changing his ecclesiastical relations. He made no secret of the fact that he knew the full force of the temptations which have lured ministers away from the Lutheran pulpits. At that time his support was $1,500 per year, of which $500 had to be paid for the rent of a small and indifferent house. He could have readily commanded in other communions a salary five or eight times that amount, and might have preached to crowds of cultured people in Boston, New York or Philadelphia; but how often was he heard to remark: "The arguments for leaving the Lutheran church are from below, not from above." Every move of that kind he considered a move to the rear, where it required less nerve and smaller sacrifices to be a soldier. "Christ," he would say, "came not to be ministered unto, but to minister;" why should His servant seek to be above Him, and lay down the cross which the Master gave him. The Lutheran church had need of him, and Providence had cast his lot in her pale; this left the path of duty unmistakable—and of other paths his heart knew nothing.

His nearness to God, finally, made him the type of a Lutheran theologian. For dogmatics, as commonly understood and taught, he had no predilections. And on accepting the call to the Seminary, his mental tastes would have chosen other branches. The Calvinistic system which he had learned at Andover was repugnant to his whole nature, and the manner in which Lutheran divines were contending about creeds and forms of doctrine gave him at first hardly a better view of Lutheran theology. As for making cast-iron formulas out of the living verities of salvation, such attempts seemed to him equivalent to stifling the truth. But he came in the course of his development to see that Lutheran dogmatics are essentially but the clear and irrefutable answer to the sinner's cry, "What must I do to be saved?" the lucid exhibition of the fulness of divine grace, which through the church is steadily dispensed to believers. The Christ who was all and in all to him, he found, is the centre around which the Lutheran system revolves, and in every radiation from that centre he recognized a ray from the Sun of Righteousness. Thus the heavenly leaven penetrated all his thinking, as well as all his activities. Every fruit of the Spirit, " goodness, righteousness and truth" as well as " love, joy and peace," had its healthy, rounded growth in him. * * * * *

What a fitting close to his earthly career that the last product of his fertile pen should have been that article on "THE GROWING LIFE," called forth, it may be remarked, by a request from the writer, who thought that some utterances on that theme from him, when so near the gate of heaven, would offer the most precious perfume with which to embalm his own blessed life in our hearts.

Farewell, thou gentle, pure and consecrated soul! Hadst thou not been so ripe, God might have spared thee a little longer to us. Our tears are not for thee, but for ourselves. And no grief of ours shall ever efface our gratitude to God for having cast our lot within the shadow of thy life, and for having brought us under the sound of thy sermons and prayers, and within the hallowing circle of thy personal influence.

MINUTE ON THE DEATH OF DR. C. A. STORK,

ADOPTED BY THE BOARD OF THE THEOLOGICAL SEMINARY OF THE GENERAL SYNOD AT GETTYSBURG.

The Rev. Charles A. Stork, D. D., was third of the name in the ministry of the Lutheran Church in this country. His father, Rev. Theophilus Stork, D. D., occupied a prominent position for a number of years, in which he attained great usefulness, and died universally beloved and lamented. His grandfather, Rev. Charles Augustus Stork (Storch) was noted for great activity, fervent piety, and abundant labors for Christ.

Thus worthily descended, Dr. Stork added new lustre to the honored name of his fathers. He was richly endowed with those grand qualities of mind and heart, which form the basis of a noble character and a useful life. To these were added the strength and finish which close application and loving service yield. Thus equipped, he entered the field to which Providence so clearly directed him with every prospect of success. In this there was no disappointment, save such only as was occasioned by physical weakness and premature exhaustion. His preparation and furnishing for the high position in which he closed his active and useful life were singularly happy and complete. His methods of study and address qualified him for great acceptability in the pulpit, on the floor of synod, and in the professor's chair. His strong grasp of mind, unswerving fidelity to the truth and to the symbols of his Church, in which he found that truth so clearly stated, and his reputation for general scholarship, pointed him out very prominently as the fitting successor of Drs. Schmucker, Krauth and Brown, in the faculty of this Theological Seminary. His service, though cut short by early decline and death, was most satisfactory and beneficial. His clear and positive convictions, flowing through the channel of a tender sympathy and unassumed affection, were calculated to exert a happy influence upon his colleagues and pupils. His removal after great bodily suffering, in which God's grace grandly triumphed, was accepted by the Church with becoming submission, but with deepest grief and lasting regret.

As an expression of our feelings upon this sad bereavement, we suggest the following action:

Resolved, That we hereby place upon record our sincere gratitude to Almighty God for bestowing upon this cherished Institution the efficient services of one so eminently qualified for the position, and also our high appreciation of the ability, faithfulness and zeal with which, ofttimes under great physical prostration, our late lamented friend and brother discharged his arduous and responsible duties.

Resolved, That we anew recognize and acknowledge the claims upon ourselves and the Church we represent, of an Institution which has been sustained and nurtured by the life-labors of so many devoted and faithful teachers.

Resolved, That a copy of this minute, with an expression of our Christian sympathy and condolence, be transmitted by the officers of this Board to the family of the deceased.

A FEEBLE TRIBUTE TO A SAINTLY SOUL.

REV. JOS. H. BARCLAY, D. D.

A saintly soul has entered into rest. "After life's fitful fever, our brother sleeps well." The learned men and great doctors of the Church have offered their tribute. Surely one who was associated intimately with ten years of his pastoral life may offer a feeble utterance at the shrine of the John whom he loved. Dr. Stork was the John of our modern Lutheran Church—a man who, if he sometimes felt to call down the fire of heaven on those who abused her, was himself so true, so devoted, so consistent, so loving, that his blows were sweeter than some men's kisses; and no living man, however much he questioned his views, ever doubted for one second his sterling integrity and rectitude of life and purpose.

On this man's scholarship and rare intellectual endowments, it will be better for the readers of this article to hear the voice of the leaders of our Church. They are most competent for the work—that is, if Elijah's mantle can be found on any living Elisha. The writer's privilege is not to write of schools and schoolmen, but of the Christly character of a God-endowed man, who always bore the sign and patent of his Christian nobility about him.

12*

Dr. Stork was such a plain, unostentatious man that the world and myriads in the Church who crave signs and love glitter instead of gold did not appreciate him. He did not draw crowds to his ministry; he did not publish books; he did not shine in mixed assemblies; he did not preach grand sermons and thrill listening multitudes; sometimes he was lethargic, even careless; occasionally needed stirring; but take him all in all, he ranks in the front, with the sweet, pure, saintly, and imperial souls that have helped the world to higher conception of life by having lived in the world. He was among the men meant by Webster, the statesman, when he said that for successful men, however crowded the lower plains, there was plenty of room at the top. And on the summit he stood, as scholar, as theologian, as philosopher, as preacher, pastor, and personal friend. It is exceptional for sons to equal a very able father—more rare for sons to surpass their fathers; yet Dr. Stork, the son, was a much stronger man than his father, and the latter was among the great leaders of our beloved faith.

In no one feature of his ministerial life do we remember our brother so well as in our Monday morning ministerial meetings in Baltimore. During ten years of the writer's pastoral life in Baltimore we met together. We had no stiff formal meetings, and rarely a set theme; we simply met and talked of Christ, and the Church, and our work. Here Dr. Stork shone as the world and hosts of the church did not know him. Conversant with books and men, possessing rare philosophical insight, he unravelled the tangled threads of theological controversy, and infused into the most abstruse subjects a sweet, personal, religious power that made his utterances like apples of gold in frame-work of silver. His thoughts weighed; his ideas convinced; his theology convicted; his church love overwhelmed. He was our leader. A small man in physique, a veritable giant in discussion; a quiet man in manner, a Boanerges in ideas; exceedingly modest and diffident, as if only giving utterance to the most trite and common-place thoughts, and yet breathing forth a richness of thought that carried conviction with every sentence.

As a personal friend, without ostentation, never loud, utterly devoid of pretension, plain-spoken, never bitter, concise in words, careful in judgment, clear as sunbeams, open as light, true to the core.

As a preacher, calm, scholarly, pungent, original in manner and matter, always fresh, powerful, and at times actually sublime. As Mr. Moody, the evangelist, said of him, "the grandest preacher in Baltimore;" *but Baltimore didn't know it.* Others who had not brains, but brass, and lived by puffing, gathered crowds; he never did; but his true monument is in the true souls he gathered into St. Mark's, the best working church of the Lutheran faith in the Monumental City.

As a scholar and theologian, let those speak who are most competent. If Dr. Stork had his superior among us, we should be glad to know the name.

As a churchman, he was as true as in his friendship; he was a thorough Lutheran, and believed, heart and soul, in the doctrines and usages of our church. He had no sympathy with imitation of other denominations. He knew that the Lutheran church, doctrinally, was sound. He knew that her usages were among the best. He stood by the old ways, and walked in them, and was a leader for others who halted, or trembled, or aimed for new paths.

We have said that Dr. Stork wrote no books. In one respect this is unfortunate. It was the custom annually in Baltimore for several of the pastors to hold meetings in the various churches, and alternately lecture on themes relating to the Lutheran church. Dr. Stork always led, and lectured from notes. Who among us will not regret that no copies exist of these lectures, especially among the last, his masterly exposition of Lutheranism *vs.* Puritanism? This was not the precise title, but the subject matter.

Our beloved disciple is dead, but he lives in the memory of his people, of his brethren in the ministry, of his students. This death is a greater loss than many realize. We sadly lack leaders in our church to-day. Nevertheless, though the workmen die, the work must go on. God's cause has never been without faithful, true, and able witnesses, in all ages of the world.

HIS FUGITIVE WRITINGS.

A literary friend writes: "In regard to his writings, I can mention a few interesting details. I remember one or two things he wrote for the New York *Independent*. One was some short verses as a parody of the hymn, 'O, to be brethren;' the refrain to which was, 'Oh, to be something.' It was intended as a rebuke in a pleasant way of certain errors of Christian teaching, as he thought.

Some notices of theological books, written by him for the *Lutheran Observer*, attracted the attention of the editor of *The Independent* (N. Y.) He received in consequence a theological work from that paper for review. He also wrote for *The Independent* some other articles.

He also wrote for *The Home Monthly*, his father's last journalistic enterprise. He also had the usual leaning to poetry and fiction common to young men of literary taste. There was, I believe, a blank verse tragedy attempted.

You know that he contributed numerous articles to various journals and church papers, some of which have been republished in a neat volume and which has received deserved commendation from competent critics. There is much more material that should be gathered and published in book form, for he was, undoubtedly, one of the most polished, thoughtful and forcible writers our church has ever had in this country. The article on Bishop Butler, in the *Lutheran Quarterly*, always struck me as in his best vein. Indeed all his Review articles display the man of genius, learning, taste and piety.

FROM A STUDENT.

It was my privilege to be for a few months, during the winter of 1882-3, under Dr. Stork's instruction. At that time the disease which caused his death was beginning to cause increasing trouble, and his work was constantly interrupted. The lectures he gave my class were on theology. The science was just being opened up to us when Dr. Stork was compelled to lay aside his pen. In these lectures the same clearness of expression, felicity of illustration and depth of original thought were observable that so eminently characterized his sermons and addresses. A wide acquaintance with the subject made his manner easy and forcible, and the lectures were delivered from copious notes, never read. The main points were dictated, and then, branching out in explanation and application, all the range of his extensive and complete knowledge was brought into play, making up a most fascinating exposition of even the deepest and most complex truths. None could listen to him without being impressed with the deep earnestness and desire to instruct that marked him. Gentle and patient to the dull student, he ever strove to bring out all that was in a man, and yet insisted on every lecture being prepared for recitation by his class in the most perfect manner possible. Well does my class recall one occasion, when, for some cause or other, the preparation not being what it should have been, Dr. Stork said: "Gentlemen, you must take this lecture for the next time, and I want it prepared correctly." In the Greek recitations which he conducted with all the students, the translation of the New Testament, many a hard point was made clear by his explanations; and in the rhetorical exercises, while he often criticised severely the oratorical flights of some ambitious student, he ever found something to praise, and never gave offense to even the most fastidious. When a debate was given on some assigned topic, after it was finished he took up each speaker's arguments, and showed the falsity and incorrectness, or the sharpness and application of each, then summing up the whole, he presented it in such a way that we never forgot it. His influence on those with whom he came in contact was always for good, and no one met him without feeling that he was in the presence of a master mind. Quiet, unobtrusive, retiring, he was a very model of a scholar, whose life, though short, will be recalled with grateful memory by those who had the opportunity of meeting and knowing him.

Thus I close the brief narrative of this remarkable man's career. A much larger volume might have been filled with the story of his life, but I was compelled to yield to an authority that could not be resisted, and it has necessarily been confined to these moderate dimensions.

The partiality of friends may often exaggerate in their estimate of those of whom they write or speak, and the reader may kindly make all allowance for personal preference while doubting the statement, but there is no difference of opinion in exalted estimate of the character of Dr. Stork. All who have ever known him agree in awarding to him the highest style of intellect, the most varied and extensive acquirements, and the most profound piety.

All sincerely deplored his early departure and mourned that our Lutheran Church should be deprived of his useful service and the world of his faultless example.

Ille extinctus amabitur.

www.ingramcontent.com/pod-product-compliance
Lightning Source LLC
Chambersburg PA
CBHW032145230426
43672CB00011B/2452